Hurricanes in Action Worldwide

Hurricanes in Action Worldwide

Adrian Stewart

Pen & Sword
AVIATION

First published in Great Britain in 2022 by
Pen & Sword Aviation
An imprint of
Pen & Sword Books Ltd
Yorkshire – Philadelphia

Copyright © Adrian Stewart 2022

ISBN 978 1 52678 868 9

The right of Adrian Stewart to be identified as Author of this work has been asserted by him in accordance with the Copyright, Designs and Patents Act 1988.

A CIP catalogue record for this book is available from the British Library.

All rights reserved. No part of this book may be reproduced or transmitted in any form or by any means, electronic or mechanical including photocopying, recording or by any information storage and retrieval system, without permission from the Publisher in writing.

Typeset by Mac Style
Printed in the UK by CPI Group (UK) Ltd, Croydon, CR0 4YY.

Pen & Sword Books Limited incorporates the imprints of Atlas, Archaeology, Aviation, Discovery, Family History, Fiction, History, Maritime, Military, Military Classics, Politics, Select, Transport, True Crime, Air World, Frontline Publishing, Leo Cooper, Remember When, Seaforth Publishing, The Praetorian Press, Wharncliffe Local History, Wharncliffe Transport, Wharncliffe True Crime and White Owl.

For a complete list of Pen & Sword titles please contact

PEN & SWORD BOOKS LIMITED
47 Church Street, Barnsley, South Yorkshire, S70 2AS, England
E-mail: enquiries@pen-and-sword.co.uk
Website: www.pen-and-sword.co.uk

Or

PEN AND SWORD BOOKS
1950 Lawrence Rd, Havertown, PA 19083, USA
E-mail: Uspen-and-sword@casematepublishers.com
Website: www.penandswordbooks.com

To Chris Shores in admiration of his brilliant researches and appreciation of his kind assistance to me.

Contents

Acknowledgements viii
Preface ix

Chapter 1   Norway 1940   1
Chapter 2   Confidence Created   14
Chapter 3   Duels with Test Group Two-Ten   27
Chapter 4   East African Achievement   41
Chapter 5   Faith, Hope and Hurricanes   55
Chapter 6   Cats v Condors   71
Chapter 7   Russian Tutorial   85
Chapter 8   Adverse Odds: Sumatra and Java   99
Chapter 9   Malta at Bay   116
Chapter 10 Two Crucial Convoys   133
Chapter 11 Jubilee   150
Chapter 12 Ground Attack in Tunisia   165
Chapter 13 Close Support: Kohima and Imphal   179

Last Word 197
Bibliography 199
Index 203

Acknowledgements

My gratitude to all who helped, in particular:

Brigadier Henry Wilson and his team at Pen & Sword Ltd, my publishers, especially my liaison officer Matt Jones.

Johnson & Alcock Ltd, my agents, especially my liaison officer Ed Wilson.

Pamela Covey, my editor.

Jon Wilkinson, who had the brilliant idea of having a Russian Hurricane on the cover as a symbol of the Hurricane's worldwide service.

The Birmingham & Midland Institute & Library, the Taylor Library and Mr Christopher Shores for the photographs.

Thank you everyone.

Preface

One of the most pleasant rewards for writing history is that you meet delightful people. Another is that you learn fascinating information. In both respects I have been especially fortunate in the contacts I have made and the 'feedback' I have received from other admirers of that most interesting of aircraft, the Hawker Hurricane.

One reason why this cannot help but be interesting is the sheer extent and variety of the service it gave. A few years ago in a book entitled *Ten Squadrons of Hurricanes* I included accounts of its part in the Battle of France, the Battle of Britain, campaigns in the Western Desert, the Balkans and the Middle East and its role as a night-fighter on the defensive and on intruder missions. Fellow enthusiasts, however, rightly told me I had not covered the Hurricane's part in campaigns in Norway, Russia, Malta, North Africa, East Africa and the Far East, its role as a naval-air fighter, catapulted from merchant vessels or launched from aircraft carriers, and some aspects of its value in the Battle of Britain.

Here then is my attempt to fill the gaps and show how the Hurricane's service can truly be called 'worldwide'. As Denis Richards and Hilary St. G. Saunders declare in the Official History *Royal Air Force 1939–1945*: 'Everywhere the ubiquitous Hurricane was to be seen.'

Chapter One

Norway 1940

On 9 April 1940 the so-called 'Phoney War' ended, though this designation had never really been applicable to the fighting at sea or in the air. Even on land, it would have been thought offensive by the Finns, subjected to a brutal assault by Russia, or the Poles, subjected to brutal assaults by both Russia and, with much more vicious efficiency, by Germany. There had, however, been almost total inactivity on the Western Front where the French army and the British Expeditionary Force on one side and Adolf Hitler's Wehrmacht on the other made little attempt to as much as inconvenience their enemies. It all seemed unreal to those who recalled the Western Front of the First World War, and so deep-rooted was their attitude that some have insisted that the Phoney War only ended on 10 May with the German onslaught in the west.

Yet the events of 9 April would provide enough action on land as well as at sea or in the air to satisfy the most experienced or the most callous. It saw charming little Denmark, so unfortunate as to have a land frontier with Germany, forcibly incorporated into the Third Reich and a dramatic invasion of Norway, the capture of which would provide naval and air bases for flanking attacks on Britain and open the North Atlantic to sorties by the German navy.

On this date a seaborne attack on Oslo was checked, but airborne troops seized the city's airfields and captured the Norwegian capital from the rear. Seaborne attacks elsewhere were completely successful and German soldiers took Kristiansand, Bergen, Trondheim and even Narvik. This last-named town lay more than 600 miles north of Oslo, but was immensely important to Germany because only through its ice-free port could the Swedish iron ore that was essential for Germany's armaments industry be shipped to her during the winter months. Accordingly ten German destroyers put ashore at Narvik the 3rd Mountain Division: 2,000 tough Austrians commanded by General Eduard Dietl, who were

2 Hurricanes in Action Worldwide

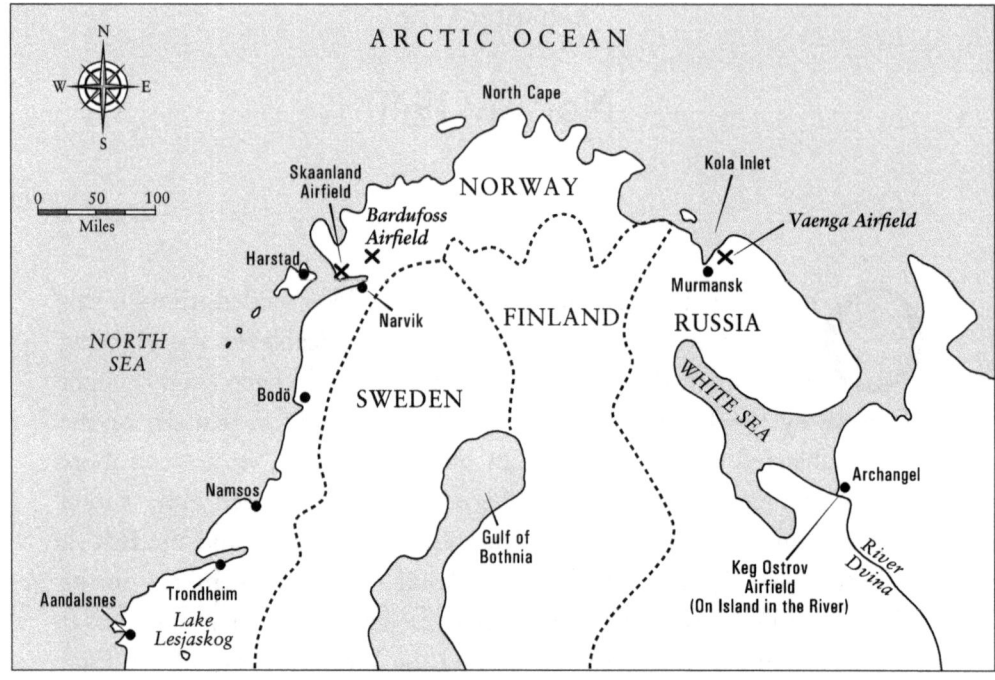

Map 1: Hurricane operations in northern Norway and north-west Russia.

specially trained to operate in snowy conditions. They secured the little town without resistance.

It was also in the far north that the first Allied counter-moves were made. In two brilliant actions on 10 and 13 April, the Royal Navy annihilated all ten German destroyers at Narvik, and on the 15th an Anglo-French force landed at the nearby port of Harstad. Unfortunately it made no move to advance on Narvik and so allowed Dietl's men, who had been understandably dismayed by the destruction of their naval support, plenty of time to recover their nerve and resolution.

This delay was partly caused because the Allies were more interested in the recapture of Trondheim in central Norway; this should enable them to check the main German forces moving northward and so retain a hold on the northern half of the country. Successful Allied landings were therefore made at Namsos and Aandalsnes, north and south of Trondheim respectively. Then, however, everything started to go wrong.

The reason for this can be stated simply: the Luftwaffe had complete command of the skies. A proposed seaborne landing directly at Trondheim was cancelled because of the threat from enemy bombers.

A force of eighteen Gladiators of 263 Squadron, flown off the aircraft carrier *Glorious* to the frozen Lake Lesjaskog near Aandalsnes, was wiped out by air attacks within seventy-two hours. On the night of 2/3 May, both Namsos and Aandalsnes were evacuated.

With Trondheim secured, the main German forces could push on towards the Allies' remaining positions in the far north, strongly supported by the Luftwaffe. Gallant attempts to oppose them were made by Blackburn Skuas from the aircraft carrier *Ark Royal* but these two-seater monoplanes, which were slower than the biplane Gladiators, were scarcely adequate for the task. A fresh batch of Gladiators from 263 Squadron was flown to Bardufoss airfield north of Narvik, but there was a growing feeling that a force of modern monoplane fighters was badly needed.

The unit chosen was No. 46 (Hurricane) Squadron which had received its Hawker fighters in March 1939 and the pilots of which had gained one of the war's earliest successes on 21 October 1939. Then based at North Coates in Lincolnshire, six of its Hurricanes, providing protection for a convoy in the North Sea, engaged nine Heinkel He 115 floatplanes attempting to attack this. The Heinkels tried to break away, but the Hurricanes were much too quick for them. One of them was shot down by Squadron Leader Barwell, while Barwell, Pilot Officers Cowles and Plummer and Flight Sergeant Shackley all contributed to the destruction of another. Pilot Officer Frost destroyed a third Heinkel and Frost aided by Pilot Officer Lefevre compelled a fourth to land on the sea with its engines stopped; it too became a total loss. All these victories are confirmed in enemy records. The Hurricanes suffered no damage.

Shortly after this encounter, Squadron Leader Barwell, who had been 46's CO for the whole time it had flown Hurricanes, was promoted to wing commander and took up other duties.[1] His successor was Squadron Leader Kenneth Cross, always known as 'Bing' after the American singer Mr Crosby, and it was he who commanded the eighteen Hurricanes of 46 Squadron that on 21 May 1940 were to be found on board the aircraft carrier HMS *Glorious*, ready to assist the Allied ground troops in northern Norway.

They had got there by a rather convoluted path. First they flew from Digby, of which North Coates was a satellite, to Abbotsinch near Glasgow. From there they taxied to and along a jetty on the River Clyde, where they were loaded onto lighters and carried 20 miles down the river to where *Glorious* was anchored. They were then hoisted aboard her in somewhat undignified fashion, and she set course for northern Norway.

It had been planned that 46 would be based at a new aerodrome being created at Skaanland, much closer than Bardufoss to both Narvik and Harstad. The squadron ground crews were taken to Harstad on 17 May and moved on to Skaanland next day. Here, though, they soon concluded that it was not yet capable of receiving Hurricanes and would not be ready to do so for several days.

Glorious therefore returned to Scapa Flow, taking 46's Hurricanes with her. The pilots, who it might be mentioned still included Cowles, Frost, Lefevre and Shackley with the first two now promoted to flying officers, may secretly have been rather relieved. Trials had suggested that Hurricanes might perhaps take off from an aircraft carrier – it was considered quite impossible for them to land on one – but none had actually done so and no 46 pilot had taken part in the experiments. They could be forgiven for wondering if it could really be achieved.

They would soon have the chance to find out. By 26 May, Skaanland was declared to be ready and *Glorious* was again on station. It must have been a testing moment for the men of 46 Squadron and for Squadron Leader Cross in particular. In *Hurricane: Victor of the Battle of Britain*, Leo McKinstry records how Cross would later declare:

> I was the first to take off, which of course had never been done before from a carrier. We did not know if the Hurricane could do it or not. In fact, with our variable-pitch airscrews and the full power of the Merlin engine, they leapt off the deck without any difficulty at all.

The Hurricanes had demonstrated a reliability and versatility soon to become legendary, but it quickly became clear that Skaanland was still unfit for them. Of the six that landed there, three were badly damaged; after this those still airborne were diverted to Bardufoss, where the three survivors from Skaanland joined them next day. The squadron strength was now only fifteen Hurricanes.

Bardufoss was not an ideal base either. It was well to the north of Narvik and the intervening miles were apt to be shrouded in cloud or fog. Nor was there any way in which the Hurricanes – or 263's Gladiators – could be given warning of enemy raids. There was no radar set in all northern Norway. Observer posts had been set up but Norway's mountains not only restricted visibility but, since they contained a high proportion of iron, disrupted or on occasions completely blocked wireless messages. This also meant that the fighters could not be controlled from the ground.

Nonetheless, the Hurricanes' arrival was a great relief to Lieutenant General Claude Auchinleck, who had been entrusted with the task of capturing Narvik. He was greatly worried about the Luftwaffe's bombing raids which had culminated on this same 26 May with the sinking of the anti-aircraft cruiser *Curlew*, particularly since in the Arctic there were no hours of darkness to provide cover for his men. Yet the presence of modern fighters reassured him and rightly so, for the whole course of the recapture of Narvik might have been designed to illustrate the Hurricanes' value.

At 2340 on 27 May, a heavy bombardment from the troops' supporting warships heralded the Allied landings at Narvik. Above circled 46's Hurricanes, the arrival of which successfully deterred the enemy bombers. In the early hours of 28 May, however, a sea-fog threatened Bardufoss. The Hurricanes returned there just in time and were grounded until the fog lifted. At once the Luftwaffe reappeared, damaging the light cruiser *Cairo*. With the warships concentrating on their own defence, Dietl was able to counter-attack and drive the Allies back to their beachhead.

For a moment the situation was critical, but luckily the fog then lifted from Bardufoss. As the first three Hurricanes arrived on the scene, the enemy bombers hastily retired. They would later make two more attempts to intervene but were driven off without difficulty, and Flying Officer Lydall gained 46's first victory by shooting down a Junkers Ju 88, one of its crew being killed and the other three taken prisoner. Under the Hurricanes' protective wings Allied reinforcements were landed, while German efforts to supply their own soldiers with artillery pieces were disrupted when a pair of Dornier Do 26 flying-boats bringing these were destroyed by three of 46's pilots led by Flight Lieutenant 'Pat' Jameson.

This was a very fine piece of airmanship since the Dorniers were moored under a steep cliff in an extremely narrow fjord. Jameson's emotions are recalled in *So Few: The Immortal Record of the Royal Air Force* by David Masters: 'It was my first action and I've never been so thrilled in my life. I've done a good deal of deer stalking and wild pig hunting in New Zealand, but they seem tame after that.'

By the evening of 28 May, Narvik was firmly in Allied hands. Dietl's men fell back into the mountains, but from these they would later emerge triumphant. On 10 May, the Western Front had finally erupted in a tremendous German assault that was followed by a series of Allied disasters vastly exceeding their misfortunes in Norway. It was quickly accepted that there was no possibility of keeping forces in northern Norway when they were so desperately needed elsewhere. The Allies therefore wrecked Narvik's port installations and industrial plants – ironically less efficiently than the Germans had done before they withdrew – and prepared for another evacuation.

In the meantime, the Luftwaffe continued its attacks on Allied troops and naval forces and the Hurricanes continued to make interceptions. Enemy records indicate that in late May and early June twenty-eight warplanes were lost in the Narvik area, though this figure included those destroyed in accidents or when not airborne like the Do 26s mentioned previously. On the other hand, the official records may not be correct; a problem that will arise more than once when recounting the exploits of the Hawker Hurricane. It may therefore be as well to deal with this here.

After the war, the 'official' figures for German losses were taken from the Luftwaffe quartermaster general's returns. These were used as a basis for getting replacements, so it was understandably argued they would not be understated. They have, however, been inaccurately interpreted by British assessors, whose own figures did not include losses that were in fact recorded in the quartermaster general's returns because these were stated as having occurred on 'war support flights' such as air-sea rescue missions. Nor did the British figures include some aircraft that returned to base only to be 'written off'. The Germans calculated their losses on a percentage basis depending on what parts could be salvaged for future use. An aircraft was considered a 'write-off' with 60 per cent or more damage, but the British assessors accepted as losses only those reported to have injuries of 80 per cent or more.

Even more significantly, it is clear that the quartermaster general's returns are incomplete. Certainly the sheer speed of aerial combat together with what the RAF understandably calls the 'enthusiasm factor' did mean that pilots exaggerated the damage they had caused or several, in perfect good faith, claimed sole credit for downing the same enemy machine. Yet after making all allowances for such errors, there are still many instances in which it cannot reasonably be doubted that enemy aircraft claimed really were destroyed despite not being confirmed in the German records.

For example, there are cases where these records are silent, even though German pilots baled out and were taken prisoner, or where German aircraft were seen to crash into the sea not only by Allied fighter pilots but by observers on land or on ships in the vicinity, or where they came down on land, their wreckage was examined and triumphantly paraded and the scars they left on the countryside were plainly visible fifty years later. Clearly then, some of the quartermaster general's returns have been mislaid or else there were other ways in which losses could be reported. Indeed, many years after the war, further Luftwaffe records came to light that showed conclusively that one or other (or both) of these situations had in fact occurred.[2]

Instances of this nature can be found in air battles fought over France, Britain, North Africa, the Balkans, Cyprus and Malta, and perhaps also Norway. On 7 June, 46 Squadron reported a number of clashes with Heinkel He 111s. In the afternoon, Flying Officer Mee and Pilot Officer Drummond shot down one Heinkel and damaged another that crash-landed at its base. This, the last success of 46 in Norway, is duly confirmed in German records, but they make no mention of two separate encounters over Narvik and Bardufoss respectively on the morning of the 7th, in which 46 claimed to have downed three more Heinkels. On the contrary, the Germans state that they flew no bomber missions that morning because the weather was too bad.

When attempting to decide which version is correct, we might start by pointing out that though the weather throughout the day was not good, in the very early hours when these clashes are supposed to have taken place it was described as 'better than usual'. Both 46's Hurricanes and 263's Gladiators flew defensive patrols, while for their part the Germans agree that flying-boats and floatplanes were sent out on reconnaissance. That their bombers were also present seems clear from the descriptions of these combats given by 46's pilots.

Thus it is related, for instance, that Squadron Leader Cross and Pilot Officer Lefevre encountered a force of four Heinkels. They both confirmed that they engaged the same enemy aircraft and between them shot it down. To this account Cross added a significant detail, recorded in Leo McKinstry's *Hurricane: Victor of the Battle of Britain*:

> I had been unable to do up my straps because we had been in such a hurry to get at the [enemy] aeroplanes. I was leaning forward up against the windscreen when I was hit by return fire. The back of my oil tank was knocked out and the windscreen shattered.

It is obvious therefore that enemy aircraft were not only present on this morning but showed a determination and ability to defend themselves. It was fortunate that Cross had been leaning close to his windscreen, since Mr McKinstry reveals that on landing, 'he found that a bullet had passed through the back of the seat where his head would normally have been.'

There is no dispute about any of the other claims submitted by 46's pilots during their time in Norway. In every instance, enemy records show that the German aircraft in question was either destroyed or so damaged that it crash-landed. It seems not unreasonable therefore that in the case of the three Heinkels claimed as destroyed on the morning of 7 June, those pilots should at least be given the benefit of the doubt.

As well as the Ju 88 shot down by Flying Officer Lydall and the two flying-boats wrecked in the fjord on the 28th, 46 Squadron definitely destroyed five more warplanes of various types during May. The most impressive victory came in the afternoon of the 29th, when Pilot Officer Banks shot down a four-engined Focke-Wulf Fw 200C, killing all its six-man crew. The mighty Condor, later to prove such a threat to Britain's Atlantic convoys, was on a bombing raid at the time, though usually the type acted most effectively as a long-range reconnaissance aircraft. Sadly, Banks was himself killed that same evening by the gunners of a Heinkel He 111.

It seems that 46's pilots were very accurate in assessing the damage they had inflicted because they pressed home their attacks to extremely close range. This, though, did mean that they came under heavy return fire, and in all three Hurricanes were lost in combat during May, including that flown by Banks. Flying Officer Lydall who had scored 46's first aerial victory was also killed, but Pilot Officer Drummond escaped by parachute. He had previously brought down a Heinkel and, with an eventual total of four victories, would become 46's most successful marksman and be awarded a Distinguished Flying Cross.

On 31 May, 46 Squadron helped to protect the evacuation from Bodø of a small force sent there to delay the German advance from the south. The principal cover on this occasion, however, was provided by 263, and the Gladiator pilots also played the greater part in frustrating a series of attacks against the Allied troops and warships in the Narvik area on 2 June. During the day nine enemy aircraft were destroyed or seriously injured and 263, at the cost of one Gladiator and its pilot, could boast four 'kills' and at least two damaged. The Hurricanes, of course, were not left entirely out of the picture and drove off a force of Junkers Ju 87 Stuka dive-bombers attacking naval vessels. Pilot Officer Drummond and Sergeant Taylor each shot down a Stuka and a third one escaped with damage and a wounded rear-gunner.

On the following day, the evacuation of Narvik began. It continued for five days, during which time the Hurricanes and Gladiators provided such effective cover that the enemy did not realize that a withdrawal was taking place until it was too late. This, though, gave little satisfaction to Squadron Leader Cross. He viewed the decision to evacuate as 'a great disappointment', not least because of the fate decreed for his by now beloved Hurricanes.

It had been decided that the protection provided by the fighters at Bardufoss was so important that 46 and 263 Squadrons must remain on duty until the evacuation was over and only leave after all other units had already done so. Then the loyal, hardworking ground staff would return home on the merchant ship *Arandora Star* and 263's surviving machines would fly to HMS *Glorious*. The Royal Navy had operated Sea Gladiators for some time and although the land-based versions lacked arrester hooks to catch the wires stretched over the deck, it was confidently and correctly predicted that their low speed combined with the wind produced by the carrier steaming at maximum power would reduce their landing run sufficiently for them to get down safely.

For the Hurricanes it was different. They had a far greater landing speed and therefore needed a far longer landing run. All expert opinions united to declare that Hurricanes could not land on a carrier. The main problem was that the pilots would have to brake so hard that the Hurricanes' tails would come up. Then, if they did not turn over completely, they would offer less resistance to the wind and would just keep going until they fell off the end of the deck. Orders were given that 46's aircraft, reduced by losses in combat and accidents in the harsh Arctic conditions to ten in number, should be destroyed on their airfield.

Squadron Leader Cross, knowing that Fighter Command needed every Hurricane it could get, was convinced that his aircrafts' strength and reliability would enable them to land on *Glorious*. On 5 June, he was flown out to the carrier in a Walrus amphibian based at Harstad for reconnaissance and air-sea rescue work, and obtained the consent of Captain D'Oyly-Hughes to his making the attempt. Cross then approached Group Captain Moore, the senior RAF officer in Norway, with a request that the previous orders be changed. That Moore gave permission showed considerable moral courage, for he would bear the responsibility if disaster should occur.

It seemed highly likely that it might. Cross was fully aware of how hazardous the operation would be for pilots who had never yet attempted anything of the kind. He therefore felt obliged to give his men a detailed explanation of his plans and the dangers they involved, after which he asked who was willing to participate. The consequences are set out succinctly in the Squadron Diary: '100% volunteered. Tests were carried out with extra weight in the tail of the Hurricanes. At 1800 hrs Flt Lt Jameson, Fg Off Knight and Sgt Taylor took off for HMS *Glorious*.'

Although squadron diaries were noted for their casual understatement, there can rarely have been a more blatant example of this trait. The 'extra weight' that was to be provided to keep the Hurricanes' tails down on the carrier's deck consisted of bags of sand strapped to the rear of their fuselages.

Unfortunately, these would also unbalance the Hurricanes and make the difficulties and perils of landing on *Glorious* even greater than they already were. Yet every man had stepped forward. Those chosen for the mission apart from Cross, Jameson, Knight and Taylor were Flight Lieutenant Stewart, Flying Officers Cowles, Frost and Mee, Pilot Officer Bunker and Flight Sergeant Shackley. The remaining pilots, who included Pilot Officers Drummond and Lefevre, joined their ground crews on the *Arandora Star*.[3]

That only Jameson, Knight and Taylor took off for the *Glorious* on the evening of 7 June was a last-minute testament to the risks involved. It was decided that it might be best if they made a preliminary trial, while their companions awaited news of its results before following. Guided to *Glorious* by one of her Swordfish, this first flight arrived over her an hour after take-off. Jameson, throttled right back at just above stalling speed, made ready for the dangerous honour of being the first man to land a Hurricane on an aircraft carrier. To his delighted relief, his unbalanced aircraft performed faultlessly: there was no bounce from its weighted tail and he came safely to a halt.

Knight and Taylor followed Jameson's example and both landed without incident. Confirmation of the success was at once sent to Bardufoss. Unhappily, as so often happened, Norway's high iron-bound mountains proved an effective bar to radio waves; the message was never received. For hours, an anxious Cross waited on tenterhooks in ignorance of the fate of his men. Finally, unable to bear the suspense any longer, he took action. It does rather seem that, having gone this far, Cross was going to attempt to reach *Glorious* whatever happened. Early on 8 June – daylight in the Arctic – his seven remaining Hurricanes took off for the carrier. All duly reached her. All landed safely.

Their bold and brilliant achievement was cruelly mocked by fate. That afternoon *Glorious* was sighted by the German battle-cruisers *Scharnhorst* and *Gneisenau* and their first hurried salvoes, though fired at long range, struck home, starting raging fires. The carrier's escorting destroyers, *Ardent* and *Acasta*, tried heroically to defend her, the latter putting a torpedo into *Scharnhorst* before both of them were sunk. *Glorious* went down as well, some two hours after first being hit. With her went more than 1,100 men, all her own aircraft, all those of the RAF, all the Gladiator pilots and all but two from 46 Squadron.

'Bing' Cross and 'Pat' Jameson were among those able to reach a life-raft, but it was three days before a Norwegian ship sighted this. By then, twenty-five of the sailors on it had died from the bitter cold and the remaining survivors were in a very bad way. Mercifully, both Cross and Jameson recovered from their ordeals and, after a spell in hospital, resumed their RAF careers. Jameson was awarded a Distinguished Flying Cross for his achievements in Norway and would retire as an Air Commodore, a Companion of the Bath and a Member of the Distinguished Service Order. 'Bing' Cross, former CO of 46 Squadron and the inspiration behind the landing on *Glorious*, would retire as Air Chief Marshal Sir

Kenneth Cross, KCB, CBE, DSO, DFC, Air Officer Commanding-in-Chief Transport Command and holder of the War Cross with Sword, Norway's highest military decoration.

Tragic as was this last episode of the Hurricanes' campaign in Norway, it could not disguise the lessons they had provided or the calibre of their performance. With regard to the former, the most important had come at the beginning and the end of the campaign. When on 26 May eighteen Hurricanes were flown off HMS *Glorious* with no mishaps and no difficulty by pilots who, although very experienced airmen, had never done this before, it showed that here was a way in which modern fighters could be supplied rapidly to areas where they were needed. When on 7 and 8 June ten Hurricanes flown by pilots untrained in this task landed safely on HMS *Glorious* despite lacking arrester hooks and unbalanced by sandbags, it showed that modern fighters could operate on aircraft carriers. Both lessons would be confirmed on many future occasions.

As for the calibre of the Hurricanes' performance in Norway, Air Marshal Sir Peter Wykeham in his *Fighter Command: A Study of Air Defence 1914–1960* says of both 46 and 263 Squadrons: 'Their conquest over conditions past describing was worthy of the hard-worked word epic.' Even Auchinleck, while shamefully traducing the British ground troops who faced similar conditions, was sufficiently impressed by the protection the RAF fighters had provided to send them what the RAF Official History calls 'a handsome message of thanks'.

The highest praise, though, comes from the official historian of another service: Captain S.W. Roskill in *The War at Sea*. First, as is right and proper, he salutes the navy's own airmen who were able 'to carry the centuries of fighting tradition into the new element'. Then he continues: 'And their comrades of the Royal Air Force showed the qualities which, a few weeks later, saved their country and made the free world ring with their fame.'

Notes

1. Barwell, who everyone called 'Dickie' though his real Christian names were Philip Reginald, served as a staff officer at the headquarters of 12 Group Fighter Command during the Battle of Britain. In July 1941 he became a group captain and station commander at Biggin Hill, where he insisted on flying intruder sorties with the resident Spitfire units. Early in 1942, he

crash-landed when his aircraft's engine cut out on take-off, severely injuring his spine which had to be put in a thick plaster cast. After its removal he resumed his operational flights, but on 1 July 1942 he was killed when his Spitfire was tragically shot down by 'friendly' fighters over the English Channel.
2. See in particular the 1987 revised and expanded version of Francis K. Mason's *The Hawker Hurricane*. See also the Appendix to *Fighters Over Tunisia* by Christopher Shores, Hans Ring and William N. Hess, in which new evidence is given about incidents related in an earlier work by Messrs Shores and Ring entitled *Fighters Over the Desert*.
3. It perhaps seems surprising that Pilot Officer Drummond, who had proved to be 46 Squadron's most successful pilot, should not have been asked to take a Hurricane to *Glorious*. It may be that it was felt he had done enough or possibly was too valuable to be risked. He would gain further victories in the Battle of Britain flying Spitfires, but was killed in action on 10 October 1940.

Chapter Two

Confidence Created

Long before the loss of HMS *Glorious*, misfortunes in Norway had resulted in a change of government in Britain. The cancellation of the direct attack on Trondheim followed by the evacuations of Namsos and Aandalsnes had led to a debate in the House of Commons that turned into a Vote of Censure. The minister most at fault was the First Lord of the Admiralty Winston Churchill. To his credit, he accepted 'complete responsibility' and recalling how the Labour and Liberal parties had constantly opposed every attempt to increase Britain's ability to defend herself, from the expansion of the Royal Air Force to the imposition of conscription, he counter-attacked them with his usual fire and vigour.

Yet the anger of the House was directed not at Churchill but at Prime Minister Neville Chamberlain who, immediately before the German invasion of Norway, had been so unwise as to announce that Hitler had 'missed the bus'. Chamberlain's own Conservative Party had come to realize that he was no wartime leader and when the House divided, thirty of them voted with the Opposition, while sixty more abstained.

Chamberlain accepted that a National Coalition Government must be formed to conduct the war and when it became clear that the Opposition would not serve under him, he resigned on 10 May 1940 to be succeeded, rather ironically in the circumstances, by Churchill.

Further ironies would soon become apparent. On this same 10 May, the German assault in the west began a series of calamities far worse than those in Norway. Churchill's own Foreign Secretary Edward Wood, Earl of Halifax, haunted by memories of the slaughter in the First World War, urged that peace negotiations must commence without delay. Churchill, rightly believing that a Europe occupied and dominated by a National Socialist Germany would have made Britain's position impossible and would not have been very pleasant for Europe either, refused even to consider such a course of action. His courage won overwhelming support from the rest of his Cabinet, including Chamberlain who had previously, though hesitatingly, supported Halifax.[1] Yet persuasive voices from men as influential as David Lloyd George and George Bernard Shaw continued to insist that ending the war was essential.

This lack of resolution must have worried Churchill, particularly after it became clear that the British Isles were facing a threat unknown since the days of Napoleon. On 2 July Hitler declared that 'a landing in England is possible', a view supported by the General Staff of his army. He added a significant rider: 'Provided that air superiority can be obtained.' Hitler's conclusion had already been reached by the British chiefs of staff, but so had his qualification. They agreed with him that 'The crux of the matter is air superiority.'

Thus, when in early July the Luftwaffe began its attempt to gain air superiority by attacking British shipping in the Channel and thereby luring RAF fighters into action, a very great deal was at stake. This included Britain's morale since these clashes were clearly visible to watchers on the shore. The confidence of Fighter Command was already high, but that of the country as a whole was immensely strengthened by the achievements of the fighters and those of one type of fighter in particular.

It is generally stated that the Battle of Britain began on 10 July. This is a somewhat arbitrary date for there had been plenty of action for more than a week previously, but it did increase noticeably on the 10th and included the first really massive dogfight involving more than 100 aircraft over a large convoy code-named BREAD in the Strait of Dover. In all, the day cost the Luftwaffe eleven warplanes: one for reasons unknown, one a victim of AA guns, two shot down by Spitfires and seven destroyed in combats with Hurricanes. The only RAF loss was a Hurricane that collided with a Dornier Do 17, its pilot being killed, as were all the four-man crew of the bomber.

A similar story could be told of 11 July, on which the Luftwaffe lost seventeen aircraft in action (and others in accidents). Of those that fell in combat, the details of one are unknown and two were victims of the fighter version of the Bristol Blenheim, of which Fighter Command had seven squadrons although one operated only at night. All the other fourteen were shot down by Hurricanes. The only RAF casualties were two Spitfires and both their pilots and four Hurricanes but only one Hurricane pilot. Even he baled out but sadly was drowned, a fate that befell many British and German airmen in these early encounters.[2]

Already, therefore, it can be seen how important the Hurricane was in creating or sustaining confidence. For a start, there were more Hurricanes on hand than any other type of fighter. In addition to the Blenheims, Fighter Command had two squadrons of Defiants, two-seater monoplanes, the only armament of which was a rear turret containing four machine guns. There were nineteen squadrons of Spitfires. All these numbers remained constant throughout the Battle of Britain. Hurricanes, however, equipped twenty-seven squadrons on 10 July 1940 and thirty-three squadrons by the time the battle ended. In addition, 245 Squadron in Northern Ireland had Hurricanes and 263, then replacing the Gladiators lost in Norway with twin-engined Westland Whirlwinds, had a Hurricane flight for airfield defence. Hurricanes made 80 per cent of the interceptions of enemy aircraft during the battle, so naturally were the fighters most often seen in action by a delighted British public.

Equally if not more important was the confidence that the Hurricane gave to its pilots. In *The Narrow Margin*, their account of the Battle of Britain, Derek Wood and Derek Dempster sum up its virtues as follows: 'A fine fighting aircraft, an excellent gun platform and it was magnificently manouevrable up to 20,000 feet. It was extremely strong and could take an extraordinary amount of punishment.'

The first sentence shows why the Hurricane pilots could rely on their machines as effective weapons of war; indeed, during the battle Hurricanes shot down more enemy aircraft than all other types of fighter and all forms of ground defence put together. Yet the second sentence was equally important. The Hurricane's reputation for coming back to base when fearfully mauled or at least for staying aloft long enough for its pilot to escape by parachute was well observed and spread rapidly. It must have strengthened the resolve of many an airman.

This confidence would soon be of crucial value. On 16 July Hitler began detailed preparations for an invasion of Britain but, encouraged by exaggerated claims made by his Luftwaffe, he still hoped it might not be necessary. On the 19th, his air force had an outstanding success when ten Messerschmitt Bf 109 fighters[3] attacked nine Defiants of 141 Squadron, shooting down six and badly damaging one more that returned minus its gunner who had presumably baled out but was never seen again. Only the timely arrival of the Hurricanes of 111 Squadron prevented the Defiants' complete annihilation. Hitler seized the opportunity to make a 'last appeal to reason', urging Britain to end the war and 'avert the sacrifices' on both sides which its continuation 'must claim'.

This was a clever move, and to reinforce it the Luftwaffe, which had rather restricted its activities over the last few days, flew a considerable number of sorties on the 20th. Had the calamities of the 19th been repeated, the arguments of those who favoured negotiations might well have been revived. In addition, another day of heavy losses with little to show for them could hardly have failed to alarm the defending pilots. Though 20 July has rarely received much mention in accounts of the Battle of Britain, it was therefore very important indeed.

It began badly for the Luftwaffe when, in the early hours of darkness, two of its massive Focke-Wulf Fw 200C Condors engaged on mine-laying missions were lost. One certainly and the other probably fell to AA fire which, incidentally, was much respected by the Luftwaffe, especially its reconnaissance pilots. Daylight saw the start of the main enemy activity, but before dealing with the resultant clashes, it may be best to explain the battle order of the Hurricane pilots' enemies.

Hermann Göring, now promoted to the newly-created rank of *Reichsmarschall* with a special king-sized baton to prove it and awarded the Second World War's only Grand Cross of the Iron Cross, had positioned three *Luftflotten* (Air Fleets) around the British Isles. These contained in all over 2,600 aircraft, though not all were serviceable. However, *Luftflotte* 5 in Denmark and Norway played no part in these early encounters and the ones concerning Fighter Command were *Luftflotte* 2 under Field Marshal Albert Kesselring in the Low Countries and north-east France and *Luftflotte* 3 under Field Marshal Hugo Sperrle in north-west France.

These *Luftflotten* were divided into *Fliegerkorps* and they in turn into *Geschwader*, the main tactical unit which contained 90 to 120 aircraft, designated according to their function. The bombers, mainly Dornier Do 17s, Heinkel He 111s and Junkers Ju 88s, were in *Kampfgeschwader* (KG for short); the Junkers Ju 87 dive-bombers in *Stukageschwader* (StG); the single-engined Messerschmitt Bf 109s in *Jagdgeschwader* (JG); and the twin-engined Bf 110s, of which Göring had high hopes and were known as *Zestörern* (Destroyers), were in *Zerstörergeschwader* (ZG). Every *Geschwader* was subdivided into *Gruppen* and they into *Staffeln* of ten to twelve machines each.

During the daylight hours of 20 July, these various Luftwaffe units, according to German records, lost a total of twelve warplanes: three to Spitfires, one to a Blenheim and eight to Hurricanes. Even this does not give the Hawker fighters their full credit, since it seems certain that they had other successes that were not recorded. Their first combat of the day came at about 0615, when three of them from 56 Squadron encountered a flight of Junkers Ju 88s from KG 4. They claimed to have downed one of these and although it is not confirmed by enemy records, its four-man crew all survived as prisoners of war. There can be no doubt therefore that this was the Hurricanes' first success on 20 July.

It appears that the Ju 88s were searching for a convoy reported by German Intelligence. There really was a convoy with the interesting code-name of BOSOM in the Channel and its protection would form the centre of a series of savage actions throughout the afternoon. The first Hurricane squadron involved was No. 238 which had the difficult and dangerous task of keeping a succession of small patrols over the convoy. At about 1330, one of them encountered some Bf 109s. These were driven away but 238 lost Sergeant Parkinson who was shot down and killed.

About half an hour later, a Heinkel He 59 floatplane appeared. These aircraft presented the RAF with a moral dilemma. They were prominently marked with red crosses and officially performed air-sea rescue duties. However, since they had a useful defensive armament, rarely carried medical personnel and frequently arrived on the scene prior to a convoy being attacked, it seemed likely that they were also used for reconnaissance purposes. Accordingly, the enemy was notified that unless they were 'engaged in the direct evacuation of sick and wounded', they would be shot down.

Since the He 59 that approached convoy BOSOM was not so engaged, 238 Squadron did shoot it down, but it may have reported its sightings first because the rest of the afternoon would see continuous action. Another He 59 was sighted and attacked by Hurricanes of 43 Squadron but this proved very capable of defending itself, shooting down Flying Officer Haworth who baled out but was drowned, and eluding the other fighters in cloud cover. Before it could return to base, however, it was intercepted by the Hurricanes of 601 Squadron and shot down in its turn.

Another Hurricane squadron in action was 501 Squadron which sighted a group of Junkers Ju 87s heading for the convoy. Before they could get at these, however, they were assaulted by the escorting Messerschmitt Bf 109s. Pilot Officer Sylvester was shot down and killed, but 501's airmen believed they had destroyed three of the 109s. They are not confirmed in German records and Squadron Leader Hogan who claimed one was a comparative novice who had seen no combat in Hurricanes before taking over 501 in mid-June, so he may have been mistaken. The end of both the others, though, was reported by a pilot who was very experienced and a very dangerous opponent.

This was Sergeant James 'Ginger' Lacey, a red-haired, sharp-eyed, quick-witted Yorkshireman who had been an instructor in a flying club before the war and had proved to be 501's finest pilot in the fighting in France, where he had earned a Croix de Guerre. At the end of 1940, he would be acknowledged as the highest-scoring 'ace' in Fighter Command. On 20 July he out-turned a 109 and poured two bursts of fire into it. He would later recall:

I can clearly remember watching him slanting down the sky at a hell of a steep angle. A beautiful little blue and grey mottled aircraft with white and black crosses standing out startlingly clear, getting smaller and smaller; and thinking what a terribly small splash he made when he went straight into the Channel.

Lacey then engaged another 109 and his account continues:

He pulled up in a climbing turn to starboard and I remember thinking he looked exactly like the other one: a beautiful blue and grey mottled effect with the sun shining on him from the south. As he pulled up in a climbing turn I pulled up inside him and as he came into my sights I was giving him an enormous amount of deflection because it was almost a ninety-degree crossing. Then as his turn continued, and I was reducing the deflection, I could see him coming back towards me; I thought for one awful moment that he was going to attempt to crash into me. Then I suddenly saw the aeroplane almost stagger as my bullets were hitting it. It didn't catch fire or break up or anything like that. Its propeller just started to slow down until I could almost see it turning over. Probably the engine had stopped and it was just windmilling. We flashed past each other, a few feet apart, going in opposite directions; and by the time I had whipped round, my new flight commander, 'Pan' Cox, latched on to this 109: he didn't fire until he was in to about twenty yards: and once again the dive of that 109 got steeper and steeper and it went in almost right beside the oily patch marking the place where my first one had gone in. I put no claim in for the half-share in that because it was 'Pan' Cox's first success. I was getting a bit blasé by that time.[4]

Lacey's account could scarcely be more clear or more definite. It would seem certain therefore that, as in the case of the Ju 88 shot down by 56 Squadron, the German records are simply incomplete.

At about 1800, the largest dogfight of the day, lasting for about half an hour, began over convoy BOSOM. This was attacked by Junkers Ju 87 dive-bombers from StG 1, escorted by Bf 110s – though these took no part in the action, being content to form a defensive circle – and Bf 109s, apparently from both JG 27 and JG 51. They were opposed first by the Hurricanes of 32 Squadron from Biggin Hill under Squadron Leader John Worrall. Attacking out of the sun, the Hurricanes burst past the defending 109s, all except Flight Lieutenant Peter Brothers. He was cut off from the rest of the squadron, but luckily he was a capable and experienced pilot who had already been credited with three 'kills', two of them 109s. He shot down one of his assailants and got away; he later became a high-scoring 'ace' with the rank of air commodore.

The remaining 32 Squadron pilots fell on the Stukas, driving them away from the convoy, shooting down two and badly damaging four others, two of which had to force-land when they got back to their base. Only after the dive-bombers had been routed did the 109s, who were supposed to defend them, attack the Hurricanes from above. Sub-Lieutenant Bulmer, one of those Fleet Air Arm pilots who had been 'loaned' to the RAF in its hour of need, was lost: he baled out but was drowned. In addition, the squadron diary reports that 'Sgt Higgins was slightly wounded in the face by splinters from bullets striking his protecting armour.' Then, however, the Hurricanes of Squadron Leader Kayll's 615 Squadron from Kenley in turn attacked the Messerschmitts, shooting down three of them without loss.

This last clash was especially encouraging. At this time the Hurricane was Fighter Command's main weapon and, apart from its 'kills', as

Francis K. Mason remarks in his *Battle Over Britain*: 'Perhaps more agreeable was the fact that the Hurricane, given the choice of combat altitude, could certainly hold its own against enemy single-seat fighters. The fillip to morale provided by this air battle was most welcome after weeks of rather inconclusive operations.'

It raised the morale of the British public in equal measure and on 22 July, Hitler's 'last appeal to reason' was unequivocally rejected. The formal reply, with more irony, was given by Halifax as Foreign Secretary. His own feelings must have been mixed and perhaps both men were relieved when the lamented death of Lord Lothian, the British ambassador to the United States, enabled Churchill to appoint Halifax to this post.[5] It is only right to record that Halifax did much to bring Britain and America closer together and regained the respect that some of his former actions had threatened to forfeit.

There would be one more trial of whether the confidence of the British public in their fighter pilots and those pilots' confidence in themselves would be shaken or confirmed. On 6 August Göring announced that the major air offensive against Britain would commence on the 10th, dramatically entitled *Adlertag* ('Eagle Day'), and the invasion would take place in mid-September. In fact, bad weather resulted in Eagle Day being postponed until the 13th, but meanwhile 8 August had marked the culmination of the Luftwaffe attacks on Britain's coastal convoys and, although not intended as such, had become a kind of 'dress rehearsal' for the 'main event'.

Of course, while the dress rehearsal might help the Luftwaffe to plan later heavy assaults, it might also show Fighter Command that its airmen were capable of dealing with these. So indeed it proved. The attacks on convoys, in particular on a large one code-named PEEWIT, caused considerable harm, but twenty-seven German warplanes were destroyed or damaged beyond repair. A Heinkel He 111 on a reconnaissance flight failed to return for reasons unknown, perhaps AA fire. At least six non-Hurricane squadrons made interceptions, downing four enemy aircraft at the cost of three Spitfires and all their pilots and one Blenheim and its three-man crew. Only four Hurricane squadrons engaged hostile formations, but what these lacked in quantity, they more than made up for in quality.

There were three major attacks on convoys on 6 August and every one of them was opposed by Hurricanes. When Squadron Leader John Peel's

145 Squadron sighted the first raid at about 0900, it was the only RAF unit on hand and was confronted by a strong force of Junkers Ju 87s from two *Gruppen* of StG 1, escorted by Messerschmitt Bf 109s from JG 27. It was Peel who had the honour of firing the first shots in the main part of the Battle of Britain and his later report can be found in Messrs Wood and Dempster's *The Narrow Margin*:

> We climbed to 16,000 feet, and looking down, saw a large formation of Ju 87s approaching from the south with Me 109s stepped up behind to 20,000 feet. We approached unobserved out of the sun and went in to attack the rear Ju 87s before the enemy fighters could interfere. I gave a five-second burst to one bomber and broke off to engage two Me 109s. There was a dogfight. The enemy fighters, which were painted silver, were half rolling, diving and zooming in climbing turns. I fired two five-second bursts at one and saw it dive into the sea. Then I followed another up in a zoom and got him as he stalled.

In all, at a cost of two of its pilots killed, 145 destroyed three 109s and two Stukas and so dispersed the remaining dive-bombers that they did no damage to the convoy. The Stuka attacked by Squadron Leader Peel returned to its base, but in a somewhat battered condition with both its pilot and its gunner wounded.

At about 1230, a huge raid was delivered by fifty-seven Junkers Ju 87s from StG 2, 3 and 77; it sank four merchantmen and damaged half a dozen more so badly that they could not continue their voyage but had to make for the nearest port. The Stukas were aided by an escort of about thirty 109s from JG 27 and some twenty Messerschmitt Bf 110s from *Lehrgeschwader* 1; *Lehr* meaning 'Development' – of operational techniques – which had been the original task of this very able formation. These aircraft provided good protection for their dive-bombers and 257, the first Hurricane squadron to attack, was driven off, though not before Flight Lieutenant Grundy had hit a 109 and watched it 'dive in a gentle turn, disappearing into the sea with a trail of black and white smoke.'

Shortly after this, the Hurricanes of 145 and 238 Squadrons reached the scene and while 238 took on the 109s and 110s, 145, again coming out of the sun, broke past the defending fighters and reached the Stukas, shooting down two, badly damaging two more and this time suffering no casualties. Sadly 238 was less fortunate, losing Flight Lieutenant Turner and Flying Officer MacCaw, but destroying two 109s and damaging a third as well as a pair of 110s.

It was well known that 238 enjoyed a tremendous team spirit, not only among the pilots but throughout the ground crews as well, mainly arising from the magnificent leadership of Squadron Leader Harold Fenton. On learning that two of his men were missing, Fenton took off again to look for them in case they had baled out into the Channel. At about 1350, he encountered a Heinkel He 59 floatplane. This he shot down but, as already seen, these aircraft could put up a good fight and Fenton was forced to 'ditch', injuring his face, chest and legs. He was, however, rescued by a navy trawler, one of only two Hurricane pilots to go down but survive on 8 August.

It seems that the He 59 had previously sent news of the battered convoy, for at about 1630 it was attacked by the final major raid of the day. It consisted of as many as eighty-two Stukas, again protected by LG 1's 110s and JG 27's 109s. Yet it made no fatal hits, thanks mainly to a pair of Hurricane squadrons. Naturally one of these was No. 145, but the experienced Peel delayed his attack until he could again make this out of the sun.

This meant that the Hurricanes of 43 Squadron were the first to see action. They were met by three times their number of 109s and three of them were shot down, two of the pilots being killed but Pilot Officer Upton baling out to be rescued unhurt. For the 'Fighting Cocks', as the airmen of 43 Squadron were invariably known, Flight Lieutenant 'Tom' Dalton-Morgan shot down one of the enemy fighters, while Sergeant James Hallowes, one of Fighter Command's most successful but unsung 'aces', destroyed a second and so damaged a third that it had to be 'written off'.

So determined was 43's resistance that some of its pilots managed to get past the 109s and attack the Ju 87s, of which two were damaged and a third was stated in the German official records as being unharmed but had both its pilot and its gunner wounded; how the bullets that struck them could have failed to harm the machine in which they were flying remains a mystery. One of those responsible for damaging a Stuka was Pilot Officer 'Tony' Woods-Scawen. Group Captain Peter Townsend, who commanded 85 (Hurricane) Squadron in the Battle of Britain but had earlier been a flight commander in No. 43, describes Woods-Scawen in *Duel of Eagles* as 'brave as a lion and blind as a bat (we called him Wombat)'. Apparently on this occasion he 'flew clean through the Stukas, firing as he went'.

Moreover, 43 so occupied the attention of the German single-engined fighters that when 145's Hurricanes swept out of the sun, they caught these completely by surprise, shooting down one of them almost in passing. The twin-engined Bf 110s of LG 1 were, however, to be found at low level with the Stukas. Their pilots engaged the Hurricanes with great determination, shooting down and killing three of the pilots, including Pilot Officer Lord Shuttleworth, a member of a family well known in aviation circles. In return No. 145 destroyed two of the 110s.

Nor could the 110s prevent 145's Hurricanes from getting at the divebombers. Flight Lieutenant Roy Dutton, a very experienced Hurricane pilot, had his engine fail but while gliding down came across a Ju 87 which he greeted with a quick burst of fire that sent it down in flames. His engine then restarted and, sighting another Ju 87 about to attack a ship, he engaged this and shot it into the sea. His engine then packed up for good, but he was able to glide back to base where he landed safely. In all, Peel's men downed five Stukas and the remainder retired in considerable haste.

So ended 8 August 1940 and with it all chance that Britain might not wish to fight on or that Fighter Command might not be able to do so. There would be setbacks and tragedies in plenty during the rest of the Battle of Britain, let alone the rest of the war, but Fighter Command's pilots would always remain confident that they could see it through whatever happened and the British public confident that all would somehow come right in the end. The Hurricane, Fighter Command's main weapon in 1940, had met its greatest test to date triumphantly.

In the first place, the Hurricane had shown that it could hold its own with Germany's splendid single-engined fighters. The German pilots would never concede this, speaking slightingly of the Hurricanes and much preferring to believe they had been shot down by the faster, more beautiful Spitfires. Group Captain Townsend delightfully calls this 'Spitfire snobbery' and its absurdity was never more clear than on the two great confidence-building days described above. On both days the

109s had had a considerable numerical advantage, yet they had shot down three Hurricanes on 20 July and seven at the most, and probably fewer on 8 August, whereas the Hurricanes had certainly shot down four, almost certainly six 109s on 20 July and ten 109s on 8 August. This hardly suggests a marked inferiority.

Indeed, on 8 August in particular, the Hurricanes' triumph over the 109s had gone far beyond the numbers shot down by each of them. The Hurricanes' greatest achievement had been their ability to disperse and chase off formations of dive-bombers, downing nine Stukas and damaging others while the German fighters had been quite unable to prevent them. This was of crucial importance. The 109s could not greatly harm Fighter Command's organization or Britain's war effort, but the German bombers certainly could. Their destruction was vital and for this role the Hurricanes were magnificently suited.

Every pilot who flew a Hurricane in the Battle of Britain could attest that it was sturdy and it was steady. If a Hurricane got on the tail of a German bomber, it would come under fire from the gunner and perhaps a crossfire from several gunners. The Hurricanes' strength enabled them to withstand a tremendous amount of punishment and usually they could soak up any hits made by the gunners and continue to pour their own fire into their target.

Moreover, that fire was aided by the fact that the Hurricanes' eight machine guns were set in tight groups of four in each thick, strong wing. This, as all pilots agreed, allowed Hurricanes to remain steadier when firing than were the Spitfires, the guns of which were spread out along the wings; it made the Hawker fighters wonderful gun-platforms and their firepower hideously effective. Peter Townsend has confessed to feeling 'utterly nauseated' when he realized what his guns had done to the crew of a German aircraft, and there is a report that on 15 September 1940, the day that Hitler decided to postpone his invasion 'indefinitely', a Hurricane pilot who had blown up a bomber at point-blank range, found on his return to base that his engine cowling was covered in blood and there were bits of splintered bone in his radiator.

Group Captain Dennis David, who flew Hurricanes with 87 Squadron in both the Battle of France and the Battle of Britain, has reported that whatever their fighter pilots may have said, many German bomber crews told him that 'the Hurricane was the aircraft they dreaded'. Well they might!

Notes

1. Chamberlain's weakness may readily be excused: he was now terminally ill from cancer. He left the government on 3 October 1940 and died on 9 November. In the House of Commons Churchill paid tribute to his sincerity and rather movingly described how Chamberlain's love of peace had led to his being 'deceived and cheated by a wicked man'.
2. Full details of the British and German losses referred to above or hereafter can be found in Francis K. Mason's *Battle Over Britain*. Unless otherwise stated, all the enemy aircraft reported as destroyed – either shot down or damaged beyond repair – can be confirmed in the German records.
3. Both the single-engined Messerschmitt Bf 109 and the twin-engined Messerschmitt Bf 110 were made by the Bayerische Flugzeugwerke (Bavarian Aircraft Company), hence the abbreviation 'Bf'. They were almost invariably given the abbreviation 'Me' by Allied pilots, but this was not officially correct until 1944.
4. Quoted in *Ginger Lacey: Fighter Pilot* by Richard Townshend Bickers.
5. It may be noticed that Churchill first offered the position to Lloyd George, whose 'outlook on the war and the events leading up to it', as Churchill tactfully expresses it, 'was from a different angle from mine.'

Chapter Three

Duels with Test Group Two-Ten

Meanwhile 'On 13 July,' reports Group Captain Townsend in *Duel of Eagles*, 'a new crowd of Me 110s made their first appearance.' These came from *Erprobungsgruppe* 210, a new autonomous unit that had been formed on 1 July and was not part of any *Geschwader*. Townsend rightly describes its pilots as 'a brave determined lot with a magnificent leader'. They were to have several memorable clashes with Fighter Command's greatest scourge of bombers, its Hawker Hurricanes.

Test Group Two-Ten, to translate its title into English, contained three *Staffeln*, the 1st and 2nd flying Messerschmitt Bf 110s but the 3rd being equipped with Messerschmitt Bf 109s. It was unusual for a *Gruppe* to hold mixed types of aircraft, but then *Erprobungsgruppe* 210 was a most unusual formation. Both its types carried bombs and its tactics were to send the 109s to attack the selected target first, drop their single small bomb, and then gain altitude quickly to cover the 110s as they came in with their two 550lb weapons.

Thus the Test Group's 109s were true fighter-bombers and were very effective, with the result that towards the end of the Battle of Britain, other bomb-carrying 109s would join in the Luftwaffe's assault. Fortunately for the defenders, these later missions were not carried out with the efficiency attained by the pilots of the Test Group's 3rd *Staffel* and proved to be little more than nuisance raiders. Despite this lack of success though, it must still be a tribute to the Luftwaffe that it could find a fighter-bomber so early in the war, whereas the RAF first gained one in April 1941, when a suitable adaptation was made to, it is tempting to say 'of course', the Hawker Hurricane.

In addition to its three *Staffeln*, *Erprobungsgruppe* 210 had a *Stabschwarm* (staff flight) of four Messerschmitt Bf 110s, flown by the *Gruppenkommandeur* and his chief administrative officers. They led from the front, the original 'brilliant leader' being *Hauptmann* (Captain)

Walter Rubensdörffer, who had been born in Switzerland but was now Germany's ablest bomber pilot. Cool, capable and chivalrous, he was both admired and respected by his men and is described as being 'always in a good temper even in the worst situations' by the eventual commander of the Test Group's 109s, *Oberleutnant* (Lieutenant) Otto Hintze.[1]

As Townsend tells us, *Erprobungsgruppe* 210 made its first strike on 13 July, but it appears that it had flown armed reconnaissance sorties on 10 July, losing one Messerschmitt Bf 110, together with its two-man crew, to anti-aircraft fire. The raid on the 13th was directed against a convoy and during it another 110 was hit by flak. It managed to return to base, but it may be mentioned that by the end of October, the Group had lost four more Bf 110s and a Bf 109 to ground fire. This was not surprising, for it specialized in low-level attacks against selected and often strongly-defended targets.

It was during another convoy raid on 29 July that *Erprobungsgruppe* 210 had its first encounter with Hurricanes. On this occasion, its eleven 110s were protected by a separate formation of thirty 110s from *Zestörergeschwader* 26. As Rubensdörffer's men went for the convoy, the Hurricanes, which came from 151 Squadron, attacked them and caused some damage before being pounced on from above and driven off by ZG 26, the pilots of which claimed to have shot down four of them. Happily, in reality no Hurricanes fell and although two were badly damaged, they got back to base and were later repaired.

This ability of the Hurricanes to survive punishment was in fact of priceless value to the RAF. It enabled the squadrons' brave, skilful and loyal ground crews to make many damaged Hurricanes battle-worthy again in a surprisingly short time. For those machines that could not be dealt with at their base, there was created the Hurricane Repair Network, which included aircraft factories, general engineering works and even furnishing companies. These proved so effective that 35 per cent of the Hurricanes received by squadrons during the Battle of Britain were repaired aircraft and in the war as a whole more than 4,000 wounded Hurricanes were restored to fly and fight again.

This durability ensured that the Luftwaffe could never overcome Fighter Command by simple attrition: at the worst stage of the Battle of Britain there were still eighty Hurricanes in reserve. Sadly, though, this durability would lead to some unfair denigration of the Hurricane.

Fighter Command's C-in-C, Air Chief Marshal Sir Hugh Dowding, has been widely quoted as having checked the average maximum speed of six Hurricanes at 305 miles per hour, more than 20 mph below the figure usually claimed. It is clear, though, that the aircraft examined were repaired machines and very battle-scarred ones at that.

Reverting to the duels between Dowding's most numerous fighters and the Luftwaffe's most capable attack formation, their first encounter, as we have seen, came on 29 July. Their second came on the 30th. Always ready to change tactics in the hope of confusing his opponents, Rubensdörffer sent out his men in ones and twos to make hit-and-run strikes on British vessels. However, these did no damage and one pair of Bf 110s was spotted by a couple of Hurricanes of 85 Squadron flown by Canadian Flight Lieutenant Hamilton and Yorkshireman Flight Sergeant Geoffrey Allard who had been 85's most successful pilot in the Battle of France. After a hectic low-level chase, the Hurricanes got within range of one of the raiders and their hasty but deadly fire sent this plunging into the sea.

On 2 August a larger raid by *Erprobungsgruppe* 210 proved more successful. It sank a Royal Navy trawler and avoided interception. Thereafter the Group ceased operations temporarily while settling down to train for and practise the precision strikes it would be called on to make when the major assault on Britain began. This was difficult and dangerous work and the Group had a number of fatal accidents, including on 7 August that of *Hauptmann* Valesi, *Staffelkapitän* of the Group's 109 unit. This was a serious blow, for Valesi was a fine pilot whose experience harked back to a stint in the German Condor Legion during the Spanish Civil War.

'Eagle Day', the start of Göring's major assault, would take place on 13 August but there were heavy preliminary raids on both the 11th and 12th, with *Erprobungsgruppe* 210 well to the fore. Early on the 11th, its pilots attacked Dover Harbour, again avoiding any interception. At midday the Group attacked convoy BOOTY off the East Anglian coast. This time it did encounter RAF fighters and two of its Bf 110s were shot down: one by Spitfires; the other by Hurricanes of 17 Squadron.

Then came 12 August and *Erprobungsgruppe* 210's most dramatic attack. The Luftwaffe chiefs planned to destroy British radar stations, thus in effect blinding Fighter Command just before 'Eagle Day'. They were small, difficult targets and inevitably the Group was entrusted with the task of knocking some of them out. Rubensdörffer had his sights on four radar stations. He intended that his three *Staffelkapitäne* should strike at different sites with four aircraft each, while he personally led the four machines of the *Stabschwarm* against the fourth one. He would take his whole force westward down the Channel with each *Staffel* in turn breaking away to deliver the individual attacks; a daring tactic that deservedly achieved complete surprise. His pilots were ordered to aim at the foot of the tall masts towering over the radar stations; this should ensure that the bombs would hit something vital on the sites.

At 1030 *Erprobungsgruppe* 210 took off and headed to the west. *Oberleutnant* Otto Hintze was the first to swing away with the 109s of his 3rd *Staffel*, heading for the radar station at Dover. Next *Oberleutnant* Wilhelm-Richard Rössiger led the 110s of 2nd *Staffel* towards the station at Rye; then *Oberleutnant* Martin Lutz and the 110s of 1st *Staffel* made for the one at Pevensey near Eastbourne. Finally, Rubensdörffer's own Staff Flight swept round to race north-eastward towards the station at Dunkirk on the north coast of Kent, covering the Thames Estuary.

As the attackers hurtled towards their objectives, the members of the Women's Auxiliary Air Force reading the messages their radar gave them began to realize that they were going to be the targets. Yet they remained stoically at their posts, relaying details of the enemy to the Operations Room at Fighter Command Headquarters, and continued to do so right up to the moment that bombs rained down all around them. While explosions shook the Operations hut at Rye, Fighter Command telephoned urgently: 'Air raid warning Red.' 'Hell's teeth!' retorted the WAAF telephonist, with admirable restraint, 'You're telling us!'

Fortunately for Fighter Command, Rubensdörffer's audacious assault did not receive the rewards that it probably deserved. Though almost every bomb dropped fell within the perimeters of the radar stations, none of them were destroyed and the damage done was less than anticipated. Even so, all except Dunkirk were put 'off the air' temporarily and once again the speed and daring of the attackers enabled them to escape without any losses.

Moreover, taking advantage of the momentary gap in the radar coverage, the Luftwaffe threw in a number of heavy raids. These knocked the radar station at Ventnor on the Isle of Wight out of action for three important days and severely damaged dockyard installations at Portsmouth and the airfields at Hawkinge and Lympne. Nor had *Erprobungsgruppe* 210 finished for 12 August. This time their sortie was intercepted by Spitfires, but only a single 110 was lost and at about 1250, the bulk of the Group made a spectacular low-level assault on the forward aerodrome at Manston, Kent, while Dornier Do 17s from KG 2 bombed from higher altitudes. Considerable damage was done and Manston briefly rendered non-operational.

After all the build-up, 'Eagle Day' proved a rather tragic farce for Göring's men. Bad weather, made worse by bad communications, led to bomber formations being sent without fighter protection and fighter units appearing without the bombers they were there to protect. *Erprobungsgruppe* 210 took no part in the day's activities, but on 14 August it was back, making another low-level attack on Manston aerodrome, destroying four hangars and three Blenheims on the ground. Anti-aircraft gunners put up a resolute resistance and shot down two Bf 110s. The gunner of one of these somehow managed to bale out and landed on the aerodrome. Though understandably shaken, he warned his captors that their annihilation was imminent.

This was certainly what Göring intended. On 15 August his Luftwaffe flew more than 2,000 sorties and for the first and last time in the battle, *Luftflotten* 2 and 3 were joined by *Luftflotte* 5 in Norway and Denmark. The fighting lasted virtually all day and covered virtually the whole of England, but everywhere Fighter Command held the attackers.

Naturally *Erprobungsgruppe* 210 was not to be left out of the fighting. Early that afternoon, the indefatigable Rubensdörffer led his men in another low-level raid, this one against the RAF base at Martlesham Heath in Suffolk. The Hurricanes of 17 Squadron had been ordered to transfer there, but luckily only three aircraft had so far arrived and these managed to take off just in time before the Test Group hurtled into the attack. Its bombing was extremely accurate, destroying or badly damaging hangars, equipment stores and workshops, wrecking the water and telephone services, putting the aerodrome out of action for forty-eight hours and leaving it 'a heap of smoking rubble'.

Though Fighter Command had directed several squadrons against the Group, only the Hurricanes of No. 1 succeeded in making contact. This unit had achieved marvels in the Battle of France, but so exhausted were its personnel that most had been sent to operational training units to rest and impart their knowledge to others. Their successors on 15 August were much less experienced and in any case had been sent off far too late.

Consequently, No. 1's Hurricanes were still climbing, at their most vulnerable, when Rubensdörffer's men attacked them from above, shooting down three of them without loss. Flight Lieutenant Brown, one of the few remaining veterans from the squadron's days in France, baled out safely but both the other pilots were killed.[2] At this moment the advantage in the duel between the Hurricane and *Erprobungsgruppe* 210 was definitely held by the latter, but the balance would change, completely and horribly, before the day was over.

For their final attacks of the day, the Luftwaffe chiefs had decided to target RAF aerodromes south of London and had entrusted this duty to various formations of Dornier Do 17s and to *Erprobungsgruppe* 210. The Group's objective was the airfield at Kenley and since it was anticipated that heavy opposition would be encountered, Rubensdörffer's fifteen Bf 110s and eight Bf 109s were supposed to have been given additional protection by further 109s from JG 52. These, unfortunately, did not make contact with their charges, but knowing that part of his task was to act as a diversion, the gallant Rubensdörffer proceeded with his mission anyway.

In order that he could both confuse the defenders and attack out of the sun, Rubensdörffer led his men in a wide sweep to the north over the London suburbs, then turned back to the south. Emerging from cloud, he found an aerodrome right in front of him. Believing this to be Kenley, he attacked immediately; his bombers, with their usual deadly efficiency, causing considerable damage and 260 casualties, 68 of them fatal.

In reality, the aerodrome sighted was Croydon, just a short distance north-west of Kenley. This was the home of No. 111, another Hurricane unit, and indeed the first to receive these then entirely new monoplanes back in December 1937. Squadron Leader John Thompson had just enough time to get nine Hurricanes airborne and away from danger before the bombs crashed down. Having got clear, he led them back to deliver one of the terrifyingly effective if highly dangerous head-on assaults in which 'Treble One', as the squadron was widely known, had come to specialize. Thompson personally encountered a 110 that was just pulling up after its attack and gave it a quick burst of fire. 'Masses of bits flew off,' he reported later and the 110 crashed in a nearby field.

At the same time, another Hurricane squadron attacked the Test Group from the flank. Warning of the raid threatening Croydon had reached 32 Squadron, based at Biggin Hill but then on patrol. Flight Lieutenant Michael Crossley, 32's finest pilot, has left a vivid report of his unit's reaction:

> We turned round and beat it for Croydon as fast as we could. Sure enough when we approached I saw a large party in progress. Masses of Me 110s were dive-bombing the place. As they did not appear to notice our approach, I steered straight past them with the object of getting between them and the sun. This was successful and we charged at them. I attacked a Dornier 17 [really a 110] from astern and opened fire at 200 yards, setting the port engine on fire. I broke away. Red Two closed in and shot some pieces off it. He then gave way to Red Three who also hit it. We followed. The fire appeared to go out, giving place to two streams of white smoke. Red Two and Three went in and knocked it about so badly that it crashed E of Sevenoaks.

Most of 32's pilots, however, attacked the Bf 109s of the Test Group's 3rd *Staffel*. Pilot Officer Anthony Barton shot down one of these, several other pilots believed that they had at least caused some damage and in any case the 109s were now dangerously low on fuel. They therefore dived away and headed for home, leaving the luckless 110s to the avenging Hurricanes from 'Treble One'.

Thompson's men found the 110s formed in a defensive circle. This in theory enabled each aircraft to give fire support to the ones in front of and behind it. In practice, it was a bad tactic to adopt if faced by the highly manoeuvrable Hurricanes and the British pilots cynically called it the 'circle of death'. Rubensdörffer tried to inch towards cloud cover in the south, but the nimble Hurricanes stayed with the 110s until they suddenly separated and raced away in different directions.

At once the Hurricanes were after them. Sergeant Craig destroyed one 110, Sergeant Dymond destroyed another, and Flight Lieutenant Connors and Sergeant Wallace accounted for a third between them. Yet another 110 fled across Surrey and part of Sussex before Squadron Leader Thompson was able to get in a lethal burst of fire that sent it flaming down to earth near Rotherfield, its blazing remains marking the funeral pyre of *Hauptmann* Rubensdörffer and his gunner *Feldwebel* (Sergeant Major) Ehekercher. The last action of the valiant Rubensdörffer was to tug his falling aircraft away from a cottage, to crash on its far side.

The Luftwaffe had its own name for 15 August: Black Thursday. To no unit could this have seemed more appropriate than to *Erprobungsgruppe* 210. It had lost more than six 110s and one 109; it had lost its *Gruppenkommandeur*, its adjutant *Oberleutnant* Fiedeler and its operations officer *Leutnant* Koch. Much to their credit, its surviving pilots did not lose heart or enthusiasm, but their efficiency seems never again to have reached the exceptional level they had achieved when directed by their remarkable first commander.

Thus on 20 August the Group, under its new leader *Hauptmann* von Boltenstern, made another attack on the aerodrome at Martlesham Heath. It clearly took the defences by surprise, but the bombing was inaccurate and caused little damage. In addition, the Group was pursued by Spitfires as it retired and lost another Bf 110. On the 22nd, it first attacked a convoy in the Channel and later the airfield at Manston, but the former raid did no damage and the latter caused only minor damage and no casualties. Moreover on the 28th, two of the Group's 109s crashed in landing accidents, one of them being 'written off'.

On 31 August, the Group again raided Croydon and resumed its duel with the Hawker Hurricane. Croydon was now the base for Peter Townsend's 85 Squadron and the Group almost caught its Hurricanes on the ground. The squadron diary tells the story:

Croydon 31/8/40. Twelve Hurricanes took off 1225 hours to intercept E/A [enemy aircraft] approaching the aerodrome. Bombs started to fall on East side of aerodrome just as aircraft were airborne.

P/O Hemingway fired a burst into an Me 109 and saw much smoke issuing from E/A.

P/O Worrall reported that before baling out a cannon shell hit his A/C [aircraft] behind the cockpit and did not get through the armour plate.

S/L Townsend reported that Jaguars [Bf 110s: this was a name by which they were often called in Fighter Command] circled when threatened by attack although withdrawing SE.

Me 109s protected Jaguars very closely.

Ten Hurricanes landed Croydon between 1340 and 1400 hours.

Once again the squadron diary is maddeningly restrained. It does not mention that other reports describe the bomb blasts 'tossing the fighters about like leaves', that all of them still took off safely only to be engaged from above by the Test Group's Bf 109s and Bf 110s, and that a ferocious fight had followed. In this, honours were about even. Pilot Officer Worrall shot down a 110 before he was hit from behind by another 110 and baled out with splinters in his thigh. In addition, two more 110s were damaged sufficiently badly to result in their force-landing at their base, and two 109s were slightly damaged. On the other hand, two Hurricanes did not come back: one was Worrall's; the other was Townsend's. In *Duel of Eagles*, he describes what happened:

> My thumb was on the firing button, but I never fired. A blast of shot splattered my Hurricane, my left foot was kicked off the rudder-bar, petrol gushed into the cockpit. The shock was so terrific that for a few instants I lost control and went into a steep dive. 'Christ,' I heard myself say, quite softly, as if I'd spilt some tea on the drawing-room carpet. Over on the right a Hurricane [Worrall's] was going down vertically, etching a black line of smoke across the sky.
> Then I straightened out. By some miracle, my Hurricane had not burst into flames… But I still had to land, and did not fancy the densely wooded country below. So I baled out and watched my poor Hurricane dive into the trees and blow up.

Townsend, like Worrall, went to hospital where part of his left big toe had to be amputated. He resumed command of 85 Squadron on 21 September, on crutches.

Early September saw no slackening in *Erprobungsgruppe* 210's attacks on targets in Britain. On the 4th, it made for the radar station at Poling near Worthing in Sussex, but was driven off by the Hurricanes of 601

Squadron. These shot down only a single 110, but this carried to his death Rubensdörffer's successor as *Gruppenkommandeur, Hauptmann* von Boltenstern. On the 6th, the Group, under Martin Lutz, the former leader of 1st *Staffel*, promoted to *Hauptmann* as its new commander, raided targets in Surrey but was again driven off by RAF fighters. Another 110 was lost, but the squadron and type of British fighter responsible are not known. Remembering, however, that if in doubt, Luftwaffe personnel almost invariably claimed they had fought Spitfires, often when there were none within miles, it would seem most probable that whatever the squadron, it was a Hurricane one.

On 7 September Göring turned his main effort against London, thereby, as it transpired, losing the Battle of Britain and ultimately the Second World War. *Erprobungsgruppe* 210 was not part of the assault on Britain's capital but did make a raid on Portsmouth, losing another aircraft, this time a Bf 109, to AA fire. Nor did it participate in the massive raids on 15 September, the defeat of which caused Hitler to postpone his invasion 'indefinitely'. It did, though, make the last attack of the day against Southampton, braving heavy AA fire and getting away before RAF fighters could intervene effectively, but causing only minimal damage.

Even after the invasion threat had lifted, the daylight raids continued, though Göring's only aim now was to reduce Britain's ability to wage war. The Test Group did its best in this respect on 24 September. *Hauptmann* Lutz led eighteen of its Bf 110s, plus others from *Zestörergeschwader* 26 against the Supermarine plant at Woolston, near Southampton. One of the Group's bombers was shot down by flak, but the others scored six hits that damaged the factory, killing almost 100 employees and injuring others. Fortunately, the Germans believed this was a bomber factory and never knew that they had struck a blow at Spitfire production.

Next day the Test Group performed a new role, its Bf 110s acting in effect as pathfinders tasked with marking the target for the benefit of the Heinkel He 111s of KG 55. This was the Bristol Aeroplane Company factory at Filton that produced not only aircraft but aero-engines; it also suffered severe damage and casualties which temporarily halted production, while some twenty new Blenheims or Beaufort torpedo-bombers were destroyed or badly damaged. KG 55 paid for its success with the loss of five Heinkels – one to Spitfires and four to the Hurricanes of 238 Squadron – but the Test Group was not harmed.

That evening, the Group made a further raid on Portsmouth; then on the 27th, nineteen of its 110s again acted as pathfinders for KG 55, which as a result of its previous mishaps had the further protection of twenty-seven more 110s from ZG 26. The target was again the Bristol works at Filton and Fighter Command was ready to defend it. The raiders were intercepted over Somerset and Dorset by both Spitfire and Hurricane squadrons, which scattered and drove away the Heinkels and destroyed six of ZG 26's 110s. Of these, two fell to Spitfires, two to the Hurricanes of 56 Squadron and two to unidentified RAF fighters which, in view of the Luftwaffe's 'Spitfire snobbery', probably again meant to Hurricanes.

Only about ten 110s from *Erprobungsgruppe* 210 fought past the defenders to the Bristol area and the Group paid for its determination with the loss of four of its aircraft. It is customary to give the credit for these to Spitfires from some unknown squadron or squadrons, but it is possible that this view reflects more snobbery than accuracy. The crews of three of the lost aircraft died, but that of the fourth survived as prisoners of war. *Gefreiter* (Sergeant) Zwik was badly wounded, but *Feldwebel* (Sergeant Major) Ebner was unhurt. He was rightly proud of his unit and proved very informative. Fighter Command Intelligence, previously unaware of the Test Group's role, now learned all about it and presumably was suitably impressed. Naturally Ebner was not prepared to admit that he or any of his comrades could possibly have been shot down by anything other than the beautiful graceful Spitfires.

There is, however, evidence to suggest that they may have been. For instance, Pilot Officer Constable-Maxwell of 56 Squadron, a very capable pilot who had previously served in the Battle of France and would later become an 'ace' and rise to the rank of wing commander, claimed to have shot down a Dornier Do 17. In fact, no Dorniers participated in this raid but *Erprobungsgruppe* 210 had in the latter part of August and throughout September flown a late Mark of 110, the Bf 110D. This bore a great resemblance to the Do 17 and was frequently mistaken for it, to the confusion of reports at the time and of subsequent historians.[3] It seems likely then that Constable-Maxwell at least attacked one of the Test Group's 110Ds. His squadron did engage ZG 26 as mentioned above, but that flew the older Bf 110Cs which were unlikely to have been so mistaken.

Furthermore, all accounts agree that it was some of the Group's 110s that fought the final actions of this sortie. Messrs Wood and Dempster tell us in *The Narrow Margin* that 'These were intercepted on the outskirts of Bristol by the Nottingham Squadron which compelled them to release their bombs unprofitably on the suburbs. The survivors were harried all the way back to the coast and out to sea.'

The 'Nottingham Squadron' was No. 504 Auxiliary Air Force, flying Hurricanes, which Dowding had personally sent to Filton aerodrome to provide a last line of defence for the Bristol factory. One of its pilots was Sergeant Charlton 'Wag' Haw who we will meet again in Russia. His Hurricane was damaged in the fight and he had to force-land it in a cornfield – the owner was not pleased – from which it was later rescued and repaired.

Prior to this, Haw believed that he had shot down one of the Test Group's Bf 110s and perhaps damaged another. In all, the pilots of 504 claimed, without loss, to have destroyed six 110s, plus a couple of 'probables'. Since the Group really lost only four aircraft, there were obviously exaggerations here; no doubt instances of more than one pilot engaging the same target. Yet it is impossible to believe that 504 had had no successes at all. Considering all the facts and adding a dash of 'Spitfire snobbery', it seems reasonable to suggest that Hurricanes were responsible for the destruction of some and perhaps all four of the machines lost by their most worthy enemy.

Whoever was responsible, *Erprobungsgruppe* 210 had again suffered grievously; among those who failed to return being its commander Martin Lutz, and the highly-experienced leader of 2nd *Staffel*, *Oberleutnant* Rössiger. A further heavy blow fell on the Group on 5 October, when eighteen of its Bf 110s attacked the airfield of West Malling in Kent. They were opposed by No. 303, a Polish Hurricane squadron commanded by British Squadron Leader Ronald Kellett. Once again the Hurricanes had much the better of the encounter, preventing any serious injury to the aerodrome, shooting down two 110s and damaging two others which had to force-land at their base. Among those lost was *Oberleutnant* Werner Weimann, the unit's fourth *Gruppenkommandeur* to die.

Yet another clash between *Erprobungsgruppe* 210 and its deadliest enemies came on 29 October, when the Group's 3rd *Staffel* of bomb-carrying Bf 109s, led by *Oberleutnant* Otto Hintze, struck at North

Weald, home of the Hurricanes of 249 and 257 Squadrons. These were just taking off when the first bombs fell just in front of them. The Hurricane of Sergeant Girdwood caught the full fury of the blast; it turned upside down, dived into the ground and exploded, killing the pilot. The Hurricane of Polish Pilot Officer Surma was badly damaged, but he was able to gain sufficient height to bale out safely. Several other Hurricanes were savagely shaken but remained intact. The Hurricanes of 249 Squadron were less affected and set off after the 109s. Flight Lieutenant Robert Barton shot down one of these and Otto Hintze became a prisoner of war.

Erprobungsgruppe 210 would make later raids – on 17 November it lost three more Bf 110s to Hurricanes, this time from 17 Squadron, during a raid in the Ipswich area – and it would later turn to night bombing, but its great period as a low-level strike specialist throughout the Battle of Britain had passed. It has been questioned whether its achievements were worth the casualties it suffered, but no one could fail to respect the skill, courage and determination of its pilots and gunners and their refusal to be daunted by the loss during the battle of so many good men, including four *Gruppenkommandeur* and its three most experienced *Staffelkapitäne*. It was a unit of which any air force in the world could justly be proud.

Yet the opposition it had faced had been too much for it and the best of that opposition had been provided by Hawker Hurricanes. Apart from those lost in accidents, twenty-eight of Test Group Two-Ten's warplanes had fallen in combat between 10 July and 29 October. Of these, British AA guns had claimed six: to those already mentioned must be added a Bf 110 brought down on a reconnaissance flight on 25 July. Spitfires had definitely destroyed three and if the one lost on 6 September and all four of those lost on 27 September fell to Spitfires – which frankly is difficult to accept – their total 'bag' was eight. Hurricanes destroyed perhaps as many as nineteen of the Group's aircraft and at the very least fourteen, which was as many as the Spitfires and the gunners put together.

Of course the Hurricanes did have one advantage: there were so many more of them about. That, though, was part of their importance. Easy to build, easy to service, easy to fly, easy to repair and very hard to hurt, the Hawker Hurricane had become the backbone of the defence of the British Isles. It was also, by this time, acknowledged to be adaptable and versatile: an aircraft that could 'go anywhere, do anything'. It would need to be.

Notes

1. Quoted in Peter Townsend's *Duel of Eagles*. As a branch of the German army, Luftwaffe personnel held army ranks and, perhaps because they were not in a separate service, the commanders of Luftwaffe units often carried a lower rank than they would have done in the Royal Air Force. Thus Rubensdörffer as a *Hauptmann* was equivalent to a flight lieutenant, but an officer in a similar RAF command would have been a squadron leader or even a wing commander; Hintze as an *Oberleutnant* was equivalent to a flying officer, but a similar RAF officer would have been a flight lieutenant or even a squadron leader.
2. After the Battle of Britain, 1 Squadron, still flying Hurricanes, gained a new reputation as a night-fighter unit, both on the defensive and on intruder missions over occupied Europe. Special mention should be made of Flight Lieutenant Karel Kuttelwascher, a Czech whose fifteen 'kills' during the hours of darkness were the most gained by any pilot of a Royal Air Force single-engined fighter.
3. There are numerous examples of this; we may take some more or less at random. As already noticed, on 15 August a pilot of the calibre of Flight Lieutenant Crossley mistook one of the Test Group's Bf 110s for a Dornier Do 17. On 15 September, the same mistake was made by the pilots of 607 (Hurricane) Squadron, the only one to sight though unable effectively to engage the Group when it raided Southampton. On 31 August, during the raid on Croydon, some reports state that bombs had been dropped by Dornier Do 17s. 'If so, I never saw them,' retorts Peter Townsend. There were in fact none to see. The bombers were Test Group Two-Ten's Messerschmitt Bf 110Ds.

Chapter Four

East African Achievement

*'Long live the Duce and the King.
The British will pay for everything.
On land and sea and in the air
They'll compensate us everywhere.'*

This piece of doggerel was found in a letter home from an Italian soldier in North Africa when it fell into the hands of Allied Intelligence; it is quoted in *The Desert War* by the Australian war correspondent Alan Moorehead. In it may be summarized the ambition of Benito Mussolini when, on 10 June 1940, he declared war on a Britain he thought was doomed to imminent and inevitable defeat.

To the Italian dictator, it must have seemed all too easy. The long peninsula of Italy, extended by the island of Sicily, flanked to the west by Sardinia and to the east by Albania which Mussolini had annexed in April 1939, seemed designed by nature to threaten the central Mediterranean with its fine modern fleet. In North Africa the Italian colony of Libya threatened the British bases in Egypt. Finally, in East Africa there was a solid block of Italian territory, with Italy's older colonies of Eritrea and Italian Somaliland enclosing Abyssinia, as Ethiopia was then generally known, which Mussolini had seized in 1936.

Though largely forgotten or ignored, Italian East Africa also posed a number of threats to British interests. Its troops could advance into the Sudan, threatening from the rear the British forces facing Libya, or alternatively could move southward to menace the British colony of Kenya, and there were more than 250,000 of them on hand, supported by 150 aircraft. In addition, warships based at the Eritrean port of Massawa could endanger the supply line to Egypt through the Red Sea.

The Italian Viceroy of Abyssinia was the Duke of Aosta, a prince of the royal House of Savoy and an honourable humane man who had done much to reconcile the local population to their conquerors, aided by the

42   Hurricanes in Action Worldwide

Map 2: Hurricane operations in East Africa.

fact that many of the different tribes were permanently hostile to their neighbours and liked the Italians better – or at least disliked them less – than they did each other. Aosta was a determined character and though ordered by his superiors in Rome to stand on the defensive, he captured the forts of Kassala and Gallabat in the Sudan and Moyale in Kenya and had overrun the whole of British Somaliland by 19 August.

Meanwhile, though, the British were building up their own strength, heartened by the news that Hurricanes were reaching East Africa; few in numbers but every one an asset of tremendous value. Hurricanes had in fact arrived in East Africa even before Mussolini had declared war, courtesy of the Union of South Africa. In May 1940, No. 1 Squadron South African Air Force was equipped with four Hurricanes and six old Hawker Fury biplanes and as the threat from Italy became more and more obvious, arrangements were made to get these aircraft to Kenya. The biplanes were shipped there, arriving on 1 June, while the Hurricanes, under the command of the splendidly-named Lieutenant Servaas van Breda Theron,[1] were flown to Nairobi, which they reached on 25 May.

Also on the 25th, eighteen Junkers Ju 86s arrived at Nairobi. Before the war, these had carried passengers for South African Airways but the Germans had originally designed them as bombers and in 1939 they were transferred to the South African Air Force along with their crews and converted back to bombers. In Kenya they were formed into two squadrons and, on 19 June, three of them were sent to raid the aerodrome at Yavello in southern Abyssinia. To escort them, a pair of 1 SAAF's Hurricanes set out on their first operational sortie.

It would be a disappointing start. The formation duly attacked the airfield, the Hurricanes strafing three Caproni Ca 133 three-engined bombers that they caught on the ground. However, the pilots were themselves taken by surprise by two Fiat CR 32 biplane fighters that dived out of the sun. One of the Junkers was damaged and one Hurricane went down in flames, 2nd Lieutenant Griffiths being killed. Happily, Captain Truter, the other Hurricane pilot, was more fortunate: he evaded all attacks made on him and downed one of the CR 32s.[2]

During late July, two extra Hurricanes, three Furies and nine Gladiators from Egypt were added to 1 SAAF's strength. In early August, however, when another nine Gladiators that had been meant to reinforce the squadron arrived at Khartoum, it was decided to retain them there to assist in the defence of the Sudan. Other fighters were sent to the Sudan later and on 30 September all aircraft there were incorporated into 1 SAAF, while the squadron's machines in Kenya, including the five Hurricanes, became No. 2 SAAF.

Kenya had now played host to two South African Air Force Hurricane squadrons and on 24 October it received No. 3 SAAF, bringing the welcome addition of nine Hurricanes and the promise of more to follow. Their pilots were inexperienced, however, so a pair of these aircraft were borrowed by 2 SAAF and flown to a landing-strip just south of the Abyssinian border by Lieutenant Loftus and Flight Lieutenant Blake; the latter, though a South African born in Pretoria, had previously served in the RAF. On the morning of 25 October, they encountered three Savoia Marchetti SM 81s – three-engined transport aircraft that could be used as bombers – and each of them shot down one of these, while Blake also badly damaged the third.

If 3 SAAF's Hurricanes had thus been able to get at the enemy, the squadron's pilots had not and were naturally disappointed. Worse, on 27 October Lieutenant Gould was killed when his Hurricane inexplicably crashed on landing. It was not until 22 November that 3 SAAF had its first clash with Italy's *Regia Aeronautica*, shooting down one Caproni Ca 133 and damaging another so badly that it crash-landed and was 'written off'.

Previously, on 6 November, had come the first modest move towards eliminating the Italian threat in East Africa. Brigadier William Slim, later commander of the Fourteenth Army in Burma, was instructed to regain the Sudanese frontier fort of Gallabat, and then capture its Italian equivalent in Abyssinia, Metemma. The forces involved were about equal in size, but the British and Commonwealth soldiers had the advantage of surprise and were supported by tanks which the Italians lacked.

Unhappily, it seems that neither Slim nor anyone else had considered the Italian aerial strength. Gallabat was taken, but Fiat CR 42 biplane fighters fell on the Gladiators protecting the British advance, shooting down five of these without loss and gaining control of the skies. Slim's move on Metemma was pounded by Italian bombers and broke down amid circumstances of disgraceful panic. Next day, the Italian bombers turned their attention to Gallabat which Slim was forced to abandon. His humiliation was completed a month or so later when he was shot in the buttocks by a strafing CR 42, which must have removed any doubts that he still held of the value of air power.

It was not a good start to the conquest of Italian East Africa and discouraged further attempts for well over a month. On 9 December, however, a British offensive in Egypt, which the Italians had invaded in September, had totally different results.

The Western Desert Force as the British and Commonwealth soldiers in Egypt were known, though vastly inferior in numbers had much better tanks, much better artillery pieces and, best of all, much better fighter aircraft. Hurricanes were now reaching the Middle East in sufficient numbers to give the British control of the air. Shielded and supported by the Hurricanes, the soldiers drove their enemies out of Egypt and then invaded Libya. By 8 February 1941, they had annihilated an Italian army and captured the whole of Cyrenaica, Libya's eastern province.

Sadly, the diversion of British military and air forces to Greece and the arrival of German military and air forces under General Erwin Rommel in North Africa quickly cancelled most of the successes of the Western Desert Force. Nonetheless, they proved an inspiration for separate but connected offensives being planned from both the Sudan and Kenya.

In the Sudan, command was in the hands of General Sir William Platt who originally controlled only the 5th Indian Division.[3] On 16 December, however, the 4th Indian Division which had been detached from the Western Desert Force landed at Port Sudan on the Red Sea, a move that proved vital for Platt's success. The two Indian divisions were intended to attack not from Gallabat into western Abyssinia but from Kassala into Eritrea.

In Kenya, Lieutenant General Sir Alan Cunningham commanded the 11th African Division containing two British-officered brigades, the 21st East African and the 23rd Nigerian, and the similar 12th African Division controlling the 22nd East African Brigade and the 24th from the Gold Coast as Ghana was then called. Attached to the 12th Division was the 1st South African Brigade, which was soon to be joined by the 2nd and 5th South African brigades to form the 1st South African Division under Major General Brink. Cunningham's plan was to strike eastward into Italian Somaliland and as a preliminary on 16 December, the fort at El Wak on the Kenya-Somaliland border was seized at the cost of just two South Africans killed.

Supporting Platt and Cunningham respectively were Air Commodore Slatter controlling 203 Group in the Sudan and Air Commodore Sowrey, the Air Officer Commanding East Africa in Kenya. Their staffs were hard at work throughout December making ready for the dual offensive. This in practice meant ensuring that there were enough Hurricanes on hand. In the Sudan, No. 1 Squadron SAAF was slowly built up to the massive strength of ten of these and also received new pilots in the more than promising persons of a couple of officers from 3 SAAF: Major Laurie Wilmot and Captain Kenneth Driver.

With the determined Wilmot taking over its leadership, 1 Squadron SAAF began to take command of the Sudanese air space. On 16 December, Captain Driver pointed the way by shooting down in flames a Savoia Marchetti SM 79: another three-engined aircraft that, having been specifically designed as a bomber, was a more capable machine than the SM 81. Over the next few days, 1 SAAF's pilots repulsed all enemy raids, damaging several more Italian aircraft including two that force-landed and may have been beyond repair. As the New Year dawned, the British and Indian soldiers were ready to take the offensive and the South African airmen were ready to provide assistance and protection.

In Kenya other South African airmen were also getting ready, though No. 2 SAAF had been having a rather unhappy time. Its Hurricanes were being transferred to the other squadrons and the delivery of a few Gauntlets – biplane fighters that were predecessors of and inferior to the Gladiators – was no consolation. On 29 December, two of its pilots, preparing to strafe an Italian airfield, were shot down by CR 42s. Flight Lieutenant Blake and Lieutenant Kok both baled out only to become prisoners of war. By 3 January 1941, 2 SAAF was no longer a Hurricane unit.

By contrast, No. 3 Squadron SAAF still was, and the mood of its pilots was very different. It had acquired seven more Hurricanes from various sources, though it had passed two of them on to 1 SAAF in the Sudan. It had also received capable pilots to replace Wilmot and Driver – Theron, now a captain, among others – and its own pilots had now gained experience on Hurricanes. Particular mention might be made of Captain John Frost – inevitably known as 'Jack' – who had been with the squadron since it was first formed and would soon prove to be not only its best pilot but the finest in the South African Air Force.

It was against Eritrea, however, that the first British thrust was delivered. The Duke of Aosta, aware that its first objective would be the recapture of Kassala, decided to abandon this and fall back to Agordat and Barentu, medium-sized towns in mountainous country that should prove excellent defensive positions, especially if strongly supported by the *Regia Aeronautica*. The British and Indian troops followed up rapidly and on 19 January 1941 took the forward Italian landing-ground at Sabdaret. To this moved the Hurricanes of 1 SAAF and thereafter there was hardly an hour of daylight during which a pair of Hurricanes were not flying protectively above the advancing soldiers.

On 22 January a flight of three Caproni Ca 133s with fighter escort attacked British motor transport, but were engaged by Hurricanes which shot down one bomber and badly damaged a second one which they later strafed and destroyed on the ground. This apparently inspired the South Africans, because for the rest of the month they concentrated on raiding the main Italian aerodromes at Asmara and Gura, inflicting so much damage that General Pietro Pinna, Aosta's Air Force chief, withdrew almost all his remaining machines from both bases.

These actions effectively gave the British air superiority: the occasional enemy air attack was easily dealt with and the Hurricanes were dominant even over the enemy aerodromes. Captain Driver again gave a fine example. On 29 January he sighted a Savoia Marchetti SM 79 over Gura airfield. This tried to escape at low level, but Driver overtook it. He later reported: 'I fired two bursts into his fuselage and then two more at his starboard engine, which then burst into flames. Two of the crew escaped by parachute before the machine crashed.'

On 31 January Driver encountered another SM 79, this time trying to bomb the British and Indian soldiers. He attacked this and his machine-gun bullets set the fuselage on fire. What happened next is vividly described in *Dust Clouds in the Middle East* by Christopher Shores: 'Four of the crew baled out, but the pilot remained in the aircraft, diving down to zero feet. Driver kept after him and fired another burst, whereupon the pilot jumped clear and the bomber crashed.'

Under cover of 1 SAAF's activities, Agordat and Barentu had both fallen by 2 February and the Hurricanes moved up to their airfields, from which they strafed other Italian air bases with gratifying results. Platt next made for Asmara, Eritrea's capital and Massawa, its main port. On 3 February, however, when halfway to Asmara, he reached Keren where the only passage through a wall of mountains rising over 2,000ft was a deep, narrow gorge held by the bulk of Aosta's reserve, including three battalions of his finest troops, the Savoia Division. Platt's advance came to an abrupt halt and for seven weeks all attempts to renew it were blocked by determined resistance.

It was perhaps little consolation to Platt's men that by drawing Aosta's best soldiers against them they had helped to prepare the way for their colleagues in Kenya. On 24 January Lieutenant General Cunningham made a diversionary attack northward into southern Abyssinia, which resulted in the capture of a number of frontier posts but his main advance was into Italian Somaliland. Like Platt's advance, it was covered and protected by South African Hurricanes, in this case those of 3 SAAF. They would quickly show their worth. On 3 February Captain 'Jack' Frost, who the day before had strafed and destroyed a Caproni Ca 133 on its airfield, sighted three more Capronis, escorted by two Fiat CR 42s, bombing an army camp. He attacked the Fiats, one of which crashed and burst into flames, and apparently he damaged the other which withdrew. Frost then turned his attention onto the Capronis and shot down all three, to the great joy of the cheering soldiers.

An odd sequel to this encounter is that the Italians confirmed the loss of the three more valuable bombers but made no mention of the loss of the CR 42. That it was destroyed is undoubted since there were scores of eyewitnesses who had seen it hit the ground and in his *Dust Clouds in the Middle East*, Christopher Shores reproduces a photograph taken of the wreckage. As a matter of interest, the claims made by the SAAF squadrons for bombers destroyed can usually be confirmed in enemy records but in several cases, those for fighters, despite being observed from the ground, cannot. It may be that this is because the Italians were not too concerned to record the losses of the biplane Fiats since they intended to replace them with more modern machines as soon as possible, or even that they were finding it difficult to get replacements to East Africa in any case. Whatever the reasons, it is impossible not to agree with the mild observation of Mr Shores that the enemy records may not be 'fully correct'.[4]

Later that day, 3 SAAF's Hurricanes demonstrated that they were equally effective in an offensive role, escorting South African Junkers Ju 86s in a raid on the Italian aerodrome at Gobwen and strafing it themselves. Considerable damage was done, several enemy aircraft were destroyed on the ground and Captain Theron shot down a Fiat CR 42 as it tried to take off. Other attacks on landing-grounds followed, one such at Afmadu on 10 February, causing such harm that the Italians abandoned it.

These actions gave 3 SAAF clear air superiority and with Hurricanes protecting and striking at the enemy ahead of them, Cunningham's men advanced on Mogadishu, the capital of Italian Somaliland. It fell without a struggle on 25 February, leaving vast quantities of stores including 350,000 gallons of petrol and 80,000 gallons of aviation fuel in the hands of the victors.

With his supplies thus augmented, on 1 March Cunningham struck northwards into eastern Abyssinia with the Hurricanes again in full support. Italian resistance was minimal on land, but as the soldiers pressed deeper into Abyssinia, the *Regia Aeronautica*, operating from a major air base at Diredawa, showed much more spirit.

Aerial conflicts began in earnest on 13 March, a day of mixed fortunes for 3 SAAF's Hurricanes. It started when Lieutenant Albertus Venter became lost and ran out of fuel, forcing him to land – successfully – in open country. Meanwhile, a pair of Savoia Marchetti SM 79s had attempted to attack 3 SAAF's landing-ground but were chased away by Captain Theron, who damaged one so badly that it force-landed at Diredawa with one crewman dead and three more wounded. In the afternoon, news of Venter's problems and whereabouts was received, so Theron took off again to go to his assistance. Landing next to Venter's Hurricane, Theron managed to siphon off some of his own Hurricane's fuel and both set off back to base.

This, they found, was again under attack from two Fiat CR 42s. Lieutenant Dudley gallantly took off to oppose them, but they pounced on him before he could gain height, shot down his Hurricane and killed him. Just at this juncture, Theron and Venter appeared overhead and on a signal from Theron, dived on the Fiats from above. Theron's first burst of fire missed, but he was more successful on his second attempt as his target pulled up. As Theron later reported: 'He then did a somersault turn and went in from about 1,000 ft.' Venter was equally successful, sending the second CR 42 down in flames. The pilot baled out and was later entertained in 3 SAAF's mess.

On 15 March 3 SAAF's Hurricanes retaliated with strikes on Diredawa aerodrome, destroying or badly damaging thirteen Italian warplanes on the ground. The sole defence was provided by a single Italian machine-gunner, but this resolute character shot down and killed Captain Harvey and also hit the Hurricane flown by the redoubtable Captain Frost. The result is graphically described in Leo McKinstry's *Hurricane: Victor of the Battle of Britain*:

> With glycol streaming from his engine, Frost had to make an emergency landing at a satellite airstrip. He then immediately jumped out of his plane, set it on fire to prevent its capture and ran for cover as he came under attack from Italian artillery and troops. Almost surrounded, his fate appeared to be sealed. But then his SAAF comrade Bob Kershaw, who had seen Frost make his emergency landing, swept down on the same airfield and yelled to Frost to leap on board. Moments later, Kershaw was airborne again, Frost on his lap and bullets racing past the Hurricane. Squeezed in the cockpit together, they were somehow able to make it back to their base, Kershaw operating the rudder's pedals and Frost the control column.

Lieutenant Kershaw's 'selfless bravery' was acknowledged with a DSO, the first awarded to a pilot in East Africa.

By this time, the Italians had decided that they would have to abandon British Somaliland. Their intention became known to British Intelligence and on 16 March a force from Aden landed at the port of Berbera. This quickly recaptured the whole colony and provided Cunningham with a nearer supply point that enabled his men to continue their rapid advance.

Platt's men, though, were still being held at Keren. The Hurricanes of 1 SAAF had not been idle: between 3 and 12 February they had destroyed three Caproni Ca 133s on the ground and shot down or caused to crash-land at least three Fiat CR 42s and a Fiat CR 32. One Hurricane had gone down but that only because Lieutenant Viljoen had run out of fuel and been compelled to force-land, luckily behind his own lines; moreover his aircraft was later retrieved and repaired. These successes, however, did not enable the British land forces to break through Keren's defences and on 12 February, mounting casualties brought their attacks to a temporary halt.

Platt then began to build up his strength for renewed assaults. This gave General Pinna's airmen a splendid chance to attack his lines of communication, but they soon found 1 SAAF's pilots were ready for the challenge. On 13 February they shot down a Fiat CR 42 and a Fiat CR

32 and damaged another three fighters, one so badly that it force-landed at its base. On the 15th, one more CR 42 was destroyed and another so damaged that it crash-landed. On neither day did 1 SAAF suffer any losses.

Indeed it was the Italian ground troops that suffered most, for Major Wilmot, 1 SAAF's aggressive CO, now directed his men in strafing attacks upon them. He was also determined to seek out the enemy airmen on their own bases and Hurricane raids on Italian landing-grounds were made on 19, 20, 21 and 23 February, causing considerable damage, though sadly they did result in South African losses. On the 21st, Lieutenant Coetzer was killed by AA fire and on the 23rd, Wilmot was brought down. He had come in at very low level to strafe a CR 32 that was on the point of taking off. This was set on fire – the pilot managed to escape – but before Wilmot could gain height he was attacked by another CR 32 that had taken off earlier. He crash-landed on the aerodrome and became a prisoner of war. One of his pilots, Lieutenant Andrew Duncan, promptly shot down the CR 32 responsible.

Not even the capture of their CO could check the ardour of 1 SAAF's pilots. They continued their attacks on enemy troop positions and aerodromes, and on 15 March, under cover of raids by them and other Air Force units, Platt resumed his efforts to break through the Keren defences. Desperately the Italian army commanders appealed for help to General Pinna, who did his best to assist. On 18 March Italian fighters and bombers struck at 1 SAAF's base at Agordat, destroying one Hurricane on the ground, badly damaging another and slightly damaging a third. It was a good effort, but it had no effect on 1 SAAF's activities.

On the contrary, the next few days saw the squadron achieve further successes. On the 21st, Captain Driver hit a Fiat CR 42 which crash-landed at its base, while Lieutenant Robin Pare shot down two others. Next day the squadron downed a further two Fiats and on the 25th, Pare destroyed one more and so damaged another that it was 'written off', while his colleagues damaged two more less seriously. On the 27th, Platt's men finally forced their way through the Keren defences. They had lost more than 500 dead and in excess of 3,000 wounded and the Italians retired in good order, but the conquest of Eritrea was at last ensured. Its capital, Asmara, fell on 1 April, by which time the Hurricanes were already strafing Italian transport fleeing down the road to the port of Massawa, which was captured on the 8th.

It is sad to have to report that in these last days of the campaign, two of 1 SAAF's pilots were killed when their Hurricanes crashed, one as he was trying to return to base after combat damage and the other in a landing accident. The South Africans were, however, delighted to learn that Platt's advancing army had liberated Major Wilmot. They flew their last sorties in East Africa on 5 April, strafing ground positions and airfields. Next day they left for Egypt, where they would add to their laurels in the seemingly endless North African campaigns.

While Platt's troops were at last moving on Asmara, the capital of Eritrea, Cunningham's men were continuing their amazing advance towards Addis Ababa, the capital of Abyssinia. This was now aided by a horrific incident that shook both the British and Italians. At Diredawa, native troops turned on the large Italian civilian population, looting, raping, murdering and mutilating. The authorities sent a frantic plea for help to the British, who by then were at Harar, 50 miles to the south-east. A South African force was rushed to Diredawa on 29 March, and after a day and a night of street-fighting, quelled these armed thugs, as well as securing Diredawa airport, which became an advance base for 3 SAAF's Hurricanes.

These were still assisting Cunningham's progress and grappling with the *Regia Aeronautica*. On 28 March, the Italians attacked British landing-grounds and the Hurricanes of Captain Theron and Lieutenant Venter hastily took off to oppose them. They had hardly become airborne before Theron's aircraft was hit by 'friendly' AA fire, and as he tried to land he was attacked by a Fiat CR 32. The Hurricane was set on fire but Theron managed to land it, sprang out and, despite a wounded leg, ran to safety. Venter's Hurricane was damaged, but he shot down a CR 32 and returned safely. Other Hurricanes were now getting aloft and the indefatigable Captain Frost overtook some CR 42s and shot down one of them.

After this, the Hurricanes acted mainly on the offensive, strafing Italian positions and motor transport, escorting the Junkers Ju 86s on bombing raids which broke up a planned Italian defence on the Awash River, and especially assaulting aerodromes, including that at Addis Ababa. The Duke of Aosta feared that resistance might cause a repetition on a larger scale of the horrors at Diredawa. He therefore abandoned the capital, which was occupied by Cunningham's men on 6 April, much to the relief of the Italian population, while the pilots of 3 SAAF turned their attention to raids on airfields elsewhere.

These strikes wrecked numbers of enemy aircraft on the ground: ten at Dessie on 6 April, for example, and eight at Jimma on the 10th. Air battles during this period cost the Italians at least two CR 42s and two CR 32s destroyed or 'written off' and another CR 42 and two SM 79s force-landed, but the South Africans suffered no further casualties until 24 April, when Lieutenant Howitson was killed by AA fire. The *Regia Aeronautica* had now been all but eliminated and it was Captain Frost, appropriately enough, who shot down the last airworthy SM 79 on 30 April.

On retiring from Addis Ababa, the Duke of Aosta had moved to the mountainous northern region of Abyssinia around Amba Alagi. Here he was attacked by British and Indian troops coming south from Eritrea, but the decisive pressure came from South African troops coming north from Addis Ababa supported by the Hurricanes of 3 SAAF, which destroyed nine Italian petrol vehicles on 7 May. Aosta surrendered to the South Africans on 19 May; they responded by giving his men a guard of honour.

Soon after this, the 1st South African Division was sent to North Africa, where it would form a valuable part of the famous Eighth Army,[5] but there were still several groups of enemies in the field even after the surrender at Amba Alagi and 3 SAAF's airmen continued to oppose these, now in a ground-attack role. On 20 May, though, the squadron lost its leading 'ace' when Captain Frost fell victim to acute appendicitis. He recovered in hospital and later fought in North Africa as CO of 5 Squadron SAAF, flying Tomahawks, adding to his reputation until he died in action on 16 June 1942.

Another notable pilot of 3 SAAF was lost while still serving with this squadron in Abyssinia. We have already observed some of Lieutenant Venter's varied experiences. On 24 May he added to these when a truck he was strafing at very low level blew up and so damaged his Hurricane that it crashed on landing. Venter was unhurt, but his luck was running out. On 3 June he was caught in bad weather and flew into the side of a mountain, being killed instantly.

In later 'mopping-up' operations in the summer of 1941, 3 SAAF lost three more Hurricanes in action or by accident but all the pilots survived.

In August, the squadron began to re-equip with Curtiss Mohawks and in early September handed over its few remaining Hurricanes to 41 Squadron SAAF which had previously flown old Hawker biplanes. This unit saw no aerial combats, but it carried out close support missions until 28 November 1941 when the fortress of Gondar in north-west Abyssinia surrendered. It was the final event of the East African campaign in which the Hurricane had played a decisive and indispensable part.

Notes

1. The members of the South African Air Force, like those of the Luftwaffe, carried army ranks. Theron would ultimately reach that of brigadier.
2. Earlier on this same 19 June, the Hurricane had made its first 'kills' of Italian aircraft in the war when Flying Officer Wykeham-Barnes of 80 Squadron had downed two CR 42s, aircraft superior to the CR 32s, over Egypt. This officer later dropped the name of 'Barnes' and we have already met him as the author of *Fighter Command*.
3. In reality, this and all other 'Indian' divisions were British-Indian divisions. Each was divided into brigades, normally three in number, and each brigade into battalions, again normally three of them. It was the usual practice for the men of one battalion in every 'Indian' brigade to be British, while those of the other two were Indians or Gurkhas.
4. Christopher Shores can speak with great authority on the air war in East Africa since the Italians paid him the high but well-deserved compliment of asking him to join General Corrado Ricci in writing their *Official History* of this. Incidentally, one of the witnesses on the ground who confirmed the destruction of the CR 42 was George Adamson, the naturalist and conservationist of *Born Free* fame.
5. It may be mentioned that when South Africa had declared war on Germany, this had been conditional on her soldiers serving only in 'Southern Africa'. This term had quickly been extended to include East Africa. It was now further extended to include North Africa and would later include Europe, with the 6th South African Armoured Division fighting valiantly in Italy until the end of hostilities.

Chapter Five

Faith, Hope and Hurricanes

Other Hurricanes had for many months been playing an equally vital role in the campaigns fought over and for the island of Malta. In the early months of 1940, a handful of them had reached Malta by way of France and Tunisia but all had been sent on to Egypt, chiefly to protect Admiral Sir Andrew Cunningham's Mediterranean Fleet. After Italy's declaration of war, however, the protection of Malta had become essential. She lay right in the path of the supply routes to North Africa and from her, aircraft, submarines and surface vessels could decimate Axis convoys, with decisive effects on the fighting in the Western Desert.

By the end of June 1940, four Hurricanes under South African Flight Lieutenant Barber had returned from Egypt to join Malta's Fighter Flight. Unfortunately, their arrival has been largely masked by the delightful legend that the island's early defence was carried out by three Sea Gladiators which 'the grateful people of Malta' named 'Faith, Hope and Charity': a phrase that gave historian Kenneth Poolman a good title for his book about the island's ordeals.

Sadly, it is only a legend. In reality, there were probably half a dozen Sea Gladiators available, with rarely more than three airborne at the same time; the names were invented by enterprising journalists in Britain, and the Air Officer Commanding, Air Commodore (later Air Vice-Marshal) Maynard only learned of them after he had left the island. It would be more accurate, as Mr Poolman gracefully implies in a chapter title, to say that Malta's survival rested on faith (in the justice of her cause), hope (that she would be able to endure her coming ordeals) and Hurricanes which for almost two years formed the backbone of her defences.

On 3 July Flying Officer John Waters shot down a Savoia Marchetti SM 79 and although he was then attacked by Fiat CR 42 fighters, he crash-landed without injury. This first Hurricane victory was followed by several others, and despite the heavy odds against them, their pilots enjoyed a seemingly miraculous immunity until 16 July.

It appears that Flight Lieutenant Peter Keeble took off on the 16th in a blind rage, having learned of the death of a brother. He attacked a group of CR 42s single-handed and although one came down and its pilot was killed, Keeble's Hurricane crashed in the same field and he also died. His loss came as a warning that if Malta was to survive, more Hurricanes must be provided.

In consequence, twelve Hurricanes of 418 Flight were hastily loaded onto the elderly aircraft carrier *Argus*, which set out for the Mediterranean. The importance of this mission, which with neat double-meaning was code-named Operation HURRY, may be judged from the fact that *Argus* was guarded by *Ark Royal*, aircraft from which made preventative attacks on airfields in Sardinia, battleships *Valiant* and *Resolution*, cruisers *Enterprise* and *Arethusa* and ten destroyers.

On 2 August, accompanied by two Fleet Air Arm Skuas as guides, the Hurricanes took off from *Argus* without any trouble and all of them reached Malta safely. Unfortunately, Sergeant 'Fred' Robertson celebrated his arrival too enthusiastically with a low-level 'beat up' of Luqa airfield. His engine cut, apparently because of a shortage of fuel and, as onlookers would recall, his Hurricane 'turned upside down and went through three stone walls'. Happily the Hurricane's strength once more proved a lifesaver. Robertson escaped with minor concussion and would become one of Malta's most successful defenders, his victories including the destruction of a Savoia Marchetti SM 79 on the night of 18 December.

Ground crews and spare parts for the Hurricanes also reached Malta in submarines and Sunderland flying-boats and the new arrivals joined the Hurricanes and Gladiators of the old Fighter Flight[1] to form 261 Squadron under Squadron Leader Balden. Later commanded by Squadron Leader Trumble in December 1940 and Squadron Leader Lambert in late February 1941, 261 would remain the sole RAF fighter squadron defending Malta until mid-May 1941, with widely varying experiences and fortunes.

During the rest of 1940, 261 would be opposed only by the Italians and would perform very creditably. It lost two pilots killed, but it shot down or badly damaged numerous Italian aircraft including at least three SM 79s at night and Italian-manned Junkers Ju 87 dive-bombers. Exactly which and how many Italian aircraft were destroyed or 'written off' is impossible to determine. All authorities agree that Italian records in 1941 are incomplete, and it would appear that they are also incomplete in 1940. On 5 September, for example, 261 claimed to have shot down three CR 42s plus one 'probable'. No Italian losses are reported on this day, but eyewitnesses on the ground confirmed that two Fiats were observed to crash into the sea and one on land, and the pilot of this last one was taken prisoner.

These achievements were the more remarkable because, with the Battle of Britain at its height, no attempt was made to repeat Operation HURRY until 17 November. This new mission, code-named Operation WHITE, was again carried out by *Argus* with a strong escort that included *Ark Royal* and the battle-cruiser *Renown*. Guided by Skuas, two sections of six Hurricanes each, under the overall command of Flight Lieutenant James MacLachlan, took off safely, and it seemed that the success of Operation HURRY was about to be repeated.

Sadly, this was not to be. The pilots had been briefed to fly not at the Hurricanes' most economical altitude of 10,000ft but at 2,000ft where the 'heavier' lower air reduced their range. In addition Vice Admiral Sir James Somerville, in command of the escorting warships, believed the Italians knew of the mission and might attack with superior forces; he therefore decided to launch the Hurricanes from a point some 40 miles west of the one previously agreed. As a crowning misfortune, a following wind veered sharply round to blow strongly against the Hurricanes, bringing with it patches of thick sea-mist.

Tragedy followed. In the first section, two pilots ran out of fuel, forcing them to take to their parachutes. A Sunderland flying-boat that had come to guide the Hurricanes on the last stage of their flight landed and picked up Sergeant Spyer who it carried to Malta, but it could find no sign of Sergeant Cunnington. Only MacLachlan and three others of the first section reached Malta, none of them with more than 4 gallons of petrol left.

The observer in the Skua guiding the second section of six Hurricanes was on his first flight out of training school. In increasingly bad weather, he became hopelessly lost and could get no help from Malta because of a fault in his radio. The Skua eventually reached Sicily, some 75 miles off course, where it was shot down by AA fire. The Hurricanes and their pilots were never seen again.

Malta received no further Hurricanes until early in 1941, when twelve of them arrived in crates on the merchantman *Essex*. These took a long time to be assembled and made serviceable and in the meantime the island sadly lost another Hurricane and its pilot through engine failure. Yet for all its lack of numbers, 261 Squadron had succeeded in gaining aerial supremacy. On 9 January, for instance, five of its Hurricanes drove off a force of sixteen Macchi MC 200 single-engined fighters of which it downed two without loss. Such was its dominance that Malta had become the base for Wellington bombers, Swordfish torpedo-planes and Glenn Martin Maryland reconnaissance aircraft. These last-named had given such detailed information about the Italian fleet that on 11 November 1940, an attack by Swordfish from HMS *Illustrious* on the naval base at Taranto had crippled three battleships and dealt a shattering blow to Italian morale.

To Italian naval disaster, there was added in December 1940 the Italian military disaster in North Africa. In January 1941 an alarmed Hitler sent the Luftwaffe's *Fliegerkorps* X to Sicily and on the 10th its airmen took revenge on *Illustrious* in a brilliant attack that scored six hits and must have sunk any carrier not possessing an armoured deck. As it was, although hit again in a later raid, she limped into Grand Harbour, Malta, where she began to make hasty temporary repairs. It was obvious that *Fliegerkorps* X would attempt to finish her off before she could complete them and that her defence would rest mainly on 261's Hurricanes, but a permanent shortage of spare parts meant that there would never be more than half a dozen of these in the air at any one time.

Nonetheless, when on 16 January a massive raid by Junkers Ju 87s and Ju 88s, heavily escorted, was directed against *Illustrious*, 261's Hurricanes, aided by some of the carrier's Fulmars and a heavy AA barrage, met this resolutely. They inflicted heavy losses on the Ju 88s, which had five aircraft shot down or crashed on landing, and they at least helped to put the Stukas off their aim, for although *Illustrious* was hit again, she was not severely hurt. Most of the bombs missed their target, but sadly they did strike dockyards and residential areas, killing almost 100 civilians.

It seems clear that the Germans realized who were their worst enemies, for on 18 January the Ju 87s and Ju 88s were back, this time directing their attention not on the carrier but on the fighters' airfields. That at Takali was already inoperable after heavy rain, but much damage was done at Luqa, and Hal Far was also attacked. Again the Hurricanes helped to disrupt the attacks and inflicted losses and damage on the enemy bombers.

Having, as they hoped, neutralized the defending fighters, on 19 January the Germans made their biggest attempt to destroy *Illustrious*. Raids by Junkers Ju 87s and Ju 88s, escorted by Messerschmitt Bf 110s, Macchi MC 200s and Fiat CR 42s, continued throughout the day, but every one was met and harried by the Hurricanes, most of the pilots flying three or four times during the day. *Illustrious* suffered only minor damage from a couple of near misses and happily this time there were few civilian casualties.

In the frenzied actions of the day there were inevitably a number of duplicated claims, but enemy records confirm that three Ju 87s, three Ju 88s, a Bf 110 and a Fiat CR 42 were shot down or crash-landed. A Cant Z 506 floatplane used for air-sea rescue work was also shot down in accordance with RAF instructions. The three days of combat saw three Fulmars destroyed or 'written off', one pilot being killed, but only on the 19th was a Hurricane and its pilot lost. For all their superior numbers, the Germans were temporarily exhausted and they made no further assaults on *Illustrious*. She left Grand Harbour after dark on 23 January and reached Alexandria, battered but intact, two days later.

The successful protection of *Illustrious* gave great confidence to Admiral Cunningham, already an admirer of the Hurricane,[2] who now ensured that submarines were based at Malta to harry Axis shipping. A few reinforcements were also sent to 261. The conquest of Cyrenaica by the Western Desert Force enabled six Hurricanes under Flight Lieutenant Whittingham to fly to Malta from newly-captured landing-grounds, while Sunderlands carried ten pilots there at various times. During January and the first days of February, seven or eight Axis aircraft including five Junkers Ju 88s were shot down or crash-landed, and when the enemy switched to night raids, Flight Lieutenant MacLachlan shot down one German bomber on 8 February and so damaged another that it got back to its base only to be 'written off'.

Despite these successes, the Hurricanes operated under many disadvantages. In the Battle of Britain there had always been plenty of aerodromes from which fresh squadrons of fighters could engage the attackers, while those squadrons whose airfields were under attack had plenty of room in which to get clear and gain sufficient height to engage advantageously. If airfields were hard hit there were always others on which to land. On a tiny island like Malta, attacks could and usually did embrace all the airfields and there were no extra squadrons to assist in any case. As the attackers, the Germans could control the timing of their strikes and the defenders were kept permanently on the alert, their problems increased by their lacking the experienced ground control and adequate radar warning system that RAF pilots had enjoyed in the assault on their homeland.

These difficulties were known to the Germans and on 9 February, their strength was increased immensely by the arrival in Sicily of a veteran fighter unit, *Jagdgeschwader* 26, whose Messerschmitt Bf 109s, less handicapped by their tropical equipment than 261's Hurricanes, could outfight these, particularly at high altitudes. Accordingly, enemy raids on Malta now saw 109s attacking the Hurricanes as they were still climbing or as they were engaged with the German bombers.

Their tactics soon bore bitter fruit. On 12 February 261's pilots were shot up as they tried to tackle some Ju 88s. Flight Lieutenant Watson was killed and Pilot Officer Thacker baled out into the sea but was picked up by a rescue launch, while Flight Lieutenant Bradbury's Hurricane, despite damage to its rudder controls and the loss of all the fabric on one side of its fuselage, got him back safely to his base where he force-landed.

On the 16th, it was the turn of Flight Lieutenant MacLachlan to be shot down. He was so badly wounded that his left arm had to be amputated at the elbow. Incredibly, he slipped out of hospital and flew a Magister training aircraft one-handed. On his return to England, he visited Queen Mary's Hospital, Roehampton, which specialized in fitting artificial limbs. He 'explained the layout of a Hurricane' and received a new arm ending in a three-pronged adjustable claw with which he could control the engine-throttle. A few months later, he became CO of No. 1 (Hurricane) Squadron, with which he destroyed five more German bombers on night-intruder missions.

For the rest of February and well into March No. 261, reinforced by five Hurricanes flown in from North Africa, had to deal with a series of raids, many of them against its own airfields. Casualties were inevitable. On 25 February the Canadian Pilot Officer Walsh baled out but tragically was struck by his Hurricane's tailplane and fatally injured. Next day, in an attack on Luqa, the Hurricanes downed three Junkers Ju 87s but were then attacked from above by 109s and three of their own pilots were killed. Another Hurricane and its pilot were lost over Hal Far on 5 March, though two Junkers Ju 87s, a Junkers Ju 88 and a Messerschmitt Bf 110 were destroyed or crash-landed. On the 7th, yet another Hurricane went down, but at least this time the pilot baled out safely.

Malta's airfields suffered badly from these raids. The one on 26 February put Luqa out of action for forty-eight hours and that on 5 March rendered Hal Far temporarily inoperable as well. Malta's Swordfish and Wellingtons had to be withdrawn to Egypt. This was an important strategic success for the Axis airmen, but happily it was balanced in late March by a strategic success gained by 261's Hurricanes. This was the protection of a convoy of four supply ships due to arrive on 23 March. Given the singularly uninspiring code-name of MC9 and perhaps for this reason generally ignored, this was in fact of great importance. Malta's servicemen and civilians alike were beginning to suffer as essential stocks fell dangerously low and a replenishment of these was vital for morale.

Certainly it appears that the Axis airmen were aware of the convoy's importance for, as at the time of the attacks on *Illustrious*, a massive raid was mounted on 22 March in an attempt to knock out Malta's fighter force before attacks were made on the merchantmen. The Junkers Ju 88s making this assault were escorted by a swarm of Bf 109s, for JG 26 had been reinforced temporarily by another 109 unit, JG 3. The eight Hurricanes sent up were simply swamped and five were shot down, at least two by JG 3, with all the pilots – including Sergeant Spyer – losing their lives.

It says much for 261's pilots that when some thirty Ju 87s, heavily escorted, did attack the merchantmen in Grand Harbour on the 23rd, fourteen Hurricanes under Squadron Leader Lambert were there to oppose them. Sergeant Robertson, closing right up to the Stukas, shot down two of them but was hit by return fire from their gunners and his Hurricane set alight. Happily, he baled out safely. A third Stuka fell and others were damaged, but more importantly the Hurricanes disrupted all their attacks. Though two of the freighters were damaged, none were sunk and Malta received 45,000 tons of precious supplies.

Early April brought further good news when twelve Hurricanes flew off *Ark Royal* and headed for Malta. The lessons of Operation WHITE had been learned, the carrier came much closer to the island and all the fighters arrived safely. They were led by Flight Lieutenant Peter 'Boy' Mould who on 30 October 1939, as a young pilot officer with No. 1 Squadron, had brought down the first German warplane destroyed by the RAF over France since 1918. Their aircraft were Hurricane Mark IIAs, still with only eight machine guns, but their improved speed and rate of climb should have made 261's task less difficult.

Unhappily, 261's pilots had now reached a state of almost complete physical and mental exhaustion. In the Battle of Britain a squadron in a similar state would have been moved to a quieter area much earlier. Some of the longest-serving pilots were transferred to more peaceful skies, including Squadron Leader Lambert – whose place was taken by the newly-promoted Squadron Leader Whittingham – and the redoubtable Sergeant Robertson. Their absence, though, was naturally felt and did nothing to raise morale.

During April the remaining pilots destroyed two Messerschmitt Bf 110s, a Junkers Ju 87, a Junkers Ju 88 and a Fiat CR 42, but the 109s continued to plague them. They had a bad day on 11 April, redeemed only by the robustness of their Hurricanes. They lost two pilots killed but although several other Hurricanes were badly damaged, only one was 'written off'.

Still more unhappy were the circumstances surrounding the death on 23 April of a very popular French-Canadian pilot, Flying Officer Auger. Shot down by 109s, he baled out and came down in the sea. Air-sea rescue launches were not sent out, apparently because it was thought they would be vulnerable to strikes by enemy aircraft, and Auger was never seen again. The 261 pilots were outraged and morale virtually collapsed: the resulting atmosphere may have contributed to a subsequent series of accidents that cost 261 three aircraft and the lives of two pilots.

Relief for 261 came only gradually. On 27 April, twenty-three Hurricanes reached Malta from *Ark Royal* and in May, their pilots and a flight from 261 came together in a new 185 Squadron, with 'Boy' Mould promoted to command it. These latest aircraft, however, were all the older Hurricane Is and in any case the formation of 185 did nothing to end the strain and exhaustion of those 261 pilots who were transferred to it. By 20 May three had been shot down, two of them being killed.

Those pilots who remained with 261 struggled on during May. On the 5th, they destroyed a Junkers Ju 88. Next day, they shot down another

Ju 88 and a Heinkel He 111, while another He 111 crashed on its return to base. However, as 261 engaged the bombers it was attacked from above by 109s. Pilot Officer Gray and Sergeant Branston fell victims to JG 26, but both baled out safely. A third Hurricane was downed by JG 27, another crack 109 unit that had come to relieve JG 26. It crashed in flames on Luqa airfield, but Pilot Officer Dredge managed to get clear and although badly burned, he made a full recovery.

This was the last combat fought by JG 26 over Malta, and its departure was greeted with relief by the RAF as its achievements had been impressive, if not so impressive as would be reported by some British historians. For example, we are assured that in two months – it was really nearer three – JG 26 had, without loss, 'claimed at least 42 Hurricanes in the air' and that 'There can hardly be a better illustration of German fighter supremacy and the woeful inadequacy of the battered Hurricane.'

This conclusion, however, is based on exaggerations. JG 26's pilots may have 'claimed at least 42 Hurricanes in the air' but their claims were simply inaccurate. If the losses of Hurricanes in combat are checked, it will be found that in reality they did not destroy half that number.[3]

As to the statement that JG 26 had suffered no losses, certainly none can be found in enemy records, but there are several cases that cast doubt on the accuracy of these. On 22 March, for instance, a pair of 261's pilots both claimed they had shot down a 109 between them. It is easy to accept that they may have exaggerated the harm they inflicted, but when one learns that no 109 is even reported as damaged, it does indicate that once more enemy records may not be complete.

Still stronger indications are given by instances where the reported destruction of 109s is supported by the evidence of personnel on the ground. On 5 March a 109 was said to have been sent down 'trailing clouds of black and white smoke' and was confirmed to have crashed into the sea by AA gunners. On 11 April, the confirmation was given by Wing Commander Allen, the station commander at Hal Far. It has been suggested that the aircraft he saw go into the sea was a Bf 110, but it appears that this was destroyed elsewhere and earlier and in any case it is hard to believe that any witness, let alone an experienced RAF officer, would have mistaken a twin-engined 110 for a single-engined 109.

Finally we may mention an incident concerning the very experienced Flying Officer Ernest Mitchelson Mason who had joined 261 in mid-March, having previously become the highest-scoring 'ace' in the Western Desert while a member of 274 (Hurricane) Squadron. On 13 April he boldly if rashly made a single-handed attack on four Messerschmitt Bf 109s. He believed he shot one down, but was then engaged by the others and forced to 'ditch'. He was rescued and evacuated to Egypt with a bullet wound in his right hand and a broken nose caused by having hit his windscreen. The point to be noted, though, is that witnesses ashore united to confirm that two aircraft had fallen into the sea. One was Mason's Hurricane. The other can only have been the 109 he had claimed.

It should also be remembered that for all the boasts of 'German fighter supremacy' and despite the disadvantages under which the defenders laboured, as mentioned earlier, the 109s had been unable to prevent the Hurricanes from harrying and disrupting the attacks of their bombers. Yet as the Luftwaffe had discovered in the Battle of Britain, defences could only be knocked out by bombers, not fighters alone, whatever their abilities. The Germans may have appreciated this, for during April *Fliegerkorps* X began an unobtrusive but steady withdrawal to the Balkans and as the bombing raids fell away, Malta quickly recovered her strength. By the end of the month, a flotilla of destroyers was based on the island and the Swordfish and Wellingtons returned.

This, though, did not end 261's troubles. A Hurricane was lost on 13 May and its pilot killed and a further Hurricane went down on the 20th but this time the pilot escaped by parachute. The squadron did have a good day on the 9th, when South African Flying Officer Laubscher and New Zealander Sergeant Jordan united to destroy a Junkers Ju 87 and Sergeant Davies damaged a second Stuka so badly that it was 'written off'. Its last 'kill' on Malta, a Savoia Marchetti SM 79, came on 15 May.

Then on 21 May, HM carriers *Ark Royal* and *Furious* flew off almost fifty Hurricanes to Malta, mainly Mark IIAs from 213, 229 and 249 Squadrons. The pilots of 213 and 229 would fly on to Egypt, but those of 249 Squadron under Canadian Squadron Leader Robert 'Butch' Barton now learned that their unit would not be going to the Middle East as previously advised but would stay on at Malta as a replacement for 261 Squadron. For the exhausted survivors of 261, this was joyful news. Their ordeals at last at an end, they too left Malta to fly to the Middle East, where the squadron was disbanded.[4]

The pilots of 249 found the news less pleasant. Their ground crews had proceeded to Egypt, as had all their personal kit; few if any of them would see either again. They further discovered that their Hurricane IIAs had been given to 261's pilots, who had left behind for 249's use their tired, often-repaired Mark Is, with the perennial shortage of spares kept serviceable only by the use of parts of other aircraft types.

It was a situation that particularly infuriated 249's senior flight commander, Flight Lieutenant Thomas Neil. A fiery character whose nickname was 'Ginger', he was already short-tempered, his passage to Malta from *Ark Royal* having proved a nightmare experience. As he took off, a large flap that covered the guns had flown up and jammed at an angle of 45 degrees. To counter the effect of this, Neil had to keep his aching leg fully extended with his foot thrust down hard on the rudder for more than five hours. By the time he had reached Malta – in the middle of an air-raid – he was in agony and definitely not in the right mood to learn that his squadron had been saddled with 261's aged aircraft, which he calls 'absolute wrecks'.

These experiences left Neil with a strong dislike of Malta: he moans endlessly of its heat, dust and mosquitoes and its inadequate roads, transport and accommodation. Rather unfairly and forgetting or ignoring his own experiences in Hurricane Is – he had shot down at least eleven enemy aircraft including six Bf 109s in two months starting on 7 September 1940 – he now decided they were all 'terrible aircraft', 'hopeless', 'out-distanced, out-performed, out-everything'.

Wing Commander Neil, as he became, lived to the age of 97 and only passed away in July 2018. He therefore had plenty of opportunities to denigrate the Hurricane, so it is fortunate that we also have the accounts of three other members of 249 Squadron: Flying Officer 'Pat' Wells and Flight Sergeant 'Fred' Etchells, both of whom flew from *Ark Royal* to Malta on the same day as Neil, and Flying Officer Graham Leggett who also reached Malta from *Ark Royal* though in his case on 30 June. Their views are all similar and all contradict that of Neil, and not only with regard to the Hurricane. Those who have read Neil's strictures on Malta may be pardoned for wondering if he served on the same island as Leggett, who recalls nostalgically that 'Here we were in this Mediterranean seaside resort, all the amenities a chap could ask for, including girlfriends from the rather posh families who lived up in Medina who used to entertain us.'

More importantly, all the three other 249 pilots entirely reject Neil's condemnation of the Hurricane. Graham Leggett agrees that some of the aged Hurricanes on Malta were 'clapped out', but he clearly regards this as exceptional, declaring: 'Personally I was perfectly happy with the Hurricane. It was a plane I knew and could rely on. You could plop it down almost anywhere. Its rigidity had saved my neck more than once.'

'Pat' Wells confirms his approval of the Hurricane equally firmly: 'It seems that every operational task was possible in a Hurricane and I believe that had the radiator not been where it was then she could have successfully carried a torpedo. An exceptionally sturdy aircraft, the Hurricane never ever let me down (except from battle damage).'

'Fred' Etchells agrees with them both. Referring to his voyage on *Ark Royal* as well as his time on Malta, he remarks:

> I had not heard of Hurricanes taking off from aircraft carriers and was very intrigued. I'm sure that a blind faith in the Hurricane must have dismissed any fears.
>
> Although slower than one would have wished, our Hurricanes were certainly reliable [and] superbly manoeuvrable despite slightly heavy controls.

It is particularly interesting that all three pilots praise the Hurricane's reliability, for it is in this area that Neil is most scathing. He insists that he was constantly worried about the possibility of engine failure, having had five such in eight weeks. Since none of them seem to have had any adverse results, it may be that his memory tricked him. If not, one can only express sympathy for his unparalleled bad luck.

It should also be emphasized that Neil's fellow pilots make it very clear that they were speaking for at least a majority of their comrades in arms. 'I never heard anybody say anything against Hurricanes,' reports Leggett. The Hurricane was a 'most famous and well-loved aeroplane,' agrees Wells, and according to Etchells: 'I don't think I ever heard a word spoken against the aircraft. Somehow one loved the Hurricane without either realizing or expressing it.'[5]

'I was in Malta eight months,' relates Neil (he left on 26 December), 'it got worse and worse.' By now it is perhaps no surprise to learn that according to Air Commodore (later Air Vice Marshal) Lloyd who succeeded

Maynard as Air Officer Commanding: 'You wouldn't have known there was a war on.' It was an exaggeration, of course, but an excusable one. Not only did the last German aircraft leave Sicily during June, but 'ferry missions' brought in large numbers of Hurricane reinforcements.

Early in the month, an entire squadron arrived from *Ark Royal*. This was No. 46 which we last met in Norway. It was now commanded by Squadron Leader 'Sandy' Rabagliati, whose senior flight commander and later successor was Flight Lieutenant Lefevre who had served in Norway but not been one of the men detailed to land on *Glorious*. Strangely, though, this squadron was disbanded at the end of June, only to re-form as a new 126 Squadron which, like 185 and 261 before it, would incorporate a Maltese Cross in its squadron badge. With three Hurricane squadrons now on Malta, a new landing-ground known as the Safi Strip was created between Luqa and Hal Far.

Faced with only Italian warplanes in June, the Hurricanes destroyed a sizeable number, though exactly how many is uncertain since all accounts agree that enemy records on several days this month are incomplete. The defenders did not escape unscathed: four of their pilots were killed in action, while Pilot Officer Saunders had to be rescued, having baled out into the sea. With many more pilots now available, however, it was possible to rest them and there was never the continuous strain that had been placed on 261's airmen.

On 27 June, *Ark Royal* flew off twenty-two more Hurricanes, though only twenty-one arrived: Sergeant Sherburne had to 'ditch', was picked up by the Italians and became a prisoner of war. On the 30th, *Ark Royal* and *Furious* prepared to send forty-two more but though twenty-six pilots, including Graham Leggett, took off safely from *Ark Royal*, on *Furious* the aircraft of Sergeant Hare swerved when halfway along the deck and crashed, fatally injuring Hare and disabling six other pilots whose machines therefore could not be launched. Only nine Hurricanes left the carrier, but at least all of them got safely to Malta, as did all those from *Ark Royal*. Moreover, the Hurricanes received in late June were Mark IIs and while 249 flew only IIAs for a time, 126 and 185 were equipped with IIBs with twelve machine guns and IICs with four 20mm cannons.

Throughout July, August and September, events followed a similar pattern. During this period four more Hurricane pilots were killed in action, but any aircraft losses were made good by the delivery of further

Hurricanes from *Ark Royal* and *Furious* in September. Sadly, though, this was at the cost of another life, for Flight Sergeant Finlay hit the superstructure of *Furious* as he took off, crashed into the sea and was killed.

For their part, the Hurricanes broke up several enemy daylight raids and shot down a number of Italian bombers: for example, a pair of Savoia Marchetti SM 79s that fell to the guns of 185 Squadron on 27 July. They also destroyed some twenty Macchi MC 200s, including two on 30 June, at least two on 4 July, three or four on 19 August and at least three, probably more, on 4 September. Among the Italian airmen who were lost was Lieutenant Colonel (a rank equivalent to wing commander) Carlo Romagnoli, a veteran of the Spanish Civil War.

In addition, at the end of July the Malta Night Fighter Unit, later 1435 Flight, was formed with four Hurricane IIBs and eight IICs. It was commanded by a full squadron leader, George Powell-Shedden, once a flight commander of Douglas Bader's 242 (Hurricane) Squadron during the Battle of Britain. It gained its first victories on the night of 5/6 August, when Pilot Officer Barnwell shot down a pair of Fiat BR 20 bombers. Powell-Shedden personally destroyed another BR 20 on the night of 11/12 August and damaged two more on the night of the 26th/27th, one so badly that it was 'written off'. His pilots downed two other bombers in early September.

Meanwhile, in the early hours of 26 July the Hurricanes of 126 and 185 Squadrons had assisted in thwarting a very different Italian raid. This was directed at six merchantmen from a convoy that had arrived at Grand Harbour carrying reinforcements and ammunition for Malta's garrison, torpedoes for her submarines, spare engines for her Hurricanes and three months' supply of food for her inhabitants. The attack force consisted of two 'chariots' or 'human torpedoes', eight one-man explosive motor-boats, two small launches and two larger craft, the equivalent of German E-boats, *MAS 451* and *MAS 452*.[6] Had they got into the harbour, they must surely have caused immense damage.

Sadly for the Italians, their plan had been revealed by British code-breakers, the famous 'Ultra' Intelligence, and Malta's defenders were ready for them. Their approach was detected by radar and as they tried to enter the harbour, they were illuminated by searchlights and shelled by shore batteries. All eight explosive craft were sunk. One of the chariots, piloted by its designer Commander Teseo Tesei, disappeared without trace and the other ran ashore, where its crew was captured. Only the larger Italian craft were unhurt, and their immunity would be a brief one.

As the light increased, fighter aircraft joined in the conflict on both sides. The Hurricanes proved more effective, shooting down two Macchis and driving the rest away. Then they attacked the MAS-boats and launches. One launch was sunk outright and *MAS 451*, hit by several Hurricanes, was left drifting helplessly. Her surviving crewmen – four had been killed – abandoned her and were taken prisoner; she later blew up and sank. *MAS 452* was apparently the target only of 126's Flight Lieutenant Lefevre, but his repeated assaults killed eight of her crew and so unnerved the remaining eleven that they hoisted a white flag. They then also abandoned their vessel and were carried to safety by the remaining launch.

Only one Hurricane was lost. Pilot Officer Denis Winton of 185 Squadron baled out. He managed to swim to and board *MAS 452* which he found manned only by her eight dead crewmen. Eventually a Swordfish with floats 'dropped in to pay him a visit' and carried him back to Malta, taking with him the MAS-boat's naval ensign as a trophy for his squadron. The MAS-boat herself was later towed into Grand Harbour.

With the convoy safely unloaded, more troops and stores brought in by warships in early August and another convoy of eight merchantmen carrying food, ammunition, spare parts and other supplies arriving in late September, Malta was more secure than she had been since the Italian declaration of war. Confidence was increased by the obvious dominance of the Hurricanes in the skies above the island. Italian raids had so declined that pilots had the luxury of complaining of inactivity. Indeed, the Hurricanes were now on the offensive, escorting British bombers against and themselves attacking targets in Sicily, including the seaplane base at Syracuse, aerodromes, railway stations and transport of all kinds. On 29 August 'Pat' Wells and another 249 pilot, Flying Officer John Beazley, even took on an Italian schooner, whereupon its crew sprang overboard.

Yet this apparent security was an illusion. Malta had again attracted the baleful attention of Adolf Hitler and in late September, he gave the first of a series of orders that would cast a grim shadow over the island's future.

Notes

1. It is a confirmation of the inaccuracy of the 'Faith, Hope and Charity' myth that at the end of the year, 261 still had four Sea Gladiators on its strength, plus others in crates as reserve. In January 1941, all of these were handed over to a Fleet Air Arm squadron which used them for meteorological flights.
2. On learning he had been made a Knight Grand Cross of the Bath, Admiral Cunningham had observed 'I would sooner have had three squadrons of Hurricanes.'
3. The most complete description of JG 26's successes will be found in *Malta: The Hurricane Years 1940–41* by Christopher Shores and Brian Cull with Nicola Malizia, on which the present account is largely based.
4. On 12 July 1941, 261 Squadron was re-formed in Iraq under the command of Ernest Mitchelson Mason. Next month, it took part in the campaign in Iran – or Persia, to use its older name – designed to secure a supply route to Russia, now Britain's ally. There was only one combat: on 26 August, Mason shot down an elderly Hawker Audax biplane. In early 1942, 261 left for the Far East, where it saw action first with Hurricane IIBs and later with Hurricane IICs until June 1944, when it converted to Thunderbolts.
5. Sources for the pilots' statements are as follows: Neil: the work by Shores and Cull to which reference has already been made; Wing Commander Neil's own *Onwards to Malta*; *Hurricane: Victor of the Battle of Britain* by Leo McKinstry; Brian Milton's *Hurricane, the Last Witnesses: Hurricane Pilots Tell the Story of the Fighter that won the Battle of Britain*. The ironic contrast of Neil's strictures and the sub-titles of these last two books needs no elaboration. Leggett: more irony; the books by McKinstry and Milton again. Wells: *Hawker Hurricane* by Peter Jacobs. Etchells: Chaz Bowyer's splendid *Hurricane at War*.
6. The initials stood for *Motoscafo Armato Silurante*, Italian for 'Motor Torpedo Boat'.

Chapter Six

Cats v Condors

Although the air attacks on Malta had lasted for many months – and there would be plenty more to come – they were vastly exceeded by the assaults on the convoy routes to the British Isles delivered by the submarine fleet of Admiral Karl Dönitz, one of Hitler's most loyal, competent and dangerous subordinates. Collectively called the Battle of the Atlantic, they lasted as long as did the war in Europe. It was perhaps only to be expected that Hurricanes would participate in the struggle, which they did in possibly the strangest of their many roles.

Their opponents would not be the U-boats but the U-boats' aerial allies, the huge four-engined Focke-Wulf Fw 200Cs, known appropriately as Condors. These could boast a top speed of 235 mph and the immensely long range of 2,210 miles at an economic cruising speed of 180 mph. They were also well able to defend themselves, for in addition to their pilot and co-pilot they carried three other crew members, whose duties included manning a useful armament of one 20mm cannon and from three to five 7.9mm machine guns. Since they were also capable of taking a lot of punishment, they were formidable opponents and it was just as well that they were only produced at the rate of one aircraft per week by a single small factory in Bremen.

Their entry into the Battle of the Atlantic began after the fall of France, when they were mustered at Bordeaux as *Kampfgeschwader* 40, and were at first used as long-range bombers or mine-layers, sinking eighty-five ships by the end of February 1941. Thereafter they proved even more dangerous, reporting details of all convoys they had sighted to the Flag Officer, Submarines at Brest, who relayed the information to Dönitz's 'wolf packs'.

Oddly, it appears that navigation was not the Condor crews' greatest skill, for there are instances where submarines directed Focke-Wulfs to a convoy, rather than the other way round. Yet once a Focke-Wulf had located a convoy it possessed the priceless ability to remain in the air for fourteen hours if necessary. It could thus stay with the convoy, sending out a steady stream of information on its composition, course, speed and progress. Its vessels had no way of shaking off their shadower, for the Condor would circle overhead safely out of range of any AA guns; indeed there is an amusing if improbable story of a convoy commodore signalling a request to a Condor to fly the other way round for a change as he was getting giddy watching it.

Naturally, thoughts turned to ways in which this menace could be mastered. The obvious answer was to provide convoys with their own fighter protection, but British aircraft carriers were few in number and it would be a long time before any of the planned small escort carriers would appear. However, at a conference of senior officers on 12 November 1940, the Air Force suggested that possibly suitable merchantmen might be converted to carry a single interceptor with which to oppose any Condor that approached their convoy.

Reactions to this idea were mixed. Churchill was strongly supportive but others were not, as is made very clear in *Afternoon Light*, the reminiscences of Australian Prime Minister Mr (later Sir) Robert Menzies. Unfortunately he gives no date for the meetings he describes, but they must have been after his arrival in London in late February 1941:

> On a Sunday night at Chequers, Winston exposed to me a great plan for dealing with the all too efficient co-operation of the U-boats and the Focke-Wulf aircraft in the Western Approaches. Briefly, the plan was that ships in convoy should each carry a fighter aircraft with a catapult mechanism. When I asked what the fighter-pilot was to do after his attack aloft Winston's reply was that he would ditch his plane as near as possible to a ship and hope to be rescued. This dashing manoeuvre was, of course, in the true Churchill tradition. Next day, Winston, in my hearing, put it to that very remarkable man, Sir Dudley Pound, the First Sea Lord. Pound added to a genial countenance the priceless advantage of deafness. So what was his reply to Churchill? 'I'm deaf, as you know, Sir, and I've missed practically all that has been said. But I did hear a rumour yesterday that there was a proposal to catapult fighters off vessels in convoy and thereafter let them take their chance. Now I don't need to tell you, Sir, *as an old Admiralty man*, that such a proposal would be nonsense.'

Churchill, we are told, chuckled, which Menzies took for acceptance but was really more likely a rather wicked reflection of his knowledge that the scheme had gone too far to be halted, with the necessary adaptations to ships and aircraft already being put in hand. Accordingly, at a War Cabinet meeting on 6 March 1941, Churchill coined the phrase 'Battle of the Atlantic' and directed: 'Extreme priority will be given to fitting out ships to catapult or otherwise launch fighter aircraft against bombers attacking our shipping.'

These ships were to be of two types. The Royal Navy arranged the conversion of a handful of auxiliary vessels which were known as Fighter Catapult Ships or FC-ships for short. They would not transport any freight, be manned entirely by naval personnel and fly the white ensign. They would carry the navy's own Fulmar fighters and the pilots would come from 804 Squadron of the Fleet Air Arm based at Sydenham, Belfast.

The other type would consist of normal freighters provided with somewhat elementary radio and radar sets and a 70ft-long steel ramp, down which their fighters would be thrust by thirteen rocket motors. They would continue to carry their usual cargoes, be manned by men of Britain's Mercantile Marine and fly the red ensign. It was originally intended that there should be 200 of them, but appreciation that it would be difficult to keep so many serviceable since corrosion from salt water would be likely to damage the fighters' engine or airframe or both resulted in their number being reduced to 35. They were known as CAM-ships, the initials standing for Catapult Aircraft Merchantmen.[1]

It had quickly been concluded that the only aircraft with the necessary performance, reliability, easy handling characteristics and sheer robust strength for the task was the Hurricane. Hawkers had confirmed that their fighter could be given the necessary adaptations and on 19 January 1941, the first Hurricane conversions began.

The Hurricanes that were adapted were old Mark Is, thus given a new lease of useful life. They received catapult spools and attachments by which they could be lifted onto the launching-ramp and lashed to it in bad weather if needed. When hurled down the ramp, they would reach a speed of 75 mph at the moment they became airborne, so their fuselages were strengthened and heavily-padded head-rests were installed against which the pilots could lean to absorb the shock of take-off. Officially

Sea Hurricane Mark IAs, they were nicknamed 'Catafighters' or, more neatly, 'Hurricats'.

Use of the Hurricane as the CAM-ships' weapon was noticed with approval by the Royal Navy, which had already discovered that its Fulmars lacked the performance needed to engage Condors. The various modifications made to the Hurricats had had the unfortunate effect of reducing their speed to 245 mph at 3,000ft, but this still gave them a narrow margin of 10 mph over the Condors. They were also very sturdy machines and their steadiness made their eight machine guns quite capable of downing a Condor; it may be recalled that Pilot Officer Banks of 46 (Hurricane) Squadron had done just that during the Norwegian campaign.

It was therefore decided that the last of the Fighter Catapult Ships, HMS *Maplin*, formerly the fast banana-boat *Erin*, would carry Sea Hurricane IAs, and when she left port on 9 May 1941 she was equipped with two of these, one on the catapult, the other on deck between mast and bridge. If the first was launched, the reserve aircraft had to be swung round the mast on the aft derrick, transferred to the forward derrick and lowered onto the ramp; an extremely difficult manoeuvre in any conditions other than a flat calm, not usually found in the North Atlantic. *Maplin*'s first mission was uneventful, but there would be other ones.

Whether carried on *Maplin* or on one of the CAM-ships, the Hurricat pilots had a hazardous existence. There was no way in which they could land back on the vessel from which they had taken off, and since the whole point of the scheme was to oppose enemy aircraft operating at a great distance from land, there was normally no chance of reaching friendly territory either. Later the Hurricats would be given an extra fuel tank under each wing, but this reduced manoeuvrability, necessitated an increase in the power of the catapult and rarely improved the aircrafts' range sufficiently in any case.

Therefore, even if successful in his duel with a Condor, a pilot would have to come down in the sea. Despite improvements in the ease with which the cockpit's sliding hood could be jettisoned and the provision of a new one-man dinghy, it was not very advisable to 'ditch' a Hurricane. The trouble was that it had a large radiator that quickly filled with water, causing the aircraft to sink literally within seconds. On the other hand, if the pilot baled out, he was more difficult to locate and the freezing waters of the North Atlantic did not allow a long survival time. Moreover, whichever course of action the pilot chose, he had to rely on a vessel in the convoy or one of the escorts to rescue him and they might well have other concerns.

With these perils in mind, Fighter Command felt obliged to call for volunteers to fly from the CAM-ships, though a surprising number of intrepid characters proved ready to come forward, perhaps looking for excitement or change; perhaps feeling that the importance of the operation justified the risks involved. This last motive must also have sustained the Fleet Air Arm pilots of 804 Squadron who were not given any choice in the matter but simply ordered to carry out catafighter duties: as Royal Navy personnel, they of all people realized how crucial the outcome of the Battle of the Atlantic was.

It was this realization, no doubt, that inspired the admirable 'team spirit' displayed by both the Royal Navy and the Royal Air Force in connection with the CAM-ships. The vast majority of the pilots were RAF volunteers who were formed into the Merchant Ship Fighter Unit (MSFU) with its headquarters at Speke, near Liverpool. It came under No. 9 Group, Fighter Command and was led first by Wing Commander Moulton-Barrett and from January 1942 by Wing Commander Pinkerton. The Royal Navy, however, provided all except two of the CAM-ships with the radio-operator who warned the pilot of the approach of enemy aircraft and the fighter direction officer who guided the pilot in his attack.

In the early days of CAM-ship operations, the Royal Navy also provided some of the CAM-ships' pilots, among whom Sub-Lieutenant Maurice Birrell deserves special mention. He had served previously with the RAF, being one of the Fleet Air Arm pilots temporarily transferred to Fighter Command at the time of the Battle of Britain, during which he had flown Hurricanes with 79 Squadron. Now a member of 804 Squadron, he was posted to the CAM-ship *Michael E*, outward bound for New York.

Birrell had already been launched in a Hurricane from a light naval catapult on the ground at Gosport and in a Fulmar from a rocket catapult on the ground at the Royal Aircraft Establishment, Farnborough, in both cases without trouble. However, neither he nor any other pilot had yet made a rocket-assisted launch from the ramp of a CAM-ship and when

Birrell became the first to do so, it proved a perilous affair, as he recounts in Ralph Barker's *The Hurricats*:

> On 18 May, I was catapulted in a Hurricane from the *Michael E* in Belfast Lough, but only half the rockets fired and disaster seemed certain. Somehow I hauled the aircraft out of the sea and got back to Sydenham. Since our destination was a neutral port I was signed on as fifth mate, and I flew in civilian clothes, with a bowler hat at the ready.

On 28 May, *Michael E* with Birrell and his Hurricat on board, joined a convoy, the first CAM-ship to do so, but ironically she would demonstrate another of the dangers facing catafighter pilots. After passing through the area where Condors might be expected without seeing any, she was sunk by a U-boat. Happily, Birrell survived.[2]

It was on 31 May that Pilot Officer Henry Davidson became the first RAF airman to be launched from a CAM-ship, the *Empire Rainbow* on the River Clyde. Davidson was an experienced pilot: he had flown Hurricanes with 249 Squadron during the Battle of Britain, assisting in the destruction of half a dozen enemy aircraft. He had, however, not made a rocket launch from the ground like Birrell, and it appears that he was rattled by a pair of staff officers, holding notebooks and stop-watches, checking his every move.

As a result, Davidson forgot to lower his flaps ready for take-off so as to increase lift or to make a correction to the rudder to counter the Hurricane's tendency to swing to port. He also allowed his throttle to slip back to only half-open when he raised his hand as the signal of his readiness and, through no fault of his, two of the rockets did not fire. All these factors caused the Hurricane to swing badly to port and its port wing brushed the water before Davidson, like Birrell before him, pulled his aircraft up and landed safely. The staff officers were understanding and when *Empire Rainbow* set out with a convoy on 8 June, Davidson was there as her Hurricat pilot for what turned out to be an uneventful voyage.

Perhaps influenced by this affair, on 6 July a rocket-catapult was erected on the airport at Speke, enabling MSFU pilots to train on Hurricats. This ramp was only 6ft off the ground. Since the Hurricane was inclined to sink slightly when launched this left little margin for error, but any doubts the pilots may have had were quickly removed by the officer placed in charge of catapult development and training.

Squadron Leader Louis Strange was a veteran of the First World War, during which he had become a member of the Distinguished Service Order and been awarded a Military Cross when in the Royal Flying Corps and a Distinguished Flying Cross after the formation of the Royal Air Force on 1 April 1918. He had also fallen out of a Martinsyde Scout, saved his life by hanging onto the drum of his Lewis gun and somehow managed to pull himself back into the cockpit. More recently, on 23 May 1940, he had added a bar to his DFC by bringing a repaired but unarmed Hurricane back from France, evading enemy fighters on the way.

Strange had never flown a Hurricane before and, after that proof of its reliability, was unconcerned about being the first man to make a Hurricat launch at Speke two months before his 50th birthday. Accompanied by a colossal roar of the rockets and a vast sheet of flame that severely damaged the blast screen, this proved an alarming experience for the onlookers but not for Strange, who merely remarked to his pilots: 'If an old boy like me can do it, it won't mean a thing to lads like you.'

Of course what the MSFU pilots really wanted was the chance to engage a Condor, and once again the way was shown to them by the Royal Navy in the person of Lieutenant Robert Everett, the senior pilot on the Fighter Catapult Ship HMS *Maplin*. Born in Australia, Everett, like Strange, had seen service in the First World War, in his case as a midshipman, and in 1941, at the age of 40, was considered a rather elderly gentleman. He had farmed for some years in South Africa and on returning to Britain had learned to fly and spent his summers as a charter pilot. He earned more money from his winter profession as a National Hunt jockey, his greatest success being his victory, out of a record field of sixty-six, in the 1929 Grand National on a big, brave, if somewhat ungainly chestnut named 'Gregalach'.[3]

Yet, as he unhesitatingly stated, everything else in Everett's life appeared tame in comparison with his experiences as a catafighter pilot. The first of these came on 18 July 1941, when *Maplin* was escorting a convoy to Halifax, Nova Scotia. Early that morning a Condor, coming in at sea level, made an unexpected appearance and bombed one of the merchantmen, causing moderate damage. Everett was at once launched to engage it, but as he was about to open fire, AA gunners on another merchantman scored a hit that blew off part of the Focke-Wulf's wing. It turned over onto its back and dived into the sea.

According to eye-witnesses, the cheers from the convoy were 'audible for miles' but Everett, thus robbed of his prey, could not help but feel somewhat disappointed. At least the lack of any combat meant that he had a full load of fuel, so he determined to fly the 300 miles separating him from the British Isles, which he did after being airborne for all but two hours. On *Maplin*'s return, guarding a convoy to Britain, he rejoined her, much to the delight of the other two pilots she carried who, until then, had not known whether or not he had survived.

With Everett again on board, *Maplin* set out on 31 July to accompany a convoy to Gibraltar, from which the merchantmen would proceed to ports in West Africa or round the Cape of Good Hope to the Middle East. Rather surprisingly, although the 'Gibraltar run' passed dangerously close to the Condors' base at Bordeaux, the voyage was uneventful, but on 8 August *Maplin*, together with three destroyers, left the southward-bound convoy to help protect one homeward-bound. This time it would be a different story.

On the afternoon of 3 August, a Focke-Wulf was sighted but it soon departed, presumably short of fuel. It had clearly reported the convoy, however, for soon another Condor was observed, shadowing at low level and obviously acting as a scout for U-boats. Since *Maplin* was 450 miles from Britain, there was no chance of Everett's Hurricat being able to get back there this time, but to save the merchantmen from Dönitz's 'wolves' it was essential that the Condor be destroyed or at least driven away. At about 1515, Everett was hurled into the air.

It appears that the Condor did not at first see Everett's Hurricane, but on doing so, it turned sharply away. Everett had to pursue it for about 35 miles, holding his fire until he was able to make an effective attack at close range, ignoring a resolute but luckily inaccurate barrage from the Condor's powerful defensive armament. Finally he was able to reach a position from which he could pour machine-gun bullets into the Condor's starboard side and cockpit, firing a series of quick bursts until his guns were empty. The Condor's gunners were still firing and, Everett later reported, 'my windshield and hood were covered with oil.' Everett believed he had been hit, but it seems probable that the oil came from his enemy which by now 'appeared to be alight inside the fuselage'. The Condor was in fact doomed: dropping a wing, it crashed into the sea.

Everett was then directed back to the convoy but his problems were not yet over, as he describes in his Combat Report:

> My forward view was very obscured owing to oil. My one idea was to get down while I still had charge of the situation. I made two rather half-hearted attempts to bale out, but the machine nosed down and caught me when half out. I changed my mind and decided to land in the sea near [the destroyer] *Wanderer*, and did so. The ship sent a boat and I was extremely well looked after.

As so often, a pilot omits to mention the full extent of his danger. The moment the Hurricane touched the water, it turned over and sank immediately. Everett was dragged down for about 30ft before he was able to struggle free, get to the surface and be picked up by *Wanderer*. His achievement was acknowledged with the award of a well-deserved DSO, but sadly it appears that he had now used up all his luck. On 26 January 1942 he was flying a Hurricane from Belfast to Abingdon on a routine mission when it came down near the Isle of Anglesey, apparently as a result of engine trouble. Everett was drowned, his body being washed ashore later.

Maplin would make one more Hurricat launch. At midday on 14 September 1941, a Condor attempted to bomb a convoy from Gibraltar but Sub-Lieutenant Cecil Walker intercepted it. He was unable to destroy it, but he damaged it and eventually drove it away, jettisoning its bombs uselessly. Walker baled out successfully and was rescued by destroyer *Rochester*. *Maplin* was converted in February 1942 so that she could carry a third Hurricane, but she saw no further action and ceased to operate as a Fighter Catapult Ship in June 1942.

So far, all catafighter combats had been fought by pilots from *Maplin*, but from 1 November 1941 onwards it would be pilots from CAM-ships who would hold centre stage. On that day, a convoy to Britain from Halifax, Nova Scotia was attacked by a Condor some 550 miles from land. Its bomb-doors were already open as it made for a straggler when it was attacked by a Hurricat from the CAM-ship *Empire Foam* flown by

Flying Officer George Varley, who had gained experience on Hurricanes with 79 and 247 Squadrons.

It appears from intercepted signals that the Condor pilot knew nothing about the catafighter scheme, so his incredulous horror at being challenged by an interceptor fighter in mid-Atlantic can be imagined. Abandoning all thoughts of aggression, he fled into cloud cover where he made good his escape. Varley continued to circle above the convoy for another two hours, during which two other Condors were reported by radar but dared not approach to observe and report on the merchantmen because of Varley's presence. Finally, with his fuel exhausted, Varley baled out and was rescued by destroyer *Broke*. Although spending only four minutes in the sea, he was stunned by how cold it was. He was quickly warmed, externally by a hot bath into which he was placed without removing his clothes, and internally by hot coffee laced with rum.

The Hurricats' deterrent effect, which Varley's sortie so well illustrates, quickly became ever more apparent. *Kampfgeschwader* 40's men now attempted few of the bombing raids that had once been so destructive and also became less effective as long-range scouts for Admiral Dönitz. They virtually abandoned their operations in the North Atlantic, concentrating on the 'Gibraltar run' which, being nearer to their base at Bordeaux, gave them more chance of getting back to it if they had been damaged by a Hurricat. Even here, they no longer dared to shadow convoys. Instead they would make a quick sighting and then depart in haste at the sight of a CAM-ship or just the fear that one might be present.

So effective had the Hurricats proved, they would be given further responsibilities elsewhere. From April to September 1942, they would be found in action defending convoys to and from Russia round the North Cape of Norway. In the course of these missions, three catafighter pilots shot down German bombers, though one of them lost his life, not because of any fault of his own or of his Hurricane but because his parachute did not open fully. None of the machines they destroyed were Condors, but the Hurricats' duels with these were far from over.

On 12 June 1942 a Condor approached a convoy homeward bound from Gibraltar. Quite obviously it was acting as a scout for U-boats and the convoy was very vulnerable since commitments elsewhere had reduced its escort to just one sloop and three corvettes. Fortunately, it was also protected by the CAM-ship *Empire Moon* and she did not even have to launch her Hurricane. Recognizing the CAM-ship for what she was, the Condor sheered away. As soon as it was out of sight, changes of course were made and for forty-eight hours the merchantmen escaped attack.

It had been a remarkable illustration of the Hurricats' deterrent value and its importance would be confirmed by subsequent events. On 14 June another Condor finally located the convoy. *Empire Moon* sent off her catafighter and Rhodesian Pilot Officer Vernon Sanders attempted to engage his enemy as it dodged in and out of cloud cover. He finally succeeded in damaging the Condor and driving it off; then 'ditched' and was picked up safely. The Condor had been able to report its sighting, however, and this time there were U-boats too near to be deceived by changes of course. Their attacks sank five ships, but this was only a fraction of the losses that might have occurred had it not been for that forty-eight-hour respite.

A more satisfying encounter above a convoy from Gibraltar to Britain took place on 1 November 1942. It was an important convoy containing sixty-five merchantmen, but the Hurricat pilot on board CAM-ship *Empire Heath* was an especially capable one. Flying Officer Norman Taylor had served with 601 (Hurricane) Squadron as a sergeant pilot in and after the Battle of Britain, destroying or helping to destroy six enemy aircraft, for which he was awarded a Distinguished Flying Medal and a commission. He would need all his ability and experience, for he would be faced with a foeman worthy of his steel.

It was Taylor's sharp eyes that spotted and identified a Condor on the morning of 1 November, flying at such a low level that it had not been detected by radar either on its approach or afterwards as it circled round the merchant vessels and their escorts, sending out a steady stream of information. It was about 5 miles astern of the convoy when *Empire Heath* flew off her Hurricat and its skilful pilot quickly turned away into the sun; then, still low over the sea, he headed for his base at Bordeaux.

There followed a lengthy chase as Taylor slowly overhauled his opponent and endeavoured to reach a favourable position from which to attack. It was an immensely difficult undertaking because the Condor kept flying only a few feet above the waves, constantly making slight adjustments of course so that Taylor was continually dazzled by the direct light of the sun and its reflection from the water. In addition, the enemy gunners kept up a steady return fire and Taylor's port wing was riddled with bullets. Taylor's own bursts of fire seemed to have no effect and the Condor's escape looked certain when its pilot at last made a mistake, pulling up sharply to make for an inviting cloud cover. Before he could reach it, however, he had to pass briefly through the Hurricat's sights and Taylor had three seconds in which to pump his bullets into the Condor's cockpit.

Taylor's aim was deadly. The Condor fell away in a shallow dive that ended only when it struck the sea, taking to their deaths *Oberleutnant* (Lieutenant) Arno Gross, *Kampfgeschwader* 40's ablest pilot, and his gallant crew. Taylor returned to the convoy, to be welcomed by the sirens of every single ship, and baled out. This was not the least perilous part of Taylor's sortie, for as if the normal hazards of catafighting were not enough, he was a non-swimmer, a handicap he had carefully omitted to mention when volunteering for this duty. When his dinghy failed to inflate his situation looked grave, but mercifully his life-jacket kept him afloat until a corvette from the escort rescued him, exhausted but unhurt. He was rewarded with a Distinguished Flying Cross and later a transfer to become a test pilot for the RAF, a career he had always wanted and in which he remained for the rest of the war and thereafter.[4]

After this, the Condors seemed to give up bothering the Gibraltar convoys completely and most of them were sent to Russia or Italy where they served as transports. Their departure and the arrival of escort carriers meant that the need for CAM-ships was passing. By the end of 1942, most had been reconverted to normal freighters with only eight remaining in service. These saw no action in the first half of 1943 and on 15 July, the Merchant Ship Fighter Unit was formally disbanded, receiving a gracious message of thanks from the Admiralty.

It was not the end of the story, however. It seems that German Intelligence had learned that the MSFU had been disbanded and the Condors eagerly took the opportunity of resuming bombing raids on the Gibraltar convoys in the belief that they would be opposed only by the ships' AA guns. On the morning of 28 July they attacked a southbound convoy, causing some damage. Then in the afternoon, they attempted to repeat their achievement on forty merchant vessels making for Britain.

Unfortunately for the Germans, those CAM-ships that had been at sea when the MSFU closed down had remained on active service until they returned to Britain and the last two were with the convoy now coming under fire. These were the *Empire Darwin* and the *Empire Tide*, the Hurricat pilots of which were Pilot Officers James Stewart and 'Paddy' Flynn respectively. They would ensure that the Hurricane's final clash with the Condor would be a memorable one.

Stewart was the first to be launched against a Condor approaching the convoy. He engaged this, 'opening fire at 300 yards and closing to almost point-blank' and 'gave a five-second burst'. His Combat Report then continues: 'I could see strikes in the sea around the nose, then a vivid white flash from near the turret. Return fire was very heavy and uncomfortably close, but I could not see any strikes on my aircraft. Having broken away to port, I repeated the attack.'

Stewart's aim had been deadly. Although to his fury his guns now jammed, the Condor was already losing height rapidly. Observers on the merchantmen watched as 'it dropped sharply, rose again for a moment, and crashed into the sea.' Stewart next made a mock attack on a second Condor which retired hastily, dropping its bombs at random. Flynn was then launched and although his Hurricat was badly hit by return fire, he left a third Condor losing height with smoke pouring from one engine. He claimed only a 'damaged', but enemy records confirm that his opponent failed to get back to its base. Both Stewart and Flynn baled out and were picked up safely.

Thus the final total of Condors shot down by Hurricats was four. This does not seem a large number, even when it is remembered that each one carried a highly-trained crew with it to its doom. Yet equally important were the times when Hurricats had driven away Condors attempting to bomb or scout for Dönitz's submarines, and the times when they had deterred Condors by their presence alone. How many ships and how many lives were thereby saved is impossible to tell. Churchill, who had been the Sea Hurricane IAs' firm supporter, best summed up their success: 'The Focke-Wulf, being challenged itself in the air, was no longer able to give the same assistance to the U-boats and gradually became the hunted rather than the hunter.'

It is also a delight to observe that of all the Hurricat pilots, whether launched from Fighter Catapult Ships or CAM-ships, not one lost his life when engaging a Condor, despite the varied dangers that they faced. One of these at least turned out to be less than had been feared. Captain

S.W. Roskill in the Official Naval History *The War at Sea* points out that 'They knew that once they had been catapulted, their patrol would probably end by a parachute descent into the sea, hoping to be picked up by a surface escort vessel.'

In fact, without exception, they were always picked up, since the escorts considered it a matter of honour to save the men who risked their lives in the convoys' defence. Nonetheless, one can only echo Captain Roskill's conclusion: 'Their sorties demanded a cold-blooded gallantry.'

Notes

1. Not, please, Catapult Assisted Merchantmen or, worse still, Catapult Armed Merchantmen as they are sometimes called. They were not assisted by, still less armed with, a catapult. They were assisted by and armed with a catapult-aircraft or aircraft on a catapult. That the 'A' stood for 'Aircraft' is confirmed in Admiralty records, in Captain Roskill's Official Naval History and in Ralph Barker's indispensable work *The Hurricats*, the most detailed account of the CAM-ships' exploits.
2. A total of twelve CAM-ships would be lost – one by accident and the rest by enemy action – although three of these met their end after they had ceased to be CAM-ships.
3. It is pleasant to record that 'Gregalach', unlike many more famous racehorses, survived the dangers of his sport to go into honourable retirement in 1934.
4. With a cruel irony, Taylor, having survived the Battle of Britain, his catafighter sortie and the risks inherent in his work as a test pilot, was killed in a flying accident on 29 April 1948 as a result of engine failure in a Harvard training aircraft.

Chapter Seven

Russian Tutorial

That the Hurricane was considered the ideal aircraft for catafighting was a tribute to its reliability, adaptability, versatility and sheer strength. It was an appreciation of those same virtues, plus memories of how well 46 Squadron had managed in northern Norway, that prompted the Hurricane's next overseas duty. Churchill had promised aid to Russia following the German invasion of 22 June 1941, and it was felt that Hurricanes would be the ideal aircraft to cope with the harsh Russian conditions.

Ironically, in June 1941 Hurricanes were already fighting in the Russian campaigns, though not for the Russians. Rumania was now Hitler's ally and her land and air forces fought alongside those of Germany. Among these, as we learn from *Hawker Hurricane* by Paul and Louise Blackah and Malcolm V. Lowe, were twelve Hurricanes originally supplied to Rumania as the result of a visit in November 1938 by King Carol, who had been much impressed by the Hurricanes he had inspected or watched in flying displays. Formed into *Escadrila* (Squadron) 53, they destroyed seven Russian warplanes in the first two days of fighting and remained in action until 1942, when a lack of spare parts caused their withdrawal from hostilities.

Finland was also an ally of Hitler, being understandably eager for revenge for a Russian assault on her during the winter of 1939–40 as unprovoked and brutal as the German onslaught on Poland. At that time Finland had also acquired twelve Hurricanes, which a group of her pilots under Lieutenant Räty flew in batches of three first to Wick in Scotland, then by way of Norway and Sweden to Finland, where they formed Detachment Räty, part of *Lentolaivue* (Squadron) 22. Unfortunately, only ten of the Hawker fighters reached Finland, since one was 'written off' at Wick and another crash-landed in Norway in bad weather.

By the time Finland joined Germany in the great invasion of Russia – she declared war on 25 June 1941 – two more Hurricanes had been lost in accidents but the remaining eight, fitted with snow-skids in place of tailwheels to assist their operation from snow-covered airfields, performed magnificently. They shot down five Russian warplanes in July and were still being used in the interceptor role as late as January 1942, in which month, incidentally, they downed another three Soviet aircraft. After this, a shortage of spares restricted them to reconnaissance missions and finally grounded them in July 1943.

It might be added that the Hurricane detachment served, at various times, with four or five different squadrons as and when needed. Clearly the Finnish pilots valued it highly, as well they might. On 16 September 1941, a Hurricane strafing Russian ground troops was shot down by AA fire and its pilot, Captain Kalaja, was killed. This, though, was the only time a Finnish Hurricane was lost through enemy action; not a single Hurricane or Hurricane pilot fell in aerial combat.

Finland's geographical position was a greater concern to the Allies than her Hurricanes. She threatened the crucial Russian ports where supplies from Britain, and later America, would have to be delivered. These were Murmansk at the head of the Kola Inlet, 200 miles east of Norway's North Cape, and Archangel, a further 400 miles to the southeast, which had far better unloading facilities but, unlike Murmansk, was ice-bound during the winter months. Accordingly it was decided that a new Fighter Command Hurricane unit would be sent to Russia with the dual task of protecting the vital ports and any convoys unloading at them, and of teaching the Russians how to fly and maintain the large numbers of Hurricanes that Britain proposed to send them.

On 12 August 1941, therefore, 151 Wing was officially formed under Wing Commander Henry Ramsbottom-Isherwood, who had been born in New Zealand but whose family, surely, had originally come from the North Country. It contained two squadrons of Hurricanes: No. 81 that had come into existence on 29 July and was based on a detached flight from 504 Squadron, and No. 134, similarly created on 31 July from a flight of 17 Squadron. These controlled a total of thirty-nine Hurricanes, almost all of them Mark IIBs with twelve machine guns, though it seems that a few were older IIAs with only eight guns.

The new squadrons were entrusted to Squadron Leaders 'Tony' Rook and 'Tony' Miller respectively. The Rook family had an interest in both of them, for Flight Lieutenant Michael Rook, a cousin of 81's CO, although

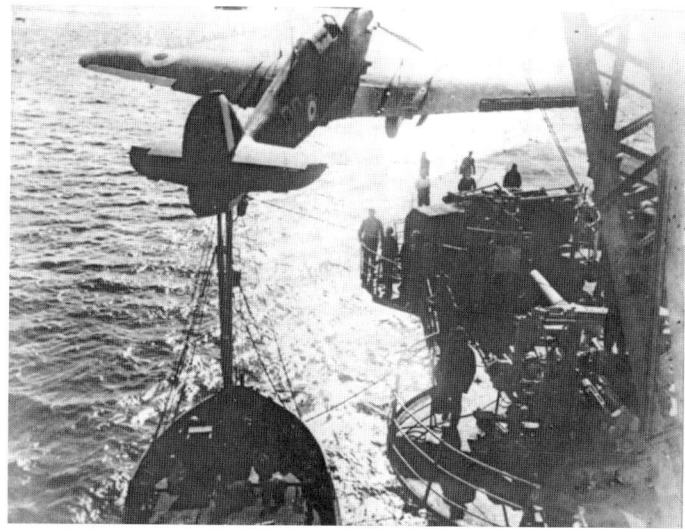

Hurricane of 46 Squadron being hoisted aboard HM aircraft carrier *Glorious* on the River Clyde. The squadron would fly off the carrier to Norway, but it was thought impossible to land on it. The pilots, however, decided otherwise.

Left: 46 Squadron's Flight Lieutenant 'Pat' Jameson who had the dangerous honour of being the first man to land a Hurricane on an aircraft carrier.

Right: Air Marshal Sir Kenneth Cross who was CO of 46 Squadron during the Norwegian campaign.

Hurricane of 32 Squadron being refuelled. Based at Biggin Hill, 32 took part in many of the early clashes in the Battle of Britain, including one on 20 July 1940.

Squadron Leader John Peel, CO of 145 Squadron, who fired the first shots on the crucial 8 August 1940.

The enemy. Top: Messerschmitt Bf 110s. Bottom: Messerschmitt Bf 109. The German precision-bombing unit *Erprobungsgruppe* (Test Group) 210 contained both these types, both carrying bombs.

Squadron Leader John Thompson, CO of 111 Squadron. This squadron inflicted a heavy defeat on *Erprobungsgruppe* 210 on 15 August 1940 and Thompson personally shot down its magnificent leader *Hauptmann* Walter Rubensdörffer.

South African Hurricanes. Top: From 1 Squadron SAAF. Left: From 3 Squadron SAAF.

Hurricanes of 1 Squadron SAAF over northern Eritrea.

The most successful pilot of the East African campaign was Captain John 'Jack' Frost of 3 SAAF. This photo shows the wreck of one of his victims, a Fiat CR 42 that he shot down over an army camp on 3 February 1941. Though confirmed by scores of eye-witnesses, its loss was never admitted by the Italians.

On 15 March 1941, Frost was himself shot down by AA fire when he was strafing Diredawa airfield. He had to force-land and his Hurricane is shown here. It is surprisingly intact.

Frost was rescued by another 3 SAAF pilot, Lieutenant 'Bob' Kershaw, who landed his Hurricane and took off again under fire with Frost sitting on his knees, a feat for which he was awarded a DSO. The two pilots are seen here together, Kershaw on the left and Frost on the right.

Operation HURRY. Above: Hurricanes of 418 Flight aboard HM carrier *Argus*. Right: A Hurricane of 418 Flight safely on Malta.

Sergeant 'Fred' Robertson had an unfortunate landing on Malta, but later became one of its most successful pilots.

Flight Lieutenant James MacLachlan was one of the few survivors of the tragic Operation WHITE. He also became one of Malta's leading pilots until he was badly wounded on 16 February 1941 and lost an arm, which did not prevent him flying and fighting again elsewhere and later.

The Hurricanes of 418 Flight joined with those of Malta's existing Fighter Flight to form 261 Squadron, aircraft of which are seen here on Takali airfield.

Hurricanes taking off from Takali airfield.

No. 261's ground crews who, despite constant problems, kept the Hurricanes airworthy.

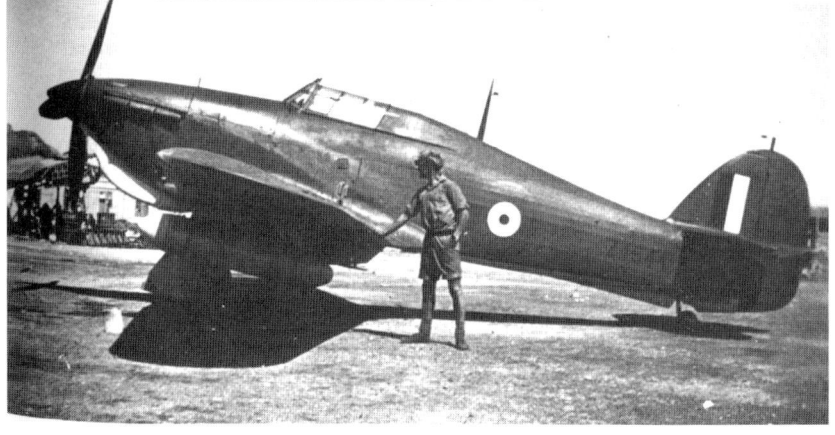

During April and May 1941 Hurricane IIs reached Malta. Top: IIAs aboard HM carrier *Ark Royal*. Bottom: A IIA on a Malta airfield.

Hurricane of 185 Squadron, formed on Malta in May 1941.

Focke-Wulf Fw 200C: the Condor. Powerful and well-armed, it was a dangerous opponent and as a bomber and a long-range scout for U-boats, a menace to Allied merchantmen.

A Sea Hurricane IA 'Hurricat' being lifted onto its CAM-ship. The same photograph, but note that in the top version the censor has blotted out vessels in the background whereas in the bottom version they have been restored.

CAM-ship pilots who engaged Condors. Top left to right: Flying Officer George Varley; Flying Officer Norman Taylor; Pilot Officer James Stewart. Left: Pilot Officer 'Paddy' Flynn.

RAF Hurricanes in Russia. Above: From 81 Squadron. Left (in the snow): From 134 Squadron.

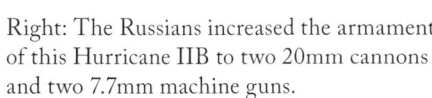

Right: The Russians increased the armament of this Hurricane IIB to two 20mm cannons and two 7.7mm machine guns.

Z2585, a Russian Hurricane IIA that crash-landed in Finnish territory, was repaired by the Finns and served them as a trainer until 31 May 1944.

Russian Hurricane pilots. Left: Lieutenant Colonel Boris Safonov, the first man to command a Hurricane Air Regiment (equivalent to a British wing). Centre: Major Petr Sgibnev, the highest-scoring Russian Hurricane 'ace' with eleven 'kills'. Right: Lieutenant General of Aviation Vasily Strelnikov had, when a captain, become the last Russian Hurricane 'ace' and always had 'special affection' for the Hawker fighter.

Air Commodore Stanley Vincent who commanded the Hurricane fighter group in Sumatra and Java, and later during the Imphal/Kohima campaign.

American Flying Officer Arthur Donahue of 258 Squadron who was wounded in an attack on Japanese troop barges on 15 February 1942 and evacuated from Sumatra.

Two views of a Hurricane being serviced at P1 airfield, Sumatra. As always, the splendid ground crews kept the Hurricanes flying in immensely difficult conditions.

Hurricanes on P1 airfield, Sumatra. They were kept widely dispersed because of the constant threat of Japanese air-raids.

Hurricane of 258 Squadron in Ceylon, where 258 re-formed after leaving Sumatra.

Hurricane on Tjililitan airfield, Java.

Hurricane of 69 Squadron which, based on Malta, carried out dangerous and essential photo-reconnaissance missions.

Hurricane in Italian hands. Hit by AA fire, it crashed onto Comiso airfield, Sicily, remaining surprisingly intact.

Sea Hurricane IBs on board a Royal Navy fleet carrier.

The three British aircraft carriers that participated in Operation PEDESTAL: in the foreground Sea Hurricanes of 885 Squadron on the deck of HMS *Victorious*; behind her HMS *Indomitable*; in the distance HMS *Eagle*.

HMS *Indomitable* carried two squadrons of Sea Hurricanes: 800 – aircraft from which are seen here preparing to take off – and 880.

Pilots of 880 Squadron. Left: Sub-Lieutenant Hugh Popham, who made a perilous landing in fading light on 11 August 1942. Right: Lieutenant Richard Cork, who shot down five enemy aircraft on 12 August 1942.

Hurricane IICs of 87 Squadron that participated in Operation JUBILEE, the raid on Dieppe on 19 August 1942.

'Hurribomber' of 241 Squadron on a Tunisian airfield.

Hurricane of 28 Squadron on reconnaissance in the vicinity of Imphal.

Tactical reconnaissance Hurricane of 28 Squadron on Imphal airfield.

Camouflaging a 42 Squadron Hurricane.

'Hurribomber' of 60 Squadron.

Anti-tank Hurricane IID of 20 Squadron.

like him formerly of 504 Squadron, was transferred not to 81 but to 134. Michael Rook, incidentally, was reckoned to be the tallest pilot in the RAF and it was felt that he did well to get into a Hurricane at all. By contrast, the other 134 flight commander Jack Ross – his name really was Jack, not John – came from 17 Squadron and at less than 5ft tall, was probably the smallest of all the men who flew Hurricanes.

At the end of August, the very first convoy to Russia, earlier even than those famous convoys with the code-letters PQ, assembled at Iceland. Given the rather odd code-name of DERVISH, this consisted of the little carrier *Argus* from which Hurricanes had once flown to Malta and on which were now twenty-four of 151 Wing's fighters, seven merchantmen carrying fifteen more Hurricanes in crates as well as their main cargo of munitions, and the remainder of the Wing's personnel in the *Llanstephan Castle*, a former luxury liner. Once again the Hurricanes' importance was emphasized by the strength of their escort: carrier *Victorious*, cruisers *Shropshire*, *Devonshire* and *Suffolk*, and six destroyers.

A voyage over the Arctic Ocean was not a pleasant one and the pilots were probably relieved when on 7 September, the Hurricanes which had been fitted with only six machine guns to reduce weight, left *Argus* for the airfield at Vaenga, north-east of Murmansk. Though none of the pilots had ever taken off from a carrier before, all got airborne safely. Flight Lieutenant Berg and Sergeant Campbell, both of 134, damaged their undercarriages in the process, but landed safely at Vaenga without injury to their aeroplanes or themselves.

Vaenga, in fact, was far from being an ideal base, having no real runways; merely a surface of rolled sand which in bad weather gave the Hurricanes plenty of opportunity to prove their ruggedness. Nor was there any radar, control system or effective communications available. On the other hand, the welcome from the Russian pilots stationed there was so enthusiastic that the RAF airmen were unfit for flying before 11 September.

It had been intended that the convoy's merchantmen would unload at Murmansk, but enemy air activity resulted in their being diverted to Archangel, thereby illustrating the need for the fighter cover that the Hurricanes would provide. The crates containing the other fifteen of these were removed to the nearby aerodrome at Keg Ostrov, after which the majority of the Wing's ground crews set off for Vaenga by rail, leaving behind only a small party charged with erecting the Hurricanes.

This was a far from easy task, since essential equipment such as spanners for the propellers were not to be found. Fortunately, the Russians had mustered a body of exceptionally able technicians for instruction on Hurricane maintenance. These now arrived at Keg Ostrov, where they improvised the missing tools, enabling the RAF contingent to have all fifteen Hurricanes assembled and airworthy in just nine days.

When the first three Hurricanes were made ready on 9 September, a delegation of Russian officers and civilian officials gathered at Keg Ostrov, keen to see the Hawker fighters for the first time. The Wing's pilots did not disappoint them, putting on a display of low-level aerobatics that could only have been performed by aircraft as tough and manoeuvrable as the Hurricane, flown by very fine and experienced airmen. They were led by Pilot Officer Raymond Holmes who had fought throughout the Battle of Britain as a sergeant pilot with 504. In his reminiscences entitled *Sky Spy* he recalls gleefully:

> If we'd flown like this at a British airfield we'd have been court-martialled. The cloud was below a thousand feet, so the three of us were able to circle the aerodrome in cloud, then spiral out at full throttle, sweeping at ground level across the grass straight at the delegation, and climbing up over their heads a hundred yards short of them. We tore out from behind hangars at them, vertically banked over their heads, until red Very lights from the control tower indicated that they had seen enough. We did a couple of rolls and went into tight formation to land in a vic of three.

The Russians were delighted, impressed and apparently enjoyably terrified. It was a happy prelude to one of the Hurricane's most successful campaigns.

At Vaenga 134 Squadron made the first patrols over enemy-occupied territory on 11 September. These encountered no opposition, but were not without their dangers, for Russian petrol was of inferior quality, being only 95 octane and not 100 as was essential for the best performance of the Hurricanes' Merlin engines. As a result, both Jack Ross and Pilot Officer Neil Cameron[1] had their engines cut out, Ross on three separate occasions. They were within a few feet of the ground before their desperate use of the priming pump restored the Merlins to life.

It was 81 Squadron that first saw combat, however. In the afternoon of 12 September, five of its Hurricanes were sent off to intercept enemy aircraft reported west of Murmansk. Though one of them was flown by Pilot Officer James Walker, the formation was led by the more experienced Flight Sergeant Charlton 'Wag' Haw, destined to become 151 Wing's most successful pilot. Sergeants Rigby, Smith and Waud completed the flight.

At about 1525, the Hurricanes sighted a Henschel Hs 126 army co-operation aircraft, apparently on an observation mission, escorted by five Messerschmitt Bf 109s. They attacked immediately and Waud fired on the Henschel which fell away, pouring out smoke though he was unable to see what happened to it as the Hurricanes were then engaged by its escort. Walker, Waud and Haw all shot down 109s, but Sergeant Norman Smith was hit; he tried to force-land but crashed and was killed. He was buried two days later in the Cemetery of Soviet Heroes on high ground overlooking Murmansk Sound, the only pilot of 151 Wing to lose his life in Russia.

This first success of the Wing was all the more commendable because all the Hurricanes involved still carried only six machine guns. It greatly encouraged the Russian pilots awaiting tuition at Vaenga, as well as leading to a flurry of congratulatory telegrams. Yet perhaps in some ways 12 September was equally important because it also saw 134 Squadron carry out two separate missions escorting Russian bombers attacking enemy positions.

From then onwards, escort duties were to be a major task for both 81 and 134 Squadrons, and a vital one since Axis ground troops were now only some 30 miles away and were spearheaded by the heroic defenders of Narvik, General Dietl's Austrians. During September and early October, Hurricanes flew about thirty-five missions on guard of Russian bombers as these struck at targets including army posts, AA batteries and aerodromes. So successful were these raids that the enemy advance was brought to a halt and so effective was the protection provided by the Hurricanes that only one Russian aircraft was lost, and that to AA fire.

Of course the Germans did try to engage the Russians, but they always found the Hurricanes waiting for them. By mid-September, all 151 Wing's Hurricane IIBs had regained their full armament of twelve machine guns and when on the afternoon of the 17th, eight of

81's fighters, led by Squadron Leader Rook, took off to meet and cover returning Russian bombers, their pilots were confident that they could cope with any eventualities.

They had good reason to be. At 1855, they sighted the bombers but also eight Messerschmitt Bf 109s preparing to attack these. Instead, they were themselves attacked by the Hurricanes. Rook damaged one Messerschmitt, oil from which covered his windscreen; he continued to fire until he ran out of ammunition, when the 109 was finished off by the combined efforts of Sergeants Anson and Sims. Pilot Officer Bush out-turned another 109 and shot it down in flames, while Flight Sergeant Haw destroyed a third, the pilot of which baled out.

Even after the remaining Messerschmitts had made a hasty departure, 81's pilots were still not out of danger, for Russian fighters had appeared and, mistaking the Hurricanes for enemy aircraft, proceeded to attack them. Sergeant Anson in particular had to take violent evasive action but happily was unhurt, and all the Hurricanes returned safely to base, as did all the bombers that 81 had protected.

A similar encounter took place on the afternoon of 26 September. Again the RAF unit involved was 81 Squadron, six of its fighters clashing with six 109s. On this occasion, the Hurricanes were acting as close escort to Russian bombers when the Messerschmitts dived down on the formation from above. Perhaps recalling an earlier incident, the Germans this time made their initial assault on the Hurricanes, but 81's pilots, despite their height disadvantage, not only prevented any attack on the bombers but out-manoeuvred, out-flew and out-fought their opponents, shooting down three of them without loss.

As might have been expected, one of the 'kills' was made by the redoubtable Flight Sergeant Haw, who used up all his ammunition in the process. He was then attacked by another 109 and dived to a low level where he was able to shake off his pursuer. Haw's 'hat-trick' was acknowledged by an award of the Order of Lenin, the only time this was ever given to a non-commissioned officer. He also received a less remarkable British decoration, the Distinguished Flying Medal. He apparently thought this entirely adequate.

Against German raids, by contrast, the Hurricanes proved largely ineffective, not through any fault of their own but because the Russian control and warning systems were frankly abysmal. A number of fruitless sorties were not only frustrating but resulted in 151 Wing's only fatal casualties apart from that of the unlucky Norman Smith.

On Vaenga's bumpy and pot-holed surface it had become the practice that two men should hold down the Hurricanes' tails as they taxied into position so as to stop them tipping forward. This they did by lying on the tailplane and rear of the fuselage. On 27 September Flight Lieutenant Berg of 134 Squadron, eager to get at a 'recce' Ju 88 reported to be approaching the airfield, tried to take off without realizing that Aircraftsmen Ridley and Thomas had not got off the tail and were pinned to it by the slipstream. The Hurricane crashed from about 50ft. Its strength enabled Berg to survive with severe injuries to his head and legs. Both the airmen died instantly.

Even a raid by fourteen Junkers Ju 88s and half a dozen Messerschmitt Bf 109s directed against Vaenga itself on 6 October caught the Russian observers by surprise and 134's Hurricanes took off amid falling bombs and machine-gun strafing. All, though, got airborne safely and scattered the Ju 88s, shooting down two, plus one 'probable' – which presumably came down since the Russians later located three wrecks on the ground – and two damaged. No Hurricanes were lost and Flight Lieutenant Michael Rook, attacked by the 109s, damaged one and then escaped at low level.

This was 151 Wing's last combat in Russia. In all, 81 Squadron had destroyed twelve enemy aircraft, while 134 had added three or four more. Each victory, incidentally, was rewarded by a bonus of 100 roubles, then worth about £20. The pilots, it should be said, were not happy about this 'blood money', masking their distaste by joking that it would infringe their 'amateur status'. They ultimately solved the problem by donating their winnings to the RAF Benevolent Fund.

Considering the minute casualties suffered, this was an achievement well deserving the message of congratulations that the Wing received from the Air Minister, Sir Archibald Sinclair. The Russians were similarly gracious and awarded the Order of Lenin not only to Haw, but also to Ramsbottom-Isherwood and Squadron Leaders Rook and Miller; a distinction not conferred on any other non-Russian airman.

There was every reason for the Russians' gratitude, for quite apart from any aerial victories, 151 Wing, particularly 134 Squadron, had done admirable work in training Russian pilots to fly the Hurricane.

On 25 September Major General Kuznetsov, who was in command not only at Vaenga but of all the air elements of the Soviet Northern Fleet, made the first Russian solo flight in a Hurricane. The general enjoyed very good relations with Ramsbottom-Isherwood, with whom his cooperation was exemplary, and he was presented with the Hurricane in question on which had been painted a red star over the RAF roundels and the Russian code-number 01.

On 26 September Captains Safonov and Kuharenko also went solo on Hurricanes and, it seems, liked them very much. Boris Safonov, who was already credited with fourteen victories in the early months of fighting on the Russian front, proved particularly 'at home' with the Hurricane and by early October was acting as an instructor to other Russian pilots. The Russians as a whole were desperately keen to learn, and in the RAF Official History, 134's Squadron Leader Miller is quoted as reporting:

They would turn up and demand training in the most appalling weather. I remember one pilot doing his first solo in a snow-storm that would have shaken any of us. It took him three shots to get down, and each time he went round again he disappeared completely from sight. I never expected to see him again. However, he made it.

On 16 and 17 October, 151 Wing flew its final sorties – bomber escort on both days – and thereafter handed over all their Hurricanes to the Russian 72nd Regiment of the Red Naval Air Fleet. Nor were the Wing's aircraft the only Hurricanes that this received. As stated earlier, it had been decided that Hurricanes would be supplied to Russia and by now about 100 had been received at Murmansk. These were sent in crates and had to be reassembled, but some sixty of them were ready for use and these were added to the ones from 81 and 134 Squadrons, enabling the Russians on 25 October to form the new 78th Air Regiment, the Russian equivalent of a Wing. Unlike 151 Wing, this contained not two but three squadrons and was commanded by Safonov, promoted to lieutenant colonel.

With their duties discharged, winter closing in and the poverty and political oppression in Russia becoming ever more apparent and depressing, 151 Wing's personnel were eager to return home. They finally sailed from Murmansk on various Royal Navy vessels, chiefly cruiser *Kenya*, in late November. As a last happy touch, they were escorted by Hurricanes flown by Major General Kuznetsov and Lieutenant Colonel Safonov.

This was not only a friendly gesture but a symbolic one, since 151 Wing's influence in Russia lasted long after its departure. Its first direct influence came from its tuition of the pilots who formed the 78th Air Regiment, some of whom, moreover, were transferred to the 152nd Air Regiment that received its first ten Hurricanes to replace aged biplanes on 16 November.

Russian Hurricane pilots had engaged enemy aircraft even before 151 Wing had left their country. Their first encounter took place on the same day that the 78th Air Regiment was formed: 25 October. The enemy was a formation of Messerschmitt Bf 110s, one of which was sent diving away steeply, with smoke pouring from it, by Lieutenant Sinev. Its destruction does not appear in German records, but since other members of Sinev's flight confirmed it had gone down, this may be another case in which the German records are incomplete or have been mislaid.

There is no doubt at all about the 78th's next claim. On 16 November, a wretched Junkers Ju 52 three-engined transport lost its way as a result of compass failure and strayed over Soviet territory. It was shot down by Lieutenant Kravchenko, eight of its passengers and crew being killed and the other six taken prisoner. The Russians suffered their first loss on 17 December when Lieutenant Volkov was shot down and killed by Messerschmitt Bf 109s, but Lieutenant Colonel Safonov gained some revenge by damaging a 109 so badly that it returned to its airfield only to be 'written off'. Boris Safonov, incidentally, is reported to have 'loved the Hurricane', in which he would fly forty-four combat missions, adding a Heinkel He 111 to his list of victories.[2]

Earlier on 24 November, Lieutenant Gavrilov shot down a 109 to record the 152nd Air Regiment's first success. In spite of his exalted rank, Major General Kuznetsov occasionally flew a Hurricane with the 152nd and is recorded as strafing a Finnish aerodrome. Most of the 152nd's combats during the winter were with Finnish warplanes, with both sides suffering losses. One particularly dramatic encounter on 4 December saw a Hurricane flown by Lieutenant Nicolay Repnikov destroyed in a collision with an enemy fighter, with both Repnikov and Finland's leading 'ace' Sergeant Toivo Tamminen losing their lives.

No account exists of a combat between a Russian and a Finnish Hurricane – this might have made interesting reading – but there was one Hurricane that served both nations. On 4 February 1942 Z2585, a Hurricane IIA of the 152nd Air Regiment, was attacked by Finnish fighters while on a reconnaissance mission. Lieutenant Feodosiy Zodorozhniy managed to evade his opponents, but his Hurricane had suffered damage to its engine and this failed while he was still over Finnish territory, forcing him to crash-land on the ice of a frozen lake. He was unhurt, managed to avoid capture and returned safely to his unit, but Z2585 was later repaired by the Finns and used as a trainer from 16 March to 31 May 1944, the last Hurricane to fly with the Finnish Air Force.

Another lesson that 151 Wing had taught was that Hurricanes could operate perfectly well in the harsh Russian conditions. Accordingly, massive numbers of the Hawker fighters were delivered to Russia by the Arctic convoys or through Persia from stocks in the Middle East and North-West India. Unfortunately, political bigotry resulted in the Soviet authorities trying to repress all mention of the aid they were receiving from the Western Allies, although protesting angrily if supplies were ever delayed. The fall of the Communist regime, however, has allowed many hidden details to emerge, sometimes casting doubts on previously accepted facts.

For example, all earlier sources agreed that the number of Hurricanes sent to Russia was 2,952, and since some were known to have been lost in transit, it was reasonable to suppose that the Russians must have received a lesser number. On the contrary, Russian sources now state that they received a greater number, with the figures ranging from 3,082 to 3,360. This is so surprising that it may be wondered if the same aircraft have been counted more than once when they changed units or were adapted, for instance.

Whatever the true position, it is unarguable that a lot of Hurricanes saw service in Russia. In *Soviet Hurricane Aces of World War 2*, Yuriy Rybin reports that Hurricanes at different times equipped twenty-seven air regiments each containing at least two and sometimes three squadrons, as well as the Free French 'Normandie' Squadron that fought alongside the Russian Air Force from the end of 1942. They performed a wide variety of tasks, including some not directly connected with wartime missions. For example, the Hurricanes' combination of strength and reliability made them ideal advanced trainers. The Russians converted several of them into two-seaters for this purpose, one of which was used by the Free French. Another was provided with a machine gun in the rear cockpit, but this adaptation does not appear to have been a success and was not repeated.

Surprisingly, the Russians have claimed that the Hurricane was difficult to maintain. It seems, though, that their ground crews simply could not match the superb standard of those in the RAF and refused to listen to British mechanics sent out to advise them. A party of Rolls-Royce experts investigating complaints about the Merlin engine found fifty of these at one depot alone allowed to rust in the open. Even despite this lack of skills, however, it is worth noting that Yuriy Rybin in his *Soviet Hurricane Aces* can still declare that Hurricanes had 'better serviceability rates' than Russian aircraft!

Some Russian pilots also criticized the Hurricane. Leo McKinstry in *Hurricane: Victor of the Battle of Britain* quotes an unpublished memoir of Colonel Igor Kaberov complaining of the aircraft's lack of speed and the lack of penetrative power of the Browning machine guns in the Mark IIAs and IIBs. The Russians remedied this latter weakness by adapting many of their Hurricanes to carry two 20mm cannons and two 12.7mm machine guns, and a few to carry all these weapons plus four of the standard Brownings, giving them a most impressive firepower.

Colonel Kaberov's unit among others used a different adaptation, replacing the Hurricanes' Brownings with 0.5in machine guns taken from American Tomahawks, Kittyhawks and Airacobras. Kaberov confirms that his Hurricanes' armament was now good, though it would have been pleasant if he had given some credit to the Hurricanes' versatility. Moreover, the reason why the Hurricane was allowed to rob the American types of their armament was because it was regarded as more reliable than they were. It may also be noticed that no mention is made of the 1,000-plus Hurricane Mark IICs supplied to Russia, which were armed with four 20mm cannons.

As for the Hurricane's lack of speed, this had always been a drawback but was compensated by its virtues, which Yuriy Rybin details as a 'sturdy construction', 'simple to fly', 'a stable gun platform' and 'an advantage over any Bf 109' in manoeuvrability. It was these virtues which had enabled 151 Wing to gain its victories over enemy fighters and bombers alike and it would be these virtues that would enable Russian Hurricane pilots to do the same.

Though Yuriy Rybin tells us that the records of five of the air regiments which contained Hurricanes cannot be found, in his *Soviet Hurricane Aces* he can still refer to 125 Hurricane pilots who between them were credited with the destruction of 281 enemy warplanes. Of course, these figures may not tell the whole story. It is fair to say that Russian pilots seem to have been particularly liable to exaggerate, and some of these claims were no doubt optimistic or duplicated. To complicate matters still further, the Russians often granted to all pilots involved in a shared claim full credit for a 'kill', not just for a fraction as did the British.

Nonetheless, certain points do become clear. Most pilots had only one or two successes, but fourteen gained the unofficial status of 'ace' by destroying five or more enemy aircraft. All of these regarded the Hurricane highly, none more so than Major Petr Sgibnev who, with eleven hostile warplanes destroyed while flying Hurricanes – and nineteen in all – was Russia's most successful Hurricane pilot and second only to Safonov as her Air Force's 'top scorer'.

While with the Hurricane unit 78th Air Regiment, Sgibnev shot down his first enemy aircraft, a Bf 109, on 3 April 1942. Thereafter, he was successful with such regularity that he became CO of the 78th's 1st Squadron on 18 June at the age of only 21. In January 1943 he became CO of the 2nd Guards Combined Air Regiment (formerly the 72nd Air Regiment). His new command also contained Kittyhawks and Airacobras, but Sgibnev continued to fly Hurricanes for some time, his attitude being that the Hurricane might be slower than some other machines but was more capable of shooting the enemy down. Sgibnev did later switch to Airacobras, but was tragically killed on 3 May 1943 when 'beating up' his airfield.

Nor was the Hurricane of value only in the fighter role, as is made clear by an article in the *Soviet War News* of 3 October 1942, quoted in Maurice Allward's *Hurricane Special*. It should also be remembered that Communist doctrine demanded that the Russian people should hear little about the aid received from the Western Allies and we do know that after the war, Stalin ordered 'hundreds of surviving Hurricanes' – and presumably other British and American types as well – to be thrown into disused mineshafts to conceal them from view. It is most unlikely, therefore, that this article would have deliberately exaggerated the Hurricanes' effect.

In the article it is stated that Hurricanes were 'successful in reconnaissance duty'; well, so they were in the North Africa and India-Burma theatres. One Hurricane unit is credited with escorting Russian bombers for three months and losing only one of them to enemy fighters; well, 151 Wing had escorted Russian bombers for much of September and October 1941 and not lost any. A combat is described in which Hurricanes had destroyed three Messerschmitt Bf 109s without loss; well, 81 Squadron had done this not once but twice. To label the article 'propaganda', as it has been, is unjust and inaccurate.

One Hurricane duty was not mentioned by the *Soviet War News* but proved increasingly important: ground attack. The Russians gave a further illustration of the Hurricanes' adaptability by fitting some of them with rails from which six rockets could be launched, but mainly they carried bombs which they used against enemy troops, motor transport, gun batteries, ammunition dumps and other targets. The Mark IICs are said to have been particularly valuable since they could use not only bombs but their four 20mm cannons with great effect.

By 1943 the Russians were employing their Hurricanes less as interceptors and more in the ground-attack role. In April Churchill arranged to send them sixty Hurricane IIDs with two 40mm anti-tank guns, and later thirty Mark IVs, similarly armed but capable of carrying a wide variety of different weapons. The IIDs at least were able to participate in perhaps Russia's most decisive victory.

It is rarely remembered that the Germans' disaster at Stalingrad did not end their attempts to subdue Russia. It was indeed followed by a brilliant German counter-offensive that culminated in their recapture of Kharkov by 15 March 1943. The spring thaw prevented further advances but on 5 July, the Battle of Kursk began. By 4 August, it had become a total German defeat and the Russians had begun an advance that ended only in Berlin, mainly because the Germans' colossal tank losses could never be made good. The Hurricane IID 'tank busters' can only have played a small part in the Russian triumph, but judging by their achievements against German armour in the Western Desert and Tunisia, it will surely have been a not unworthy one.

Moreover, even in 1943, Russian Hurricane pilots were still gaining occasional victories over enemy aircraft, though at a high cost. Among the successful airmen, mention should be made of Captain Vasiliy Strelnikov, who flew Hurricanes with the 78th Air Regiment from December 1942 to September 1943, becoming the last Russian Hurricane pilot to destroy or damage beyond repair five German warplanes. In return, his Hurricane was twice set on fire. On the first occasion he baled out; on the second he had to 'ditch', luckily close to shore. Both times he suffered burns and other injuries, but he survived and indeed lived to see the end of the Second World War and enjoy a distinguished career thereafter. Yuriy Rybin ends his book on *Soviet Hurricane Aces* with an extract from Strelnikov's memoirs which may also serve to end this chapter:

> I began my service in 1940 as a graduate of the naval aviation academy and left in 1981 as a Lieutenant General of Aviation. During my years of service I became familiar with the greatest variety of aircraft types, from training biplanes to supersonic bombers. But I remember with special affection the one which was simple by today's standards: the Hurricane. It was in this very aircraft that I encountered war at a time when the combat potential of the Luftwaffe was at its zenith during the most difficult years for our country, 1942–43. I recorded victories in it and stayed alive when I was shot down. This is undoubtedly due to this rugged and reliable British aircraft.

Notes

1. Neil Cameron deserves much more than just a passing reference. Flying with 17 Squadron, from which it will be remembered 134 had been formed, he had assisted in the destruction of four enemy aircraft during November 1940. After his time in Russia, he flew Hurricanes in North Africa, first with 213 Squadron, downing a Savoia Marchetti SM 79 on 14 November 1942, and later with the Greek 335 Squadron. In February 1945 he commanded a Thunderbolt squadron in Burma. After the war, he rose to become Air Chief Marshal Sir Neil Cameron, Chief of the Air Staff, and later Marshal of the Royal Air Force and Chief of the Defence Staff. On retirement he was created Baron Cameron of Balhousie. He died on 30 January 1985.
2. Safonov would later gain four more successes while commanding a Kittyhawk wing, thereby becoming Russia's highest-scoring fighter 'ace'. He was killed in action when engaging German bombers on 30 May 1942.

Chapter Eight

Adverse Odds: Sumatra and Java

While the vessels carrying the men of 151 Wing back from Russia were moving in a great semi-circle across the Arctic Ocean, a Japanese Task Force, built around six splendid aircraft carriers, was heading eastward through the cold waters of the North Pacific. On 3 December – their second 3 December as they had just crossed the International Date Line – the carriers turned south-east to race towards Hawaii. Early on the 7th, their aircraft took off and in a ruthlessly efficient assault lasting just over an hour and a half they crippled the United States Pacific Fleet and added America to the number of Britain's allies.

That same 7 December was also the moment that Britain faced a new enemy, all the more dangerous because very little was known of her capabilities, which were fatally underestimated. This ignorance was especially prevalent with regard to Japan's warplanes, which even official publications described as being mere imitations of Western types, only five years out of date.

To add to the Allies' confusion, the Japanese system of aircraft classification was one of extraordinary complexity, made worse by Japan's Army and Navy Air Forces using different and alternative methods of identification. The Allies attempted to avoid these difficulties by deciding upon arbitrary code-names for each type, the bombers being given ladies' names and the fighters men's names with, in practice, one important exception.

Probably the most famous of Japanese warplanes was known to them as the A6M or Navy Fighter Type 00 or Zero-Sen.[1] The Allies followed the Japanese example and although given the code-name of 'Zeke', this aircraft was almost always called the Zero or, by Royal Air Force pilots, the Navy 0 or Navy Nought. With a top speed of about 350 mph at its preferred altitude, a good rate of climb, an exceptionally long range and an armament of two 20mm cannons and two 7.7mm machine guns,

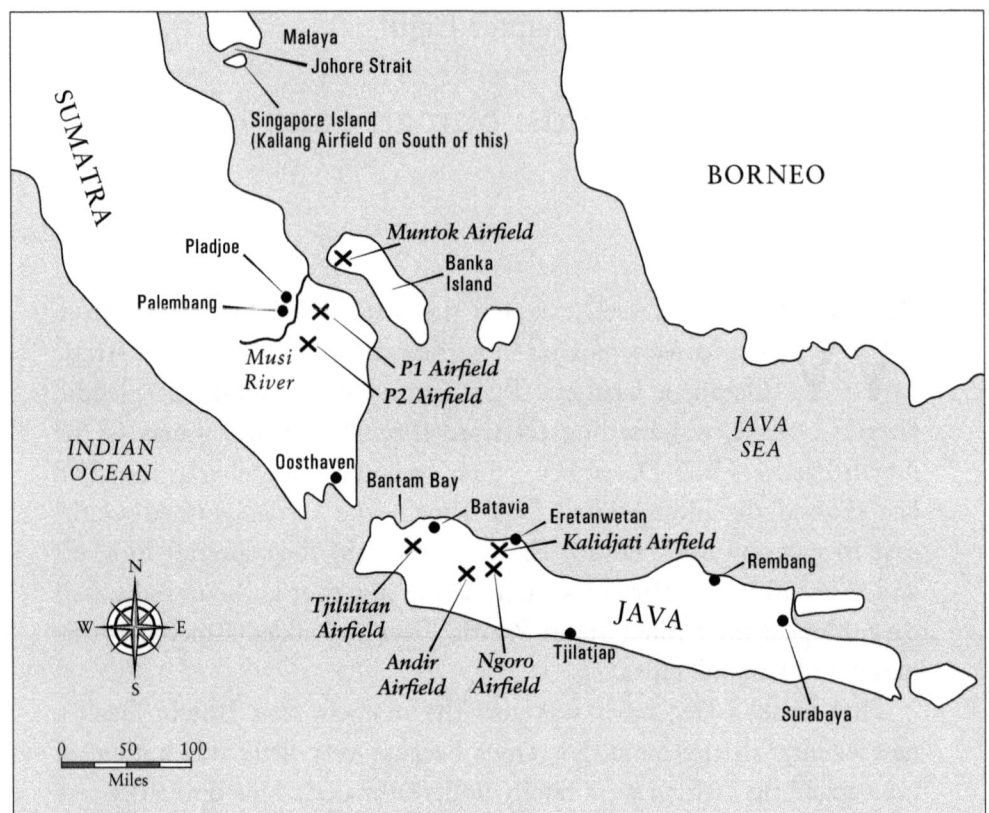

Map 3: Hurricane operations in Sumatra and Java.

the Zero was a formidable antagonist. So much was this the case that accounts during the war and for many years afterwards would refer to every Japanese fighter as a Zero, perhaps in unconscious tribute to its excellence.

It was, however, a navy fighter and consequently when Hurricanes were sent to the Far East, as inevitably they were, they rarely encountered Zeros, their main opponents being Army Nakajima Ki-27 'Nates' or Nakajima Ki-43 'Oscars'. These had a lesser speed of at most 310 mph and a smaller armament of just two 7.7mm machine guns, though the Oscars would later increase this to two 12.7mms. Nonetheless, they also proved dangerous opponents since they were mostly flown by men who had become very skilful and experienced in Japan's long war with China.

Unfortunately, the woeful ignorance of Japanese capabilities that has already been mentioned meant that the RAF pilots sent to the Far East were quite unaware of the dangers and difficulties they would have to face. In particular, they had no notion of the virtues and defects of Japanese fighter aircraft. Their early clashes with these provided some unpleasant surprises and have led to more denigration of the unlucky Hurricane.

The problem and its solution have been well summed up by Terence Kelly, a sergeant in No. 258, the second Hurricane squadron to appear in the Far East, in his book *Nine Lives of a Fighter Pilot*. The main trouble, he points out, was that the RAF airmen had been 'led to believe that the Hurricane was the most manoeuvrable modern fighter aircraft (which in Europe it certainly was).' They quickly learned that, on the contrary, the enemy fighters would not only 'vastly outnumber us' but also 'could out-turn us. So getting involved in dog-fighting was no more than a short cut to suicide.'

> 'On the other hand,' Kelly continues, 'we could fly to heights which the Japanese fighters simply could not reach, we had the better firepower and we could subject our Hurricanes to stresses which the Navy 0s could not tolerate...
>
> 'So, we reasoned, the intelligent thing for us to do on "Scramble!" was to get up to 30,000 feet or so as quickly as we could and wait for the enemy fighters and bombers to appear below us and then, at our leisure, pick on a target, have a shot at it and then with no more ado break off and dive, calculating that no Navy 0 could follow us far down without the gravest risk that it would disintegrate when pulling out of a power dive which a Hurricane could cope with without difficulty.'

Not all high officials or even all Hurricane pilots would agree with Kelly at the time or afterwards. Yet it might be noticed that as late as May 1943, by which time the Hurricanes in Europe and the Middle East were increasingly changing from interceptor to ground-attack duties, Wing Commander Paul Richey, who had flown Hurricanes with No. 1 Squadron in the Battle of France, would prepare a report on fighter tactics and strategy, quoted by Christopher Shores in his *Air War For Burma*, which reached the following conclusions:

The Japs can dog-fight better than we can; however, they are lightly armed and need to get in good long bursts against our heavily armoured aircraft before they can shoot them down. Their manoeuvrability enables them to do this if we try and dog-fight them. On the other hand, one short accurate burst from a Hurricane usually causes the disintegration of an 01 [the Oscar] – and the Hurricane is faster. All this being so, the obvious thing to do is to work out tactics to give ourselves the maximum advantage. We won't dog-fight. We will only attack from above, diving and firing a short burst before climbing again. If we are caught out and are below the Japs or at their level we will immediately take steps to reverse this situation by diving away and climbing up again before attacking.

In other words, Richey entirely agreed with Kelly as to the relative merits of the Hurricane and the Japanese fighters, and the best means of using the Hurricane's merits to greatest effect. It is surely disgraceful that it apparently took so long for these lessons to be learned at the cost of the lives of so many good men.

Yet even if the lessons had already been appreciated, the Hurricane's first campaign in the Far East, the defence of Malaya and Singapore, would still have been unsuccessful because it had become hopeless before it started. On 8 December 1941, Japan had attacked Malaya and also Thailand which surrendered forthwith. During that day and the next, her Army Air Force now based in Thailand effectively wrecked the RAF's airfields in northern Malaya. On the 10th, her Navy Air Force based in Indo-China sank the British battleship *Prince of Wales* and battle-cruiser *Repulse*, leaving Malaya without naval protection. On the 11th, her Twenty-Fifth Army fell on Malaya's land defenders, with its light tanks, though pitiable by European standards, routing Indian troops, most of whom had never seen one before. A series of panic-stricken retreats followed.

It was not until 13 January 1942, by which time three-quarters of Malaya including all her advanced radar stations had been overrun, that fifty-one Hurricanes in crates and twenty-four pilots arrived by convoy. The aircraft were old Mark Is or early IIAs and, having originally been destined for the Middle East, were further handicapped by having desert filters. The pilots, who were formed into 232 Squadron, were newly-trained and came from four different previously unconnected sources. The ground crews had no experience of the type and, as if all this was not enough, the odds in favour of the Japanese airmen were usually eight to one and sometimes as high as ten to one.

Despite all their disadvantages, however, the Hurricanes did manage to achieve successes, especially against Japanese bombers. A particularly dramatic instance came on 21 January, when Flight Lieutenant Farthing attacked a Mitsubishi Nell. Clearly this had not dropped its bombs, for it vanished in a colossal explosion that brought down two other bombers in flames and filled the Hurricane's engine intake with 'bits and pieces of Japanese aircraft'. The Hurricanes also proved effective in hampering the Japanese land forces as Colonel Masanobu Tsuji, the enemy's director of military operations, generously acknowledges in his *Singapore: The Japanese Version*. Inevitably, though, 232 Squadron suffered heavy losses, including those of Farthing and its CO, Squadron Leader Landels.

On 31 January Hurricanes of 258 Squadron arrived to support 232, but once more these were too few and too late to change the tide of events. On the 27th, sixteen Mark IIBs had flown from HM Carrier *Indomitable* to Java, whence they moved on to Sumatra and then to Singapore. Unfortunately, the inadequate Indonesian landing-grounds had taken their toll and only thirteen reached their final destination. Here their long-range tanks had to be removed and the guns stripped of protective grease and reassembled. Consequently, only eight of them were ready for action on the 31st.

In any case, 31 January was the day when all the British and Commonwealth troops who could do so retired to Singapore Island and the causeway connecting it with the mainland was blown up. By 3 February the Japanese had wrecked Singapore's three military aerodromes, all in the north of the island within easy range of the enemy's artillery; this forced the Hurricanes to retire to the mud-soaked civilian airport at Kallang. The Japanese crossed the Johore Strait on the 8th, the surviving Hurricanes left for Sumatra on the 10th and on the 15th, Singapore and 70,000 troops surrendered: the largest military capitulation in British history.

By that time, a useful force of Hurricanes, on paper at least, had already been built up in Sumatra. These aircraft had arrived in batches during late January and early February, either flying off HMS *Indomitable* or being carried in crates aboard merchant vessels. All of them had been sent originally to Java but most had proceeded to Sumatra, as did thirty-five new pilots who had been carried to Batavia (as it was then called), the capital of Java, on the troopship *City of Canterbury*.

Some Hurricanes, however, remained in Java, where they were handed over to the Dutch, to whom at that time the East Indies belonged. At first they received twenty-four aged Mark Is[2] but these were soon followed by some Mark IIAs and IIBs. They also gained the assistance of about forty British ground personnel and an engineer officer, Flying Officer (later Squadron Leader) John David. The formal handing-over ceremony was enlivened when Lieutenant Colonel Zomer, who was accepting the Hurricanes on behalf of the Dutch Java Air Force, accidentally fired the guns of one of them. Mercifully, nobody was hurt.

However, it was not an encouraging omen for the future and the Dutch Hurricane pilots did indeed operate under several handicaps. They faced heavy adverse odds. They were completely without any spare parts. Worst of all, the RAF pilots had no time to train them in the use of their new aircraft. Fortunately Lieutenant Jan Brunier, who acted as second-in-command to the Hurricane unit's CO Lieutenant Anemaet, had served with the RAF during 1941 and was able to impart his knowledge to his men, even if one or two Hurricanes were 'written off' in the process. Moreover, the Dutch, most of whose former aged fighters had been wiped out in a Japanese air-raid on Surabaya on 3 February, were delighted with their Hurricanes' strength, firepower, speed and rate of climb. Their enthusiasm would triumph over all obstacles.

Meanwhile in southern Sumatra, the Royal Air Force was doing its best to get organized. A bomber group, No. 225, was created, officially with four squadrons of Blenheims and three of Hudsons, but all had been mangled in Malaya and contained less than fifty aircraft in total. A new fighter group, No. 226, also came into being under Air Commodore Stanley Vincent, who had been station commander at Northolt in the Battle of Britain, during which he had frequently taken off in a Hurricane to strike personally at the enemy. His Group contained 232, 258 and 488 Squadrons, the last-named being a former New Zealand Buffalo unit that had lost all its aircraft in Malaya but whose surviving pilots had been given Hurricanes. There were about thirty-five Hurricanes on hand and they were formed into 266 Wing under Wing Commander Harold Maguire one of the pilots to have arrived on the *City of Canterbury*.

All the RAF aircraft operated from two airfields: P1 just north of Sumatra's capital Palembang, and P2, a secret base hacked out of dense jungle some 20 miles to the south with clumps of trees growing in the middle. At neither was there proper ground control; indeed in the absence of Very High Frequency radio sets, there was virtually no ground-to-air communication and not much between individual aircraft. There were no radar sets in Sumatra and its Observer Corps posts were scattered far too widely. There were hardly any tool kits, let alone spare parts. The airfields' surfaces were so bad that five Hurricanes were 'written off' in landing accidents before the Japanese attacked. Despite heroic efforts of the ground crews under Flight Sergeants Barber and Slee, two-thirds of the bombers and half the Hurricanes were usually unserviceable.

On 3 February the Japanese turned their attention to Sumatra and by nightfall on the 8th, a series of attacks on P1 had caused immense losses to its Blenheims and Hurricanes. The Hawker fighters received no warning of these raids, so were invariably engaged as they took off or before they could gain height. They downed only two Oscars and lost a dozen Hurricanes shot down or damaged beyond repair in aerial combat, plus three more on the airfield. In 258 Squadron, four pilots were killed either on the ground or in the air battles, while 232 lost two dead and a third in hospital. The fate of 258's Canadian Pilot Officer Roy Keedwell was particularly tragic. Although wounded, he brought his damaged machine back to base, but on landing collided with a burning Blenheim. The Hurricane caught fire as well and its pilot died of burns three days later.

On the 13th, however, the Hurricanes had the better of an extraordinarily confused encounter. Another batch of Hurricane IIBs had arrived in Java, carried in crates aboard the aircraft transport *Athene*. By now eight of these had been assembled and were flown to P1 by pilots from both 232 and 258, led by Wing Commander Maguire. As they approached the airfield, so too did a group of Kawasaki Lily bombers, escorted by Oscars. Whether this was a coincidence or the result of good Japanese Intelligence has not been determined.

Since most of the Hurricanes from Java were short of fuel they attempted to land, but Maguire and Sergeant Henry Nicholls of 232 Squadron gallantly remained airborne in an effort to provide some protection. As the other new arrivals neared the runway, an Oscar tried to attack them. The result gave a graphic indication of the comparative strengths of the Hurricane and the Japanese fighters. Japanese accounts, quoted by Terence Kelly in another of his books, *Battle for Palembang*, tell us that

> On the 13th, 29 Hyabusas [Oscars] escorted 7 light bombers to Palembang, where Lt Masabumi Kunii, a veteran and great 'strafer', pounced on a Hurricane and shot it down, but pulling out of his dive the wings of his Hyabusa folded like a butterfly and he fell to his death.

Still greater emphasis is given to the comparison by the fact that the Hurricane that Kunii attacked, though damaged and pouring out smoke, was able to pull up sharply and steeply in order to give its pilot, Sergeant Scott of 258 Squadron, a chance to bale out, which he did safely.

In the meantime, Maguire and Nicholls had shot down another Oscar that crashed at the end of the runway. An examination of this gave grim evidence of a further weakness of Japanese fighters: their lack of protection for the pilot whose head and back were riddled with bullets. Nicholls was then shot down himself, but baled out safely. Under cover of all this activity, Squadron Leader Richard Brooker was able to get his 232 Squadron into the air. Pilot Officer Watson crashed on take-off and his Hurricane was 'written off' and Pilot Officer Emmerton was killed in action, but two Lily bombers and one more Oscar were destroyed or badly damaged.

The Hurricane pilots, as resilient as their aircraft, were greatly encouraged by these indications of the Japanese fighters' weak points. News from Java that a further nine of *Athene*'s Hurricanes were ready for collection gave more encouragement; a mixed body of pilots from 266 Wing led by Flight Lieutenant Hutcheson of 488 Squadron was sent to Java to deliver them. No one was aware that the RAF units in Sumatra were under far greater threats than enemy air-raids.

On 14 February part of a large Japanese convoy, strongly escorted and carrying two regiments of Japan's 38th Infantry Division that had earlier been responsible for the capture of Hong Kong, seized Banka Island where 10 per cent of the world's tin was produced and there was a valuable aerodrome at Muntok. The main body of this force pressed on to the mouth of the Musi River on which Palembang stands. It was attacked by Blenheims and Hudsons but, sadly, these inflicted much less damage than was thought at the time. Still more sadly, on orders from Java, contrary to the wishes of Air Commodore Vincent whose Battle of Britain experience told him that his fighters' most important task was guarding their own bases, every available Hurricane under 258's CO Squadron Leader Thomson had been sent out to escort their bombers.

Vincent's protests would soon prove abundantly justified. At about 1130, P1 was attacked by Mitsubishi Sally bombers dropping anti-personnel weapons and Oscar fighters strafing. Close behind these came Mitsubishi Topsy transports from which poured Japanese parachute troops, part onto the oil refineries at Pladjoe just outside Palembang and part close to P1. Immediately afterwards, Thomson's flight returned and was warned to make for P2 instead. The pilots mistook the enemy transports for Hudsons – with every excuse, as these were the same aircraft built under licence – but Pilot Officer Lockwood of 232 shot down a Sally and there were several clashes with Oscars, Flying Officer Macnamara of 258 crash-landing at P1 and 'writing off' his already damaged aircraft.

Next to land at P1 were Sergeants Kelly and Lambert of Thomson's flight, who were unaware of the situation as their radios were inoperative. The Duty Control Officer, Pilot Officer Nash, at considerable personal risk, ran out to warn them and they hastily left for P2. Then the replacement Hurricanes from Java appeared. Desperately short of fuel, they were set upon by a swarm of Oscars and five of them, including Hutcheson's, crash-landed in the jungle, although amazingly all the pilots survived. The other four landed at P1, where Nash rushed to refuel them with a petrol tanker. They also got away to P2.

After all serviceable aircraft had left P1, the RAF personnel under Wing Commander Maguire resisted the Japanese paratroopers gallantly, but eventually were compelled to destroy a number of disabled machines and withdraw from the airfield. Some casualties were suffered, but many of P1's defenders, including Maguire, Squadron Leader Brooker, Hutcheson, Macnamara and a badly-wounded Nash were able to escape, ultimately to Java.

All surviving RAF aircraft – Blenheims, Hudsons and Hurricanes – were now mustered at their secret base of P2. From here, throughout 15 February, they were in almost constant action, especially against the barges that were carrying Japanese soldiers up the Musi River to

Palembang. The Hawker fighters got off to a bad start when fog caused an early sortie to be abandoned, two of them crashing when landing on P2's terrible surface and being 'written off'. Happily, neither pilot was seriously hurt. Thereafter, though, the Hurricanes, flown alternately by pilots of 232 and 258 so as to exert continuous pressure, strafed the barges unmercifully, causing casualties that the Japanese would admit ran into hundreds and remained for a long time an evil memory. Only one Hurricane pilot was hit by AA fire and the American Flying Officer Arthur Donahue, despite a wounded leg and consequent loss of blood returned to P2 and safety. He was evacuated to Britain via Java and Ceylon, but was killed in action over the Channel on 11 September 1942.

Also throughout 15 February the Hurricanes escorted British bombers in attacks on Japanese shipping at the mouth of the Musi River. Their final mission saw 232 Squadron strafe a number of enemy machines sighted on the ground at Muntok airfield on Banka Island and rake the decks of a couple of enemy destroyers from masthead height. Moreover, when some Nakajima Nate fighters tried to intervene the Hurricanes drove them off, damaging two so badly that they crashed on landing.

Yet despite the fact that the Japanese had been halted in their tracks and P2 remained undetected, it had still been decided that Sumatra was to be evacuated. Already on the morning of the 15th, several leading figures, including to his disgust Air Commodore Vincent, had retired to the port of Oosthaven in the extreme south-east of Sumatra and that evening the RAF ground crews followed them. The remaining Hurricanes were flown out as well, mostly by airmen of 232 Squadron, though three pilots of 258 risked boarding allegedly unserviceable aircraft, all of which they managed to get safely to Java.

By 18 February, all surviving RAF aircraft and most RAF personnel were back in Java, though much vital equipment, such as spare Merlin engines for the Hurricanes, was left behind. That the evacuation had been premature was confirmed on the 19th by Group Captain Nicholetts who returned to Oosthaven with a party of fifty volunteers; they spent twelve hours salvaging a large quantity of stores, quite unhindered by the enemy.

Once in Java, the Hurricanes were reorganized. They now became West Group, still under Air Commodore Vincent, and acquired those aircraft from *Athene* that were still available. By this time, ground crews but no pilots from 242 and 605 Squadrons had reached Java. It was decided that the ground crews of the existing fighter squadrons who were badly in need of a rest should be evacuated and the flying personnel should join 242 and 605. Squadron Leader Brooker and the pilots of 232 became part of 242, except for Flight Lieutenant Wright who was promoted and took charge of 605. Those 488 pilots who had gained experience on Hurricanes also went to 605, as did some of 258's pilots, though most of them now left Java for Ceylon.[3]

Between them, 242 and 605 possessed twenty-five Hurricanes, of which the unprecedented number of eighteen were ready for combat. Their new base at Tjililitan near Batavia had admirable control facilities and communications and was well served by radar stations, supported by a network of observers on smaller islands to the north. In consequence the Hurricanes, although still dreadfully outnumbered, were able to receive warning of enemy activity and were soon making successful interceptions of Japanese formations; on 20 February, for instance, they downed, without loss, two Nates and a wretched reconnaissance floatplane.

Unfortunately, although there was a surplus of fighter pilots, there were no aircraft in reserve and virtually no spare parts. Inevitably, therefore, for all the toil of the ground crews, the number of serviceable Hurricanes gradually declined. Attempts were made to persuade the Dutch to give up some of their Hurricanes, but having finally got machines of this calibre, understandably they refused. This caused some bitterness, but while their pilots were less experienced than those in the RAF, the Dutch Hurricanes, based at Ngoro in central Java, were put to good use, on one occasion slaughtering a formation of Nakajima Kate carrier-based bombers that they caught without an escort.

On 24 February, aerial activity over Java was almost continuous. The Hurricanes of 242 and 605 shot down or badly damaged three Japanese bombers and three Oscars. They lost two of their own number, but both pilots baled out and a third force-landed without injury to the pilot. On the same day, incidentally, two Dutch Hurricanes were 'written off' after combat damage.

By this time, we learn from *Bloody Shambles*[4] by Christopher Shores and Brian Cull with Yasuho Izawa, the Hurricane pilots 'had devised tactics to combat the manoeuvrability of the opposing Japanese fighters by climbing to maximum height, diving to attack and then continuing in the dive, either to head for home or up to regain altitude.' They were tactics that would please Terence Kelly and Paul Richey, but in the excitement of the moment, of course, they were sometimes forgotten, as happened on 25 February.

On this day, and on some later occasions, the Hurricane pilots encountered Japanese Navy Air Force machines: this time genuine Zero fighters escorting a Mitsubishi Babs naval reconnaissance aircraft. Sergeant James Sandeman Allen of 242 shot down the Babs, but two of 605's airmen – Flight Lieutenant 'Harry' Dobbyn and the American Pilot Officer 'Red' Campbell – made the mistake of 'mixing it' with the Zeros in a typical dogfight. Dobbyn was shot down and killed. The Zero responsible was promptly shot down by Campbell, but his Hurricane was then hit by cannon shells from another Zero and he was forced to bale out. He came down in a paddy field and suffered injuries which prevented him flying again before the campaign ended and he became a prisoner of war.

Normally, however, the Hurricane pilots stuck to their diving tactics and although these meant that it was often impossible to assess the harm they had done with any accuracy, there is little doubt that they did destroy a few Japanese fighters during the last part of February. Their situation, though, was about to become hopeless as the Japanese prepared to seize Java, the richest of the Indonesian Islands. On 27 February invasion convoys headed for both western and eastern Java. A combined ABDA Fleet – American, British, Dutch, Australian – under the Dutch Rear Admiral Doorman did its best to intercept these, but was routed by their strong covering forces, its surviving ships afterwards being hunted down individually. On the same day, all hope of receiving fighter reinforcements disappeared when the American aircraft transport *Langley* making for the port of Tjilatjap in the south of Java with thirty-two Kittyhawks on board was sunk by shore-based bombers.

As darkness fell on 28 February, the invasion forces closed in. The eastern one landed near Rembang in north-eastern Java; the western one mainly at Bantam Bay in the extreme west of Java, while a detachment of this broke away to come ashore at Eretanwetan, 100 miles east of Batavia. The demoralized Dutch land forces offered scarcely any resistance and by the morning of 1 March, the Japanese had secured all their beachheads.

At least the British and Dutch airmen did everything possible to hamper the invaders. The RAF Hurricanes made very effective low-level attacks at both Bantam Bay and Eretanwetan, strafing troops already ashore and barges bringing them there, as well as setting on fire six of the landing craft and three light tanks. They also engaged Japanese reconnaissance seaplanes spotted on the water and destroyed or badly damaged at least three of them. Later that morning and in the afternoon, they turned their attention to columns of troops already moving inland. The Japanese proved resolute opponents as we learn from Messrs Shores and Cull, quoting New Zealand Pilot Officer 'Harry' Pettit formerly of 488, now of 605 Squadron, in *Bloody Shambles*:

> We were flying very low during this operation and in fact probably would have done better if we had used a bit more height and attacked more steeply. The Japanese were remarkably steady under fire and continued to use their rifles against the low-flying aircraft, on many occasions not even attempting to take cover. The accuracy of their fire was evidenced by a few holes in my Hurricane.

Several other Hurricanes suffered more than just 'a few holes' from the rifle-fire of the dauntless Japanese soldiers. Flying Officer Sharp of 605 Squadron had to force-land and was not seen again; apparently he was killed by the enemy. Sergeant Young of 242 Squadron also force-landed, though he was unhurt, while Sergeant McIntosh of 605 got back to his airfield but his machine was 'written off'.

In eastern Java, the Dutch Hurricanes made similar strikes on the landing beaches at Rembang, once again proving particularly effective against barges carrying troops. They came under heavy AA fire, two being so damaged that they had to force-land and were subsequently destroyed to prevent capture by the advancing enemy, while a third was able to return to its base at Ngoro only to be 'written off'. Worse still, as the Dutchmen landed back at Ngoro, they were spotted by a patrol of Zeros which strafed the base so effectively that almost all those Hurricanes that were not destroyed were crippled and unable to get airborne before they were eliminated by further raids next day. By 3 March only two remained serviceable and on that day both were 'written off' after aerial combats.

Another Hurricane unit had also ceased to be. The RAF's shortage of aircraft was now such that in the late afternoon of 1 March, four of 605's pilots transferred their allegiance – and 605's four remaining Hurricanes

– to 242, while Squadron Leader Wright and all his other men prepared to be shipped off the island. Air Commodore Vincent and his staff had already been ordered to evacuate, handing over control of the RAF fighters to Wing Commander Maguire who had only recently reached Java after a tortuous voyage from Sumatra in a small coaster. Vincent was most distressed at having to leave his men, but he was not finished with the Japanese and would later command Hurricanes again in another famous campaign.

Now only Squadron Leader Brooker's 242 Squadron was left to provide fighter cover, and for almost another week its Hurricanes continued to oppose the Japanese whenever and however possible. The enemy occupied Kalidjati airfield inland from Eretanwetan early on 2 March, and this was promptly strafed by three of 242's pilots, the Canadian Sergeant Fleming setting fire to three Lily bombers. He was then attacked by Nate fighters and forced to bale out. He landed safely, but was then shot at and wounded by one of the Nates. He was brought to a hospital but this was taken by the Japanese next day and he became a prisoner of war. Another three 242 Hurricanes strafed advancing columns of Japanese soldiers. These again fearlessly returned their fire and Pilot Officer Watson was hit. He had to crash-land, but was later able to get back to his squadron.

Later that day, 242 withdrew eastward from Tjililitan to Andir in the centre of western Java. From here they continued to make repeated attacks on Kalidjati over the next few days, a petrol bowser being set on fire and several enemy aircraft destroyed or damaged. Japanese troops were also attacked and there were a number of clashes with enemy fighters. By now the Hurricane pilots were clear as to the best tactics to be used and they destroyed or badly damaged ten of their opponents at much less cost than might have been expected. The Hurricanes' strength once again reduced losses, though the Canadian Pilot Officer Mendizabal was shot down on 3 March – at least he baled out unhurt – and on the 4th the South African 2nd Lieutenant Anderson was badly wounded and taken prisoner, dying of his injuries two days later.

Anderson was brought down in a combat with Zeros that were armed with cannons as well as machine guns, but, as Messrs Shores and Cull point out, all the other Hurricanes involved returned safely despite most of them having suffered 'varying degrees of damage'. This was particularly the case with the Hurricane of Sergeant Allen, whose account is thus quoted in *Bloody Shambles*:

> The 'Zeros' came in underneath and we had a simple target for the first few vital moments, after which we were so heavily outnumbered that we got into serious trouble. I was credited with two 'Zeros' destroyed, one probable and one damaged but crawled back to the aerodrome with 28 cannon shell and 43 bullet holes in the machine (Z5584), and with slight wounds to my head and legs.
>
> I remember being given a cup of tea and I was shaking so badly it stirred itself! However, I took off in a fresh plane 10 minutes later so that I was able to recover my nerve.

Not, unfortunately, that any achievements could now do more than hamper the relentless Japanese advance. On 5 March, Batavia fell. On the same day, any morale that still existed in Java was destroyed by a raid of Japanese carrier aircraft on the port of Tjilatjap that completely wrecked the harbour together with the twenty-three merchant vessels therein. Still the Hurricanes kept up their forlorn fight. Also on 5 March, Flight Lieutenant Parker shot down a Lily bomber. He was then attacked by four enemy fighters, but evaded these and returned safely to base. Next day 242's Hurricanes had several encounters with Japanese bombers, four of which they destroyed or damaged, but by nightfall they were left with only two of their own fighters still serviceable.

All that could now be done was to evacuate valuable personnel if possible. Dutch transport aircraft were provided to rescue Wing Commander Maguire, Squadron Leader Brooker and a few other pilots, some of them wounded. Brooker and the others did get away, but as Messrs Shores and Cull report in *Bloody Shambles*, Maguire discovered that luggage was being loaded on the aircraft and got out to see if this could be removed to make room for more passengers. While the wing commander was arguing with the ground crews, someone closed the door of his aircraft, whereupon this took off without him.[5]

Thereafter the end came with a speed that perhaps was merciful. At dawn on 8 March, the two remaining Hurricanes took off on a final reconnaissance mission. On their return, the squadron received orders that they were to be destroyed on the airfield and this distasteful task was duly carried out. At 1300, the Dutch authorities began negotiating for a surrender. At noon on the 9th, hostilities ceased.

Most of the RAF personnel in Java, pilots and ground crews alike, fell into Japanese hands, spent several months in camps in Java and were then taken to Japan in prison ships that were hardly fit to go to sea and were utterly disgusting. On reaching Japan, they were kept in camps set in beautiful scenery that only emphasized that their conditions were desperately poor, food was desperately short and they had to toil endlessly in the local dockyards. It is some consolation, though, that unlike many elsewhere, particularly those on the infamous Burma-Siam railway, the great majority of RAF prisoners survived their torments and lived to return home at the end of the war.

One of the survivors was Sergeant Terence Kelly. He had seen action in Singapore, Sumatra – where he had been the last man to fly a Hurricane out of P2 airfield – and Java, and he had been successively on the strength of 258, 605 and 242 Squadrons. As mentioned earlier, he would write several accounts of his experiences, and his views on tactics and aircraft comparisons have already been quoted. In his *Nine Lives of a Fighter Pilot* (and earlier in *Hurricane over the Jungle*), he records an amazing incident with which the story of the Hurricane in Indonesia may fittingly end.

Kelly could not recall the exact date, only that it was 'somewhere between 24 and 28 February 1942'. By this time, the Hurricanes had perfected their tactics of dive, engage and dive on. The flight from 605 Squadron of which he was a member sighted a group of enemy fighters – he calls them Navy 0s but most probably they were Oscars – and promptly fell on them. Kelly was first into the attack, dived away and, looking back, saw the other three Hurricanes and then the Japanese fighters following him down between 'two enormous towers of cumulous clouds'.

So fascinating was the sight that Kelly forgot what he was doing and when he recollected himself, he was in a power dive at 'terminal velocity'. He managed to recover from this with the help of the tail trim, minute strips of metal fixed to the trailing edge of the elevators to give perfect fore-and-aft balance. Having done so, he found his airspeed indicator had 'gone right round the clock not once, but twice!' He reflects that

> Even by the time I had pulled out to straight and level I had to have been flying at more than 590 miles an hour, and in the vertical I

was certainly knocking the speed of sound if, in fact, I hadn't been through it. I do not know if any other Hurricane pilot has actually claimed to have flown through the sound barrier. I am not now claiming to have done so myself. But I put it forward as a possibility, for I have so much respect for the sturdiness of that wonderful aircraft, the Hurricane, to believe it could well be able to take the strain.

Notes

1. The ways in which these designations were reached gives some idea of the difficulties faced by Europeans or Americans trying to fathom them. The 'A' was the letter arbitrarily chosen by the Japanese to indicate a fighter that could operate from aircraft carriers. This was the sixth type to fill this role, hence the '6'. The 'M' stood for its manufacturer, Mitsubishi. The type number came from the last two numbers of the year when the aircraft had gone into production, counting from 660 BC, the legendary date for the foundation of Japan by her first Emperor Jimmu Tennō. This was 1940 AD or 2600 by Japanese reckoning.
2. Another Hurricane I was delivered to Australia at about this time: the only one to reach this country. It was used for fast communications as well as for testing a suit designed by Professor Cotton of Melbourne University to reduce the effect on pilots of the gravitational forces experienced at high speeds.
3. On 30 March, 258 Squadron was re-formed with fresh Hurricanes in Ceylon. In April, these helped to defend the island against attacks from Japanese carrier-based aircraft, incurring heavy casualties but putting up a resistance sufficient to persuade the enemy to give up any thoughts of invasion. The high loss of Hurricanes was caused because most of their pilots unwisely engaged in dogfights. There were four Hurricanes that were flown by men who had fought the Japanese in Sumatra and Java. They knew better and all emerged unscathed.
4. This work is subtitled *The First Comprehensive Account of Air Operations over South-East Asia December 1941–May 1942*. It appears in two volumes: *The Drift to War to the Fall of Singapore* and *The Defence of Sumatra to the Fall of Burma*.
5. Wing Commander Maguire was taken prisoner by the Japanese but after the war enjoyed a brilliant career in the RAF, retiring as Air Marshal Sir Harold Maguire KCB, DSO, OBE. Squadron Leader Brooker was flown to Australia, where he formed and took command of a Kittyhawk squadron. On returning to Britain, he commanded first a Typhoon wing and then a Tempest wing, the latter during the fighting leading up to and including the crossing of the Rhine. He was killed in action on 16 April 1945.

Chapter Nine

Malta at Bay

From the large important islands of Indonesia which the Japanese had so quickly captured, it is a relief to turn to one, small but strategically vital, the armed services and civilians of which had defied the European members of the Axis Pact for more than a year and would continue to do so despite greater dangers, disadvantages and difficulties in the future: Malta GC.

We left Malta and her protectors in late September 1941, at which time the future appeared reasonably secure. The Luftwaffe was involved in the titanic struggle in Russia and the *Regia Aeronautica* made few bombing raids which were effectively dealt with by Malta's Hurricanes. Her three day-fighter squadrons – 126, 185 and 249 – were now at full strength and could even supply an occasional machine to 69 Squadron to support its Martin Marylands on photo-reconnaissance missions.

Malta's night-fighter unit was also in action, so impressively that on 2 December it was expanded to become 1435 Flight under Squadron Leader (later Wing Commander) Innes Westmacott, a former flight commander in 185 Squadron. He is quoted in Terence Kelly's *Hurricane and Spitfire Pilots at War* as declaring that 'The Italians were also impressed, most unfavourably, to the extent that some of them would drop their bombs in the sea and head for home without crossing the coast.'

At the end of September, however, there came the first signs of the difficulties that lay ahead. On the 29th, Pilot Officer Lintern of 185 Squadron was shot down and although he baled out, he came down in the sea and drowned. On 1 October Lintern's commanding officer, Squadron Leader 'Boy' Mould, was also shot down and killed. Both fell victim to a new type of Italian fighter, the Macchi MC 202, which had a top speed of 370 mph, though its armament was only two 12.7mm and two 7.7mm machine guns. During October and November, MC 202s would shoot down five other Hurricanes over Malta; Flight Sergeant Owen baled out, but the other four pilots were killed. Macchis also destroyed one of 69 Squadron's 'photo-recce' Hurricanes on 21 November. Happily, Wing Commander Dowland, the unit's CO, baled out and was rescued from the sea by a Swordfish fitted with floats.

MC 202s also appeared on night missions. In the early hours of 14 October, Pilot Officer Barnwell damaged one so badly that it crash-landed at its base, but was himself attacked by another pair of MC 202s and forced to bale out. He was never seen again and it is suggested that his parachute failed to open.

It seems that the Hurricane pilots, used to their machines being much superior to any flown by the Italians, were caught out by the MC 202s' fine performance. Fortunately, they soon learned to cope with them. The first MC 202 to be destroyed by a Hurricane fell to the guns of Sergeant Hunton of 185 Squadron on 25 October, and carried with it to his death Lieutenant Colonel (equivalent to Wing Commander) Eugenio Leotta, one of Italy's leading airmen. At least five other Macchis were downed in November.

A particularly revealing clash took place on 8 November, when four Hurricanes of 126 Squadron took on a far greater number of MC 202s. The Australian Sergeant Haley fatally injured one Macchi, but then collided with it. The Macchi disintegrated, its pilot being killed, but Haley was able to escape safely by parachute. Pilot Officer Lardner-Burke engaged another Macchi. This he shot down, its pilot also dying, but the Hurricane was hit as well and Lardner-Burke wounded so seriously that he was taken to hospital. Nonetheless, he flew his damaged aircraft back to base and landed perfectly.

Nor were Malta's Hurricanes content to act in a purely defensive role. As mentioned previously, they had begun to make raids over Sicily and in late September some of 185's aircraft were fitted with racks to carry four 40lb bombs under each wing, as were some from 126 and 249 later. With these or with smaller 20lb fragmentation bombs, these Hurribombers, as they were called, made strikes on Comiso airfield, the seaplane base at Syracuse, troop movements, trains, petrol lorries and fuel dumps.

Assaults by Hurribombers and strafing raids by fighter Hurricanes continued at intervals for the rest of the year, though not without casualties. Canadian Wing Commander Mark Henry 'Hilly' Brown had come to Malta in a Sunderland: he was a distinguished Hurricane 'ace' who had risen from pilot officer to squadron leader in the celebrated

No. 1 Squadron. On 12 November he led 'Sandy' Rabagliati, now also a wing commander, and American Pilot Officer Tedford in a strafing attack on Gela aerodrome. In addition, Rabagliati sighted and shot down a Junkers Ju 87. Brown, however, was hit by AA fire and killed. The Italians buried him with full military honours.

Also on 12 November, Australian Sergeant Simpson was shot down by Macchi MC 202s during a Hurribomber raid on Comiso aerodrome. He baled out into the sea, was rescued by the Italians and became a prisoner of war. Sergeant Greenhalgh was taken prisoner as well after another attack on Comiso. Hit by AA fire when flying at a very low level, he crashed onto the airfield and skidded right across it before coming to a halt. He was unhurt and, amazingly, the Italians found his Hurricane to be intact and almost undamaged.[1]

In any case, these Hurricane strikes formed only a small part of the aggressive activities of Malta's forces, most of which were directed against Axis convoys carrying supplies to the German and Italian soldiers under General Erwin Rommel in North Africa. Blenheims, Wellingtons and Swordfish all took part in attacking enemy merchantmen at sea or in harbour, day and night, regardless of casualties. Malta's submarines also played an effective part and the island now received a unit of surface warships to inflict further destruction.

In September 1941, 28 per cent of all supplies sent to Rommel failed to reach him. In October, 21 per cent was lost. In November, an astonishing 63 per cent was destroyed in transit. The importance of these activities became crystal clear on 18 November when the British and Commonwealth troops in North Africa, now expanded to become the Eighth Army, commenced a major offensive code-named Operation CRUSADER. After a series of confused encounters marked by blunders on both sides, the Eighth Army was able to relieve besieged Tobruk and regain the whole of Cyrenaica.

It is extraordinary, therefore, that General Sir Claude Auchinleck, who as Commander-in-Chief, Middle East was the main beneficiary of Malta's efforts, showed neither appreciation of nor gratitude for these. As late as August 1942, he could announce that the retention of the island was not absolutely necessary. It was fortunate that Churchill and his naval and Air Force commanders had greater strategic insight. Unhappily, so did Hitler. As was mentioned earlier, the Führer had already taken steps that he hoped would cripple Malta and just before CRUSADER began his first blow against the island-fortress was delivered.

Ironically, this was triggered by an episode that initially seemed highly beneficial for Malta. During early November, three squadrons of Hurricane IIBs – 242, 258 and 605 – had been ferried to Gibraltar and on 12 November, thirty-seven of these from 242 and 605 were on board carriers *Ark Royal* and *Argus* preparing to fly to Malta, guided by Blenheims from Gibraltar.

One of the airmen was Pilot Officer 'Sonny' Ormrod of 605 who was on *Argus* where, incidentally, he says he was almost choked by the fumes from her funnel as he waited to take off.[2] In his diary, quoted by Kenneth Poolman in *Faith, Hope and Charity*, he reports that Pilot Officer Lowe 'had never flown a long-range Hurricane before' and 'swung violently to port' as he left the flight deck. Ormrod peered over the side, 'expecting to see Lowe in the sea, but he wasn't, he was flying and his wheels were retracting too. Very lucky, for he'd broken the flag flying from the *Argus*, and had almost knocked off his tail wheel, which came off when he landed at Malta.'

It was one more instance of the Hurricane's remarkable strength and reliability, but three other aircraft failed to reach Malta because they ran out of fuel, all their pilots becoming prisoners of war. Even so, the addition of thirty-four fighters to the island's defenders was obviously most welcome, and the vessels responsible headed back to Gibraltar to collect the Hurricanes of 258 Squadron as well. Sadly, they would never do so. The first of those steps taken by Hitler had been to order submarines to the Mediterranean in the hope that they might disrupt Malta's supply lines. His hopes would not be in vain.

On 13 November – a Thursday, not a Friday – *U-81* torpedoed *Ark Royal* as she made for Gibraltar, and although attempts were made to tow her there, she finally capsized and went down. Only one man, Able Seaman Mitchell who was killed when the torpedo struck, was lost but *U-81* had indeed sorely hampered the supply route to Malta.[3] There was no question of the slow old *Argus* carrying 258's Hurricanes to the island on her own. For a time they flew as a defensive shield for Gibraltar; then, as we have seen, they were sent to the Far East, where 258 would fight in Singapore, Sumatra, Java and Ceylon.

Nor were the ground crews of 242 and 605 ever sent to Malta. As we have seen they also went to the Far East, presenting the confusing spectacle of 242 and 605 Squadrons apparently serving in two different places at the same time. In reality, though, the pilots of both in Malta, while officially retaining their old identities for another four months, were in practice incorporated into the existing Hurricane squadrons.

The success of Operation CRUSADER only increased Hitler's determination to eliminate the thorn in Rommel's side.

On 2 December 1941, *Fliegerkorps* II, previously conducting operations on the Moscow front, was ordered to Sicily, joining with *Fliegerkorps* X in the Balkans to form *Luftflotte* (Air Fleet) 2. Also transferred from Russia to command this came Field Marshal Kesselring who was in addition given control over the Luftwaffe in North Africa and in practice over the *Regia Aeronautica* as well. This put 2,000 warplanes at his disposal and his Führer had given precise orders on how to employ them. He was to 'ensure safe lines of communication' to Rommel, in which connection 'the suppression of Malta' by attacks on her and her supply convoys was, said Hitler, 'particularly important'.

Kesselring was a fine strategist and, for all the cheerful good nature that had earned him the nickname of 'Smiling Albert', a ruthlessly resolute opponent. He shared Hitler's views and set out to follow Hitler's instructions to the best of his very considerable ability, intending to batter Malta into impotence while at the same time starving her to the point of surrender. His actions against Malta's supply routes will be examined later, but it may be noticed now that by February 1942, these had increased the Hurricanes' many difficulties by causing shortages of fuel and ammunition. His direct assault on Malta took time to prepare, and for much of December 1941 the Hurricanes were still opposed only by the Italians, but this situation would not long continue.

On 19 December, *Fliegerkorps* II entered the fight with Junkers Ju 88s. The Hurricanes of 126 Squadron shot down two of these, but return fire from their gunners killed Pilot Officer Edward Steele, the first but not last citizen of the United States to die in the defence of Malta. Next day, the Ju 88s were back and they were escorted by the latest Messerschmitt Bf 109Fs. This time it was 249 Squadron that opposed them. Its Hurricanes damaged several of the bombers and one was destroyed but as it fell, it collided with Sergeant Moran's Hurricane which also came down, killing the pilot. The Hurricanes with their slow rate of climb found it difficult to engage the 109Fs and these shot down and killed Flying Officer Cavan.

Malta's greatest ordeals had begun. Kesselring, rather nicely, gave Malta – and his own hard-worked airmen – a break on Christmas Day, but apart from that, pressure on the defenders was continuous by day and frequent by night. Despite the Christmas 'holiday', Malta was attacked by more than 200 warplanes in the last eleven days of the year. The Hurricane pilots were constantly faced with enemy forces that far outnumbered them. It was a grim situation and during this time six Hurricane pilots died in action. In addition, a pair of Hurricanes collided on 29 December. Pilot Officer Macnamara baled out and was later rescued from the sea, but Canadian Pilot Officer Blanchard was killed.

Nonetheless, the Hurricane pilots stuck to their task. During this period, half a dozen Junkers Ju 88s were destroyed or so damaged that they crashed on landing, two Bf 109s were shot down, and several enemy formations were sufficiently disrupted to reduce the effectiveness of their bombing. Moreover, the Hurricane's strength did limit fatal casualties: in late December, five more were very hard hit but two of them force-landed without injury to the pilots, while the other three at least remained airborne long enough for the pilots to escape safely by parachute.

On 27 December the Hurricanes destroyed one Junkers Ju 88 during daylight and one after dark. The former fell victim to Flight Lieutenant Carpenter of 126 Squadron who sent it into the sea with one engine on fire. The latter was downed by Pilot Officer Denis Winton who we last met as a member of 185 at the time of the Italian attack on Valletta Harbour, but was now with the Hurricane night-fighter 1435 Flight. His victory was witnessed by an American member of 126, the ominously-named Pilot Officer Howard Coffin, who recorded it in his diary: 'It [the Ju 88] burst into flames and you could see the pilot bale out. The searchlights did a wonderful job of illumination. What a sight! And did the Maltese cheer! The lights followed him down until he landed in the water and then they snapped off.'[4]

January 1942 saw no change in the situation. A typical clash came on the 3rd. The Hurricanes were able to get at the Junkers Ju 88s, shooting down two of them, but were then attacked themselves by 109s. Sergeant Westcott was forced to bale out, which he did safely, while the American pilot Howard Coffin was wounded and his Hurricane 'riddled with holes' but still managed to return to base where he crash-landed and was taken to hospital.

German raids continued unabated throughout the rest of the month, with more than 1,800 tons of bombs being dropped, a large proportion of them on Malta's airfields. Heavy rain made matters worse, except at Luqa which was well-drained. It required tremendous efforts at all hours of the day and night by ground crews, soldiers and civilians to keep the runways operational and the Hurricanes airborne.

Nevertheless, they did get airborne and continued to engage overwhelmingly superior numbers of German warplanes. They destroyed at least three Junkers Ju 88s, damaged others and disrupted some hostile formations, but could not hope to do more than hinder the Luftwaffe's operations. The most valuable asset of the Hurricanes remained their strength. They did not lose a man until 22 January, and then only as the result of an ugly accident. As well as the bombing raids, the airfields were often strafed by Bf 109s and on this day the AA gunners at Takali mistook returning Hurricanes for Messerschmitts. They opened fire and hit two of them. Sergeant Harvey was able to land his damaged machine, but Sergeant Neale was killed.

On 25 January the Hurricanes were attacked from above by 109s and suffered heavy losses, though not as heavy as some British commentators would have us believe. We are told that 'seven of the British fighters were shot down', with no mention of the pilots. More detailed accounts, however, tell a less horrific story. In fact, three of the aircraft supposedly shot down got back to their base where they crash-landed without injury to the pilots, while of those airmen who were really shot down, three baled out safely and only Pilot Officer Russell of 126 Squadron died, and he was the only pilot of a day-fighter squadron to be killed by enemy aircraft in January 1942.

Sadly, though, it must be recorded that other Hurricane units also lost good men in late January. On the 28th one of 69 Squadron's 'recce' Hurricanes was hit by Italian AA fire. Sergeant Ballantine baled out, but became a prisoner of war. Just before dusk on the previous day, Pilot Officer Mackie of the night-fighter 1435 Flight was 'jumped' by 109s as he took off on a practice mission. He fought back and watchers on the ground saw one Messerschmitt go into the sea, but he was badly wounded and died later in hospital.

Undaunted by this tragic event, seven more of 1435 Flight's Hurricanes went out that night on intruder sorties over Sicily, for even as Malta reeled under Kesselring's assaults, the flight's CO, Squadron Leader Westmacott, was determined on aggressive action. In Terence Kelly's *Hurricane and Spitfire Pilots at War*, Westmacott explains:

> I...suddenly remembered we had a large number of long-range tanks removed from Hurricanes flown to the island. They were not jettisonable but I thought that at night, flying very low, there was no reason why we should not fit these and operate as 'intruders' round Comiso and Catania, the two German bomber bases. I visualised one Hurricane at each remaining there for one hour and being relieved by another to fly home.

Night-intruder sorties duly began on 24 January, continuing through early February and adding to the list of the Hurricanes' successes the destruction of two Junkers Ju 88s, a floatplane and an aged biplane (perhaps a communications aircraft) and the strafing of trucks, trains and a staff car. Moreover, as Westmacott delightedly reports: 'Apart from some "kills" we sometimes so disorganised the enemy night-flying programme that they packed it up for the night with many bombers not setting out for Malta at all.'

Unfortunately, however, operations of this kind could not harm the Axis convoy routes to North Africa, and as Malta's other striking forces were driven onto the defensive, supplies and reinforcements at last began to reach Rommel. Encouraged by these, on 21 January he launched a daring counterstrike against the Eighth Army that achieved complete surprise, regained half of Cyrenaica and captured the great complex of airfields at Martuba, just south of Derna, from which the RAF provided fighter cover for convoys making for Malta and could now be used by the Luftwaffe to attack these.

Kesselring, well aware that his aerial offensive by blunting Malta's capabilities had made Rommel's land offensive possible, was equally encouraged. He redoubled his efforts and throughout February and in the first week of March Malta's defenders and her people could only endure continuous misery and hold on as best they might. Her fighter squadrons as the principal defenders came under particularly severe pressure, on the ground as well as in the air, for in February alone 222 raids were made on their airfields. At the start of February, only twenty-eight Hurricanes were still serviceable and by the middle of the month, the number was down to eleven. Fortunately, the magnificent ground crews, through their herculean endeavours, brought this back up to twenty-one by the end of February and to thirty by mid-March.

The pressure on the Hurricane pilots was perhaps eased slightly by the infusion of welcome 'new blood' to replace some of those who had served longest on Malta. On 16 February a Sunderland flying boat brought in a batch of fresh pilots, headed by Canadian Squadron Leader Stanley Turner, a very aggressive character with the unnerving habit of firing a large revolver in public, who had flown Hurricanes in the Battle of Britain with Douglas Bader's 242 Squadron and now took command of 249. On the 21st, ten more 'fighter boys' arrived by Sunderland, including a new CO for 185, Squadron Leader Ronald Chaffe. The experiences of the replacement squadron commanders, however, would adequately summarize the perils that the defence of Malta entailed.

On 22 February, 185 was engaged in a fight with Bf 109s. Squadron Leader Chaffe damaged one of these but, intent on finishing it off, he did not see another Messerschmitt diving onto him from behind. His Hurricane was fatally hit and he baled out into the sea. His pilots confirmed that he had been able to get into his dinghy, but a later search by air-sea rescue services found no trace of him. It had been Chaffe's first operational sortie from Malta.

On 24 February, Turner and the American Pilot Officer Donald Tedford were directed against a hostile formation that they were told was immediately ahead of them. It appears that the flight controller had confused the two plots on his radar screen, for in reality the enemy aircraft – four Messerschmitt Bf 109s – were close behind, and the 249 pilots were taken completely by surprise. Cannon shells hit Turner's Hurricane in the engine which caught fire and on the cockpit which was jammed and prevented him from baling out. Mercifully, Turner dived away steeply and was able to blow out the flames. He crash-landed with only minor injuries: one more pilot to owe his life to the strength and reliability of his Hurricane.

Tedford, sadly, was shot down and killed. It was believed, incorrectly, that he might have baled out into the sea, and when this information reached Tedford's friend and fellow American Howard Coffin, he promptly took off without any orders or permission in a vain search for the missing airman. Nobody ever blamed him for his impulsive action.

In contrast to the comparatively small loss of life in January, six Hurricane pilots besides Chaffe and Tedford were killed in action during February, among them Pilot Officer Lowe whose dramatic take-off from *Argus* was described earlier. Another airman died when his Hurricane dived into the ground on a test flight. Then in the first week of March, the day-fighter squadrons lost three more pilots dead and another in hospital.

Yet for all the great odds against them, the Hurricane pilots still managed to harry the Junkers Ju 88s, thirteen of which were shot down, crashed on landing or 'written off' during daylight raids at this time. Another Ju 88 was shot down in flames by Sergeant Wood of 1435 Flight on the night of 4/5 March. The pilots were also becoming more skilful at dealing with the formidable Bf 109s, of which twelve were destroyed or crash-landed. As Pilot Officer Howard Coffin cheerfully noted in his diary: 'The 109s aren't so hot when you can see them.'

Then on 7 March two groups of reinforcements arrived. From Egypt came four radar-equipped Beaufighters, trained to operate at night. They would give some support to 1435 Flight, making their first 'kill', a Junkers Ju 88, on the night of 8/9 March, though only after this had been crippled by 1435's CO, Squadron Leader Westmacott. From HM aircraft carrier *Eagle* came fifteen day-fighters and these were not Hurricanes but Spitfires. It is an illustration of the importance of Malta and of the unsupported burden that the Hurricanes had carried worldwide for two and a half years of war that these were the first Spitfires (apart from an occasional reconnaissance machine) to operate outside the British Isles. Their arrival caused great jubilation among the Maltese.

The Spitfires were attached to Turner's 249 Squadron, but it took some time to make them ready for combat which they first saw on 10 March. Meanwhile on the 9th, the Hurricanes of 126 and 185 had had a typically savage clash with Junkers Ju 88s escorted by Messerschmitt Bf 109s. In accordance with their usual practice, the Hurricanes concentrated on the bombers. Australian Flight Sergeant Gordon Tweedale shot down one and others were damaged, but Pilot Officer Coffin was hit by return fire from their gunners. His Hurricane was so badly damaged that it was 'written off', but it got him back to base all the same. Then the 109s dived down, one of them badly damaging Tweedale's Hurricane and wounding him in the heel, which put him in hospital for a time. Again the Hurricane brought its pilot back safely. The Messerschmitt responsible was itself shot down by Pilot Officer 'Archie' Steele.

On 10 March, enemy raiders were met by both Spitfires and Hurricanes. At first the Spitfires – faster and with a better rate of climb – engaged the German fighters, leaving the bombers to the Hawker fighters. However, their pilots quickly came to realize, as had the Hurricane pilots, that their first objectives must be the bombers because these could do far more damage, and thereafter they joined in the attacks on these and like the Hurricanes were themselves swooped on from above by the 109s. A number of enemy aircraft were claimed, but by the end of 20 March four Spitfire pilots had died and the Hurricane squadrons had lost two pilots killed, with a third rescued, badly wounded, from the sea and a fourth crash-landed but unhurt.

In these circumstances the Spitfires, for all their excellent performance, had one great disadvantage compared with the Hurricanes: they were simply not as strong. Not only could they take less punishment in air combat, but when attacked on their airfields they could be put out of action more easily, being harder to maintain and repair. By the end of 20 March, of the fifteen Spitfires received from *Eagle*, only two were still operational. During March and April, as Kenneth Poolman neatly puts it in *Faith, Hope and Charity*: 'Once again the Hurricanes took the main defence upon their strong backs.'

They certainly did so to some effect on 21 March, when four of them from 185 Squadron surprised a group of Messerschmitt Bf 110s attempting to bomb and strafe Malta's airfields. Diving out of the sun, the Hurricanes sent four of them hurtling into the sea, and then pursued the rest as they retired, shooting down a couple more. German records admit the loss of just a single Bf 110, but in this instance there is no doubt that these are incomplete. Watchers on the ground, including a Spitfire 'ace', Sergeant (later Squadron Leader) Roy Hesselyn, confirmed the certain destruction of four 110s and the probable destruction of all six. The Germans would also give an implied confirmation themselves. No 110s were never again seen over Malta in daylight; a somewhat extreme reaction if only one had really been lost.

Also on 21 March, nine more Spitfires flew to Malta from HMS *Eagle*, and she delivered another seven on the 29th; these aircraft joined 126 Squadron as well as 249. The Hurricanes also received reinforcements in the form of 229 Squadron: ten Mark IICs on 27 March, nine others on 6 April and six more on the 19th. These, though, proved less effective than had been hoped. Few of the pilots had any experience of combat and Malta was definitely 'no place for beginners'. They did their best, having their first engagement on 1 April. On the 5th, Pilot Officer Andrews was Mentioned in Despatches for bringing back a Hurricane when badly wounded and on the 9th they lost their first aircraft, the pilot of which baled out safely.

Again, though, what was most discouraging was the wastage of Spitfires. Although several Hurricanes had been destroyed on the ground, there were always enough serviceable to allow 185 and 229 Squadrons to send up a reasonable number to confront enemy raids, but this was not the case with the Spitfires of 126 and 249 Squadrons. On 9 April, for instance, a huge formation of fifty German bombers escorted by fifty fighters was opposed by ten Hurricanes and two Spitfires. By the 10th, the ground crews, working continuously, had improved the situation, but only to the extent that there were now twelve Hurricanes and four Spitfires to oppose the attackers.

Nor could such small numbers of Spitfires hope to reverse the growing German superiority in the air. The raids in March doubled those in February. The raids in April almost doubled those in March, dropping more than 6,700 tons of bombs. Not that they were unopposed. During the last ten days of March and the first twenty days of April, despite the odds against them, Hurricanes alone destroyed or caused to crash-land ten Junkers Ju 88s, two Junkers Ju 87s and a Messerschmitt Bf 109 in daylight and possibly other enemy aircraft at night. For that matter they may have gained other victories by day which have not been mentioned in the German records since, as the Bf 110 affair on 21 March shows, these are surely incomplete.

In any case, though, the cost was high: three pilots of Spitfires and two from 185 Squadron were killed by 109s or the gunners of Junkers Ju 88s. Losses would undoubtedly have been worse but for the strength of the Hurricanes. On 10 April five of them were badly hit, but two of 185's airmen baled out safely and two from 229 crash-landed without injury. The most remarkable escape was that of 185's Pilot Officer Ormrod. His

Hurricane was already in flames when he crash-landed at Luqa airfield, but Corporal Clawson and Leading Aircraftman Mitchison rushed to his aid despite bombs and strafing and pulled him out of the cockpit. Their courage was recognized by awards of the George Medal.

On 15 April, the courage of the Maltese people was also recognized in the award – unique in the case of a community – of the George Cross. It was an honour richly deserved and must have rallied flagging morale. It could not, however, hide a brutal truth. Field Marshal Kesselring had succeeded in one of this aims. His men had battered Malta into temporary impotence as a base. First Malta's surface warships, then her bomber force and finally the gallant submarines that had defied all previous assaults had to retire to less perilous areas. Malta could no longer perform her vital task of savaging Axis convoys to North Africa.

Urgent action was essential and on an appeal from Churchill, President Roosevelt generously sent the US fleet carrier *Wasp* to the Clyde. She was the first American 'flat top' to enter the European theatre and with her broad lifts and long flight deck she could carry far larger numbers of Spitfires than any British carrier. On 20 April forty-seven of them left her deck for Malta, all except one arriving safely.

It seemed that air superiority would be regained, but this was not to be. Only a need to record the facts makes it bearable to repeat that again the precious Spitfires proved a wasting asset. Perhaps because of the speed with which the operation had been mounted, they were not in a very good condition when they reached Malta, their guns and wireless sets in particular being faulty. Arrangements to receive them were muddled and there was a delay in servicing and refuelling them that enabled the enemy to pounce on them before they could commence operations. Worst of all, it again proved difficult to keep them flying in the harsh conditions that existed on Malta.

Consequently, though the Spitfire pilots, many of whom were comparatively inexperienced, engaged the enemy with unflinching resolution – six of them had been killed in action by the end of the first week of May – there was nothing they could do to halt the rapid disappearance of their aircraft. By the end of 20 April, only twenty-seven remained serviceable. By the end of the 21st, this number was down to seventeen. By the end of the 22nd, every one was grounded. Desperate endeavours were able to restore some to combat-worthiness, but as late as 7 May only six were fit for action.

This catastrophe once more placed a great burden on the Hurricane pilots, but still they kept up their stubborn resistance. They even continued to strike at enemy territory, though this could now be done only by 1435 Flight. On the night of 26/27 April, for instance, Squadron Leader Westmacott shot up a train, but one of his best pilots, Sergeant Wood, was killed by anti-aircraft fire.

Against the daylight raiders, the ruggedness of their aircraft and the experience of their ground crews enabled the two Hurricane squadrons to continue sending up a useful force of interceptors. The odds against the Hurricanes were awesome: eight to one was considered fairly reasonable. Nonetheless, in the last days of April and the first week of May, Hurricanes shot down, caused to crash-land or severely damaged three Junkers Ju 88s, four Junkers Ju 87s and four Messerschmitt Bf 109s.

Inevitably, though, a high price had to be paid for this resistance and many fine men paid it. We first met Pilot Officer 'Sonny' Ormrod as a pilot of 605 Squadron flying off *Argus*. He had later transferred to 185 Squadron and some of his experiences have already been recounted. On 22 April his luck ran out, finally and horribly, for he was brought down, it would seem, by Malta's anti-aircraft guns. Ormrod baled out, but his parachute did not open. His body was found on a rooftop several weeks later.

On 28 April 185 Squadron lost another very capable airman in similarly tragic circumstances. The Canadian Pilot Officer John Fletcher, like Ormrod, had earlier been a member of 605 Squadron and had flown to Malta from *Argus* at the same time. He was then a sergeant pilot, but had received a commission in late March. On 28 April he had to bale out, but apparently opened his parachute too quickly. It streamed back over his Hurricane's tailplane which ripped it open, rendering it useless.

If experienced 185 pilots could fall to the heavy odds against them, it is not surprising that the inexperienced 229 Squadron should have suffered badly. During the last week of April and first week of May, it lost four pilots killed in action and a fifth when his Hurricane crashed on a test flight, while its CO Squadron Leader Dafforn was badly wounded. On 6 May, however, another 229 pilot, Flight Sergeant Roy, probably owed his life to his Hurricane's robustness. Hit by return fire from enemy bombers, he crash-landed at Hal Far and skidded into a large building at the end of the runway with such force that great chunks of stone rained down on the Hurricane. Its pilot suffered only minor injuries.

Yet the Hurricanes and their pilots had held on just long enough. As the RAF Official History rather unkindly explains:

> Hitler, with that improvidence characteristic of the master-plotters of war, was short of aircraft. A new campaign presented its demands in Russia; Rommel was due to attack in Cyrenaica; the Luftwaffe must exact revenge for Bomber Command's raids on the Reich. Each of these projects seemed more important to Hitler than bombing Malta. So in the opening days of May, to Russia, to Cyrenaica and to France the greater part of Kesselring's bombers departed.[5]

In his *Faith, Hope and Charity*, Kenneth Poolman relates that one elderly Maltese lady used to pray constantly: 'O Lord, send over the Italians!' This was not out of any fondness for them, but because they were much less murderously efficient than the Germans. On 30 April her prayers were granted as Italian bombers appeared, flying at high altitudes. They would repeat their raids through the early days of May, on the 8th of which month the Malta Hurricanes made their last 'kills', a Junkers Ju 88 and a Messerschmitt Bf 109.

This comparative lull gave Malta a chance to prepare for another big reinforcement mission. Early on 9 May, USS *Wasp* was again ready to fly off forty-seven Spitfires, on this occasion being joined by HMS *Eagle* with seventeen more. When the fighters took off, one from *Wasp* crashed into the sea to be trampled under by the carrier, while two others also failed to reach Malta, all three pilots losing their lives. For the remainder, however, their reception was magnificently arranged.

Every Spitfire and Hurricane already on the island took off to protect the new arrivals as they landed, and as soon as each touched down it was rushed to one of the numerous storage pens that had been erected around all the airfields. Here a highly-trained ground crew took on average only seven minutes and sometimes less than five minutes to remove the Spitfire's long-range tanks, refuel it, check its radio and guns and get it back into the air. So rapid was the turnaround that this time there was no fear of the Spitfires being shot up on their airfields.

Since there were on Malta several Spitfire pilots whose aircraft had already been destroyed or crippled, they took off in these new machines in place of men exhausted by their long trip to the island. A number of 185's Hurricane pilots did so as well, with not entirely happy results. Mention has already been made of Australian Flight Sergeant Gordon Tweedale. He had now become one of Malta's most successful 'aces', having been at least partly responsible for the destruction of seven enemy aircraft including both those shot down on the previous day. When he took off on 9 May, however, it was on his first flight in a Spitfire and his last, for he was one of three Spitfire pilots killed in air combat on this day. Sadly, two other 185 pilots who had earlier been very successful with Hurricanes, Pilot Officer Boyd and Sergeant Finlay, would also die in Spitfires before another week had elapsed.[6]

On 10 May Malta sent up an unprecedented total of fifty fighters to protect the fast mine-layer *Welshman*, which had reached Grand Harbour with a valuable cargo that included ammunition. Of these, thirty-seven were Spitfires and thirteen Hurricanes. Thereafter the changeover came quickly. USS *Wasp* left for the South-West Pacific, but if British carriers could not cope with as many Spitfires as she had done, experience enabled them to handle larger groups than had previously been thought possible. Not all the Spitfires sent from them reached Malta – on two separate occasions four of them failed to do so – but more than enough did: seventeen more in May, fifty-nine in June, sixty-one in July, sixty-five in August and twenty-eight in October.

As the number of Spitfires increased, that of the Hurricanes dwindled away. First 185 Squadron converted to Spitfires. Later 1435 Flight re-formed as a daylight unit, also with Spitfires. The unlucky 229 Squadron briefly provided protection for air-sea rescue vessels, losing another Hurricane and its pilot, and then flew back to Egypt. Its ill luck continued, for three pilots lost their way and came down in enemy-held territory. Sergeant Willcox was able to reach the British lines. Sergeant Ganes and Pilot Officer Lee were captured, but Lee escaped and also got back to safety and the award of a Mention in Despatches.

So rapid was the process that a number of Hurricanes remained on various airfields, and it says much for their robustness and the attitude of Malta's airmen that in July a few Hurribomber raids were made on Sicily by pilots who had previously flown Hurricane fighters. Then in August these were repeated on several occasions, both day and night, by Royal Navy pilots who were without aircraft. These later Hurribombers, incidentally, carried two 250lb bombs, one under each wing. Even as late as October, Hurricanes manned by naval pilots were still serving Malta on undramatic but essential air-sea rescue duties.

Thus the Hurricanes' activities on Malta did not end in May 1942, but then nor did other more unwelcome factors. As the RAF Official History points out: 'Malta's troubles…were still far from over. All too close ahead lay…the day when, failing the arrival of a convoy, the last slender reserves of fuel, food and ammunition would be exhausted.'

Notes

1. It seems that for some reason news of Greenhalgh's capture was not received in Malta and it was believed he had perished. Flight Sergeant 'Fred' Etchells, whose account in Chaz Bowyer's *Hurricane at War* has been mentioned earlier, met Greenhalgh again at a golf club dinner ten years later and came to 'a fully sober condition in one second flat!' 'A very joyful reunion' followed.
2. On *Argus* the upright funnel had been replaced by ducts that ran under the flight deck to discharge the gases over the stern. She had in fact no superstructure at all since her bridge had also been replaced by a small charthouse that could be raised or lowered hydraulically, hence her nickname of 'The Flat Iron'.
3. On 25 November, another German submarine *U-331* hit the British battleship *Barham* with three torpedoes, causing her to capsize and then disintegrate in an explosion that killed 56 officers and 812 ratings. Horrific as these casualties were, however, this loss was strategically less serious than that of the noble *Ark*.
4. Quoted in *Malta: The Hurricane Years 1940–41* by Christopher Shores and Brian Cull with Nicola Malizia. They also combined to produce *Malta: The Spitfire Year 1942* (though in fact Spitfires did not reach Malta until March or take over the main defensive role until May).
5. *Royal Air Force 1939–1945, Volume II: The Fight Avails* by Denis Richards and Hilary St. G. Saunders. Kesselring had advised Hitler that Malta had been neutralized, but it appears that the Führer had already made his decision before receiving this information.
6. The Spitfire, being smaller and faster than the Hurricane, was probably less easy to hit but certainly less able to protect its pilot when it was hit. During the siege of Malta Hurricanes flew in defence of the island-fortress for twenty-four months, though admittedly in many of these they faced only Italians. They had seventy-nine pilots killed, not counting losses on ferry trips. Their worst loss in a single month was ten in December 1941. Spitfires formed part or all of the defenders for nine months and had eighty-seven pilots killed, again not counting losses on ferry trips. In both May and August 1942, thirteen Spitfire pilots died and in both July and October 1942 their fatal casualties were as high as twenty.

Chapter Ten

Two Crucial Convoys

Malta's reserves of fuel, food and ammunition had been in danger since the appearance in the Mediterranean of Field Marshal Kesselring and *Fliegerkorps* II in December 1941. They were ready to carry out Hitler's commands to harry Allied supply convoys to Malta as well as assist Axis convoys to North Africa, and in the former task their mere arrival struck an initial blow.

Situated in the centre of the Mediterranean, Malta had to be supplied by vessels sailing either from Gibraltar in the west or from Egypt's great port of Alexandria in the east. The presence of a powerful, experienced and well-led force of German warplanes made the passage of convoys from the west unduly hazardous. There were enemy aircraft in Sardinia as well as Sicily so these convoys could be attacked when still distant from Malta, but the real problem was 'the Narrows' between Sicily and Cape Bon, Tunisia. These waters were so restricted that it was the practice for major warships to turn back when they were reached. Moreover, Force H at Gibraltar had been sorely hampered by the loss of *Ark Royal*. In February 1942 the British chiefs of staff advised Admiral Cunningham that replenishing Malta from the west was impracticable.

It was far from welcome news to Cunningham, on whose Mediterranean Fleet at Alexandria now fell the burden of protecting convoys to Malta, for in the first week of February, as we have seen, Rommel had captured the great airfield complex at Martuba near Derna. This not only deprived the Allies of a base from which fighters could cover convoys to Malta from Alexandria, but provided the Luftwaffe with one from which its warplanes could assault them. In January three merchantmen from Alexandria had delivered 30,000 tons of supplies to Malta while her Hurricanes drove off enemy aircraft trying to attack them, but the loss of the Martuba airfields created a very different situation. It would not be long before the seas between Crete and North Africa acquired a new name: 'Bomb Alley'.

This designation was entirely justified. In February a convoy to Malta of three big freighters was attacked by Kesselring's airmen who sank two of them and so damaged the third that she had to return to Alexandria. No supplies reached Malta in February.

In March Cunningham tried again. Once more the convoy contained three merchant ships, plus this time HMS *Breconshire*, an Auxiliary Supply Ship manned by a Royal Navy crew that had already made half a dozen successful trips to Malta. Its small escort of light cruisers and destroyers under the inspirational leadership of Rear Admiral Sir Philip Vian amazingly drove off a strong force of Italian warships that included battleship *Littorio*, but the supply ships had to be diverted southward away from the Italian threat and could not reach Malta under cover of darkness as planned. Next morning the Luftwaffe fell on them, sinking one freighter and so disabling *Breconshire* that she had to be towed to a small port on the south side of Malta, where she was finished off by subsequent air-raids.

Thus only two freighters reached Grand Harbour and, inexplicably, the work of unloading them proceeded with no sense of urgency in the daylight hours and not at all at night. For three days bad weather provided protection, but on 26 March it cleared and Kesselring sent 326 of *Fliegerkorps* II's warplanes to attack the merchantmen. Every serviceable Hurricane on Malta – and by this time every serviceable Spitfire as well – attempted to defend them, but sheer weight of numbers prevailed and both vessels were sunk. Of the 16,000 tons of supplies they had carried, less than 2,000 tons had been unloaded.

It was a tragedy, made greater because it proved impossible to assemble sufficient forces to run another convoy until June. For Malta it resulted in great hardships. Food had to be strictly rationed with communal feeding centres set up. An almost total absence of fruit and vegetables caused unpleasant skin diseases to appear and the medical authorities to warn of the possibility of scurvy. Ammunition, aviation fuel and kerosene – source of all heat and light on a treeless island – and oil – source of all power for the flour mills, the pumps drawing water from Malta's deep wells, the cranes in Grand Harbour – had to be tightly controlled. Malta's governor, General Sir William Dobbie, warned his people that they must be prepared for hardship and his superiors that the island's 'chance of survival' was being steadily eroded.

Governor Dobbie's own health was also being steadily eroded by his responsibilities and perhaps he felt some relief when on 7 May he was succeeded by General Lord Gort VC. Admiral Cunningham had also been recalled, ultimately to Washington as head of the British Naval Mission there. His replacement was Admiral Sir Henry Harwood, victor of the Battle of the River Plate who arrived in Egypt on 20 May.

By early June reinforcements from the Home Fleet were arriving at Gibraltar, while others from the Eastern Fleet, based in the Indian Ocean, were arriving at Alexandria. It was therefore decided to send not one convoy but two in the hope that this would divide the enemy's attention and resources. The larger convoy of eleven merchantmen left Alexandria in two sections in the evening of 11 June and at noon on the 12th, with an escort commanded by the redoubtable Rear Admiral Vian: this was Operation VIGOROUS. In the early hours of the 12th, another convoy of six ships passed through the Straits of Gibraltar and headed to Malta from the west: this was Operation HARPOON. 'Events were to prove, however,' remarks Ian Cameron in his account of the Malta convoys *Red Duster, White Ensign*, 'that two nibbles at a problem are less effective than one good bite'.

Both convoys began their run under fighter cover, but VIGOROUS did not enjoy this for long. Its protection came from Hurricanes and Kittyhawks operating from bases in the Western Desert, but the loss of Martuba meant that when 'Bomb Alley' was reached it was beyond their range. The enemy mounted continuous air-raids and to make matters worse an Italian naval force that included battleships *Littorio* and *Vittorio Veneto* threatened the convoy. It was attacked by RAF bombers but conflicting reports gave no indication whether it was still a danger or not.

In consequence, Admiral Harwood, who had unwisely decided to control the convoy from Cairo, ordered it to steam backwards and forwards in 'Bomb Alley' until the situation was clarified. By the time it was confirmed that the Italians were retiring, two merchantmen and two destroyers had been sunk by air attacks and a third destroyer by E-boats (German motor torpedo-boats), and the escort vessels had expended two-thirds of their AA ammunition. Harwood therefore ordered the convoy to return to Alexandria, losing light cruiser *Hermione* to the torpedoes of one of Hitler's U-boats on the way.

The total failure of the VIGOROUS convoy made it essential that the HARPOON one succeeded. This contained five freighters: the British *Troilus*, *Orari* and *Burdwan*, the Dutch *Tanimbar* and the American *Chant*. The Americans had also provided a new 9,300-ton tanker, the *Kentucky*, a generous and welcome gesture as at that time no British tanker was capable of making the 14 knots needed to stay with the convoy. The mine-layer *Welshman* at first accompanied the convoy but then broke away, using her superior speed to make for Malta independently with a cargo of ammunition and spares for the island's vulnerable Spitfires. She got there safely early on 15 June.

Escorting HARPOON were the battleship *Malaya*, four cruisers, seventeen destroyers, four minesweepers and, most vital of all, the aircraft carriers *Eagle* and *Argus*. On the aged *Argus* was a Fulmar squadron, No. 807. On *Eagle* were sixteen Sea Hurricanes which, unlike the Mark IA Catafighters described earlier, were true carrier-based aircraft since they had arrester hooks to catch the crosswires on their warships' decks.

It had never been intended that the Hurricane should operate as a naval fighter and in several respects it was not suitable for this role, at least on paper. In practice though, its reliability and adaptability enabled it to triumph over its disadvantages and the Fleet Air Arm's greatest test pilot, Captain Eric 'Winkle' Brown, is on record as stating that 'The Hurricane was to take to the nautical environment extraordinarily well.'[1]

During its seaborne career, the Hurricane would serve aboard six fleet carriers and seven escort carriers. It would fly over the Arctic Ocean where the Sea Hurricane's first 'kill' was made on 31 July 1941 when Lieutenant Commander Judd and Sub-Lieutenant Howarth of 880 Squadron from the carrier *Furious* shot down a Dornier Do 18. It would fly over the Atlantic Ocean where the Sea Hurricane's last 'kills' would be made on 26 May 1944, two four-engined Junkers Ju 290s being destroyed over the Bay of Biscay, one by Sub-Lieutenant Burgham and the other by Sub-Lieutenants Mearns and Wallis, all of 835 Squadron from the escort carrier *Nairana*. It would fly over the Indian Ocean protecting Allied landings at Diego Suarez in Vichy French Madagascar, which island was occupied to deny it to the Japanese, and it would fly over the Mediterranean protecting Allied landings in Vichy French North Africa and guarding two crucial convoys to Malta, the first of which was HARPOON.

There were several versions of Sea Hurricanes, the last and best being the Sea Hurricane Mark IIC which, like its RAF equivalent, had a Merlin XX engine and four 20mm cannons. However, those on *Eagle* to defend HARPOON – twelve of them from 801 Squadron, the other four from 813 – were older Mark IBs converted from RAF Hurricane Is with Merlin III engines, boosted to increase their speed, and eight Browning machine guns.

HARPOON was sighted and tracked by enemy reconnaissance aircraft during the afternoon and evening of 13 June, and the Fleet Air Arm Hurricanes gained their first success when Sub-Lieutenant Michael Crosley of 813 Squadron shot down a Cant Z 1007. Other aerial scouts appeared early on the 14th, and Crosley was soon in action again. A Junkers Ju 88 was damaged by Lieutenant King-Joyce and Crosley finished this off.

By now, though, the enemy knew exactly where the HARPOON convoy was and for the rest of the 14th it was consistently attacked by a total of almost 150 bombers and torpedo-planes escorted by more than 100 fighters. The first raid was a small one, mounted by the *Regia Aeronautica* from Sardinia. A formation of about ten Savoia Marchetti SM 79 torpedo-planes was intercepted by a couple of 801's Sea Hurricanes flown by Lieutenant 'Dick' Turnbull and Sub-Lieutenant 'Red' Duthie, who between them shot down one and drove away the others. A flight of eight Fiat CR 42 fighter-bombers did get through to attack *Argus*, but they had no success and lost two of their number to the carrier's Fulmars, while two more, short of fuel, had to land in Vichy French Tunisia where their pilots were interned.

Soon afterwards, the biggest raid of the day was delivered by Italian high-level and torpedo-bombers, strongly escorted by Macchi MC 200s and Fiat CR 42s. By ill luck the wind was blowing from astern, which meant that the carriers had to reverse course in order to send off their fighters. Though these did everything in their power to thwart the raiders, inevitably some broke past them to attack the convoy, putting one torpedo into the 6in-gunned cruiser *Liverpool* and two into the unlucky freighter *Tanimbar*. She caught fire, blew up and sank in ten minutes, but *Liverpool* was towed safely back to Gibraltar by the destroyer *Antelope*.

It proved a costly success for the Italians. The defenders claimed that three Italian fighters had been shot down and three were indeed destroyed or crash-landed. As for their bombers, it was said that four SM 79s had been downed by the Fleet Air Arm fighters and three more SM 79s by the convoy's AA gunners. HARPOON's protectors seem to have been too modest, though perhaps not very good at aircraft recognition. In fact, eleven Italian bombers were shot down or crash-landed: four SM 79s, six Savoia Marchetti SM 84s and one Cant Z 1007,[2] and among the airmen lost was Lieutenant Colonel (Wing Commander) Giovanni Farina. It was in this raid, however, that the Sea Hurricanes lost their only pilot: Lieutenant Tickner of 801 was shot down and killed by a Macchi MC 200.

That was the last enemy attack from Sardinia, but the German and Italian airmen on Sicily had yet to make their appearance. The Germans did so at 1820 that evening, when nine Junkers Ju 88s bombed *Argus*. Luckily they inflicted no damage or casualties and two of them were shot down by a Hurricane flown by 801's Sub-Lieutenant Peter Hutton. Shortly afterwards, a big raid was made by Savoia Marchetti SM 79 torpedo-bombers and Junkers Ju 87s escorted by Macchi MC 200s, Macchi MC 202s and Reggiane Re 2001 fighters. Torpedoes from the SM 79s were avoided by *Argus* just in time, but the Junkers Ju 87s, which were flown by Italian pilots, did not even manage a near miss.

By this time the defending fighter pilots were coming close to exhaustion, but they still proved able to intercept these raiders. Lieutenant Turnbull and Sub-Lieutenant Duthie were again in action against torpedo-planes, shooting down one and so damaging another that it returned to its base only to be 'written off' as a total loss. Turnbull's Hurricane was badly damaged by return fire, but despite its injuries returned safely to *Eagle*.

The pilots of 813 Squadron were also in action, Sub-Lieutenant Spedding shooting down a Reggiane Re 2001 and Sub-Lieutenant Crosley damaging another so badly that it force-landed in Tunisia. A couple of 813's Hurricanes were also lost. Lieutenant Bullivant had to bale out but was rescued by a destroyer, while Spedding's Hurricane was 'written off' after being mauled in a fight with three Italian fighters and crash-landing on *Eagle*; the pilot was unhurt. Sadly, during the day 807 Squadron lost four Fulmars and five of their crewmen. They were not as rugged as the Hurricanes.

Of the enemy aircraft that were shot down or damaged beyond repair on 14 June, the Sea Hurricanes were responsible for ten and the Fulmars for four. There were also some ten or twelve cases where the success was probably gained by HARPOON's anti-aircraft gunners but perhaps by HARPOON's protecting fighters or a combination of both. If fighters were involved, probably they were Sea Hurricanes, if only because there were more of these on hand. Not that it really matters. The value of the Fleet Air Arm pilots lay not in the number of their aerial victories but in their having so hampered and disrupted the enemy's air attacks that only one of the precious merchantmen had been sunk.

This was immensely important because at 2100 on 14 June HARPOON reached the Narrows, whereupon, as was customary in the case of convoys approaching Malta from the west, the major escort units turned back. They naturally included the aircraft carriers and next morning these were attacked by a small force of Savoia Marchetti SM 79s. They were, however, driven off by 801's Sea Hurricanes, Lieutenant Turnbull and Sub-Lieutenant Duthie again combining to shoot down one of them, and all the warships got back to Gibraltar safely.

The convoy was less fortunate. Its five remaining merchantmen, now guarded by anti-aircraft cruiser *Cairo*, nine destroyers and four minesweepers, passed through the Narrows that night before making a final dash for Malta. It was realized that losses then would be inevitable, but it was hoped that the 'good start' HARPOON had been given by the carrier fighters would enable the bulk of its supplies to get through.

Unhappily, 15 June was a long series of misfortunes. An Italian squadron of cruisers and destroyers was driven off, but the British destroyers *Bedouin* and *Partridge* were badly damaged and the former sunk later by Italian torpedo-bombers. Axis air attacks concentrated on the merchant ships, sinking *Chant* outright and so disabling *Burdwan* and the tanker *Kentucky* that they had to be abandoned after their crews had been taken off. They were eventually finished off, rather ingloriously, by the Italian destroyers. Even when Malta was reached, the Polish destroyer *Kujawiak* hit a mine and sank. Early on 16 June, however, *Troilus* and *Orari* came safely into Grand Harbour.

So ended Operation HARPOON. It has rarely received much notice, still less much praise, but it was absolutely crucial. Its effects have best been summed up in Ian Cameron's *Red Duster, White Ensign*:

> As good fortune would have it, the two merchantmen that survived – the *Troilus* and *Orari* – were unusually large and heavily loaded.

Within a few hours of berthing they had discharged 20,000 tons of vitally needed supplies, including the flour and ack-ack ammunition on which the fate of the island depended. In view of the complete failure of the convoy from Alexandria, the arrival of these two merchantmen assumed a massive significance. For it was their cargo which tipped the scales that hung so precariously between survival and defeat; with the help of what they had brought, Malta was able to tighten her belt and survive until another and larger convoy could be fought through; but if the *Troilus* and *Orari* had been sunk, Malta would almost certainly have fallen. That is the measure of the achievement.

At the same time it was appreciated that Malta's fate had only been postponed unless that other and larger convoy could arrive. The supplies brought by HARPOON would last only for a limited period and there was no way in which they could be extended since the rations issued to service personnel and civilians alike had already been cut to the barest minimum.

Moreover, the most worrying aspect of the HARPOON convoy had been the loss of *Kentucky*. This meant that the shortage of oil and kerosene was desperate, and to give his people an example – and a warning – Lord Gort travelled through Valletta on a bicycle. It had been customary for the authorities to decide on a 'Target Date' when food and fuel supplies would run out and surrender would be inevitable. This was now determined to be 7 September at the latest.

It was obvious from the lessons of HARPOON and VIGOROUS that no convoy could reach Malta from the east until the Martuba airfields were retaken and that a convoy from the west must be given the protection of carrier-based fighters for much of the way to ensure its 'good start'. It also soon became clear that it would not be possible for the necessary preparations to be made before mid-August and there would be no time to mount a second convoy before the fatal 7 September. If the August convoy – it was code-named Operation PEDESTAL – succeeded, this could bring about Malta's salvation. If it failed, this would certainly ensure Malta's surrender.

So a tremendous responsibility rested on the crews of thirteen big fast freighters – two of them American – that were assembled for Operation

PEDESTAL and loaded with a total of 85,000 tons of supplies: an odd and extremely dangerous mixture of flour, ammunition and aviation fuel in cans. To join them, the United States again generously provided a tanker fast enough to stay with the convoy. The *Ohio*, with her cargo of 11,000 tons of oil and kerosene, was taken over by the Ministry of War Transport, which provided her with additional AA guns, the gunners to man them and a new British crew under Captain Dudley Williams Mason.

To escort the convoy and ensure the necessary 'good start', Vice Admiral Sir Neville Syfret, the South African officer who had succeeded Somerville in command of Force H, was given battleships *Nelson* and *Rodney*, seven cruisers, twenty-six destroyers and, most importantly, three aircraft carriers. *Eagle* was back, again carrying twelve Sea Hurricanes of 801 Squadron and four of 813 Squadron, and this time with four extra Sea Hurricanes as a reserve. *Indomitable*, which had a large forward lift and a large hangar area, carried twelve Sea Hurricanes from 800 Squadron and ten from 880, as well as 806, a squadron of Grumman Martlets. *Victorious*, which lacked *Indomitable*'s advantages, relied mainly on the Fulmars of 809 and 884 Squadrons, though she did also have five Hurricanes from 885 Squadron.[3]

Since this was the first time the Royal Navy had had three fleet carriers in one task group, these spent three days in the Atlantic getting used to operating together and rectifying any problems that were revealed. They joined the convoy for a final practice on 9 August; then all vessels entered the Mediterranean after dark on the 10th.

Axis Intelligence knew all about PEDESTAL and its importance. On aerodromes in Sicily, Sardinia and Italy's own island-fortress Pantelleria between Sicily and Tunisia, the Luftwaffe and *Regia Aeronautica* had gathered almost 250 bombers or fighter-bombers of various kinds and about the same number of interceptor fighters, plus reconnaissance machines. Their plans were well coordinated and, as will be seen, included the use of new, if as it transpired, not very effective secret weapons.

On 11 August the Axis air forces did little except keep PEDESTAL under observation by reconnaissance aircraft, chiefly Junkers Ju 88s. In the morning, the Sea Hurricanes made their first interception of one of these, the naval airman responsible being Lieutenant Richard Cork of 880 Squadron, a veteran Hurricane pilot who had been seconded to

Douglas Bader's 242 Squadron during the Battle of Britain and been awarded a Distinguished Flying Cross, later amended to a Distinguished Service Cross by order of the Admiralty. He was flying Hurricane Z4642 which had been 'unofficially' converted to carry four 20mm cannons, thus increasing its firepower at the cost of reducing its speed. He claimed a 'probable', but in fact the Ju 88 got back to base on one engine with a dead gunner in the rear cockpit.

That afternoon the pilots of 880 intercepted another Junkers Ju 88. It put up a sturdy defence and badly damaged the Hurricane of Lieutenant Forrest who was compelled to 'ditch' but happily was rescued quickly. His CO, the aggressive red-bearded Lieutenant Commander Francis Judd, who it may be recalled had made the first 'kill' by a Sea Hurricane back in July 1941, now made the first one by a Sea Hurricane in Operation PEDESTAL: he sent the Ju 88 down in flames.

These minor achievements, unfortunately, could do little to disguise the fact that 11 August was a terrible day for the PEDESTAL convoy. The most serious blow fell at 1315, when *U-73* put four torpedoes into HMS *Eagle*. Half a mile away on *Indomitable*, Sub-Lieutenant Hugh Popham of 880 Squadron was preparing to take off when his attention was attracted by the explosions of the torpedoes. In his book *Sea Flight* he describes *Eagle*'s horrifyingly quick end:

> Listing to port, she swung outwards in a slow, agonised circle, and in seven minutes turned abruptly over. For a few seconds longer her bottom remained visible, and then the trapped air in her hull escaped, and with a last gust of steam and bubbles she vanished. All that remained was the troubled water, a spreading stain of oil, and the clustered black dots of her ship's company.

Mercifully, prompt work by destroyers saved about 900 of *Eagle*'s crew, but some 260 went down with her. So did sixteen of the Hurricanes she carried; only four from 801 Squadron that were already airborne were able to land on the other 'flat tops'.

Then at dusk, a small force of Junkers Ju 88s and Heinkel He 111 torpedo-bombers attacked. They caused no harm, though two bombs came close to *Victorious* and were chased away by Hurricanes and Fulmars. Unfortunately, the Fleet Air Arm pilots, few of whom were experienced in night operations, found it hard to locate their carriers in the gathering darkness. Furthermore, they were getting very low on fuel. Hugh Popham was one of those in this predicament and in desperation decided to land on the first carrier he sighted, with perilous consequences as he relates in *Sea Flight*:

> I could see the deck, swinging away to starboard under me. It was my last chance. I crammed the nose down, cut the throttle, and with the last bit of extra speed, tried to kick the aircraft into a turn to match the ship's. She was swinging too fast. The wheels touched, and the skid wiped off the undercarriage and the aircraft hit the deck and [went] slithering and screeching up towards the island on its belly. I hung on and waited. It stopped at last, just short of the island, on the centre-line – what was left of it.

Once again the strength of the Hurricane had saved a pilot's life. Popham hastily scrambled out just before it burst into flames. He was less embarrassed at having 'written off' his aircraft than at having to admit he had no idea what ship he was on; it was in fact *Victorious*. Several of her own aircraft in return landed on Popham's *Indomitable* for Captain Troubridge had risked showing lights to assist his pilots and consequently assisted other pilots as well.

Nor was Popham the only pilot to crash when landing on a carrier, and those that did wrecked or badly damaged several machines other than their own. PEDESTAL had begun 11 August with three carriers on which were about seventy fighters. It began on 12 August with two carriers on which the number of serviceable fighters was fewer than fifty.

It was not a promising situation but at least no pilots had been lost, and 12 August would tell a very different story. Throughout the day, the Axis airmen posed a continuous threat. They could decide when and in what form attacks would be made and their already high superiority in numbers had been further increased by PEDESTAL's misfortunes on the 11th. As a result, the convoy's defenders had to be permanently on the alert, unable to relax for a moment, ready to battle against heavy odds at any time and without much warning. In the circumstances, their achievements were remarkable.

Throughout the day, the Fleet Air Arm pilots shot down occasional Italian aircraft attempting to track the convoy, one of these becoming another victim of the ever eager Lieutenant Commander Judd, but their main concern was dealing with the three major raids the enemy delivered. The first and smallest of these was carried out by Junkers Ju 88s escorted by Bf 109s and came in at about 0900. It was also the least successful since it was intercepted some distance from the convoy by Hurricanes from *Indomitable*: first those of 800 Squadron led by their CO Lieutenant Commander Bruen; then those of 880, on this occasion commanded by Lieutenant Cork.

Surprisingly, the 109s seem to have made no attempt to protect the Junkers, but the gunners of these proved worthy adversaries, hitting two of 800's aircraft. Sub-Lieutenant Roberts had to 'ditch', being rescued safely by a destroyer, and Lieutenant Martyn got back to *Indomitable* only to crash-land, so damaging his Hurricane that it was assessed as being beyond repair. The victory, however, clearly lay with the Hurricanes, which destroyed several Ju 88s, Cork personally downing two. Better than any individual success, though, was the fact that the Hurricanes so harried and dispersed the Junkers that only four got through to the convoy and these bombed ineffectually.

As the enemy retired, more Hurricanes from *Victorious* joined in the fight. The Junkers' gunners again gave a good account of themselves, killing Sub-Lieutenant Hankey, one of the 801 pilots who had survived the sinking of *Eagle* and landed on *Victorious*. On the other hand, Lieutenant Carver who led 885's Hurricanes shot down two more Ju 88s, a particularly fine achievement since he was flying with an arm in plaster, having fractured it in an accident earlier.

At noon the largest raid was delivered. It came from Sardinia in a series of waves that contained virtually every aircraft available to the enemy: Savoia Marchetti SM 79s and SM 84s, Cant Z 1007s, Macchi MC 202s, Reggiane Re 2001s, Junkers Ju 88s, Heinkel He 111s, Messerschmitt Bf 109s and Bf 110s. It was also this raid that revealed the new weapons prepared by the ingenious Italians. One was a Savoia Marchetti SM 79 packed with explosives, the pilot of which had baled out as planned, leaving it to be steered by a radio guidance system. Another was the use of 'motobomba' which were dropped by some of the SM 84s. These were torpedoes that came down by parachute, and on hitting the water set off on a zigzag course that could not be predicted.

Fortunately for PEDESTAL, these ideas worked better on paper than in practice. The radio-controlled SM 79 failed to obey its controls and flew past the convoy to crash in Algeria, much to the annoyance of the Vichy French authorities. The 'motobomba' were dropped in front of the convoy in the hope that they would disperse the merchantmen and make them easier targets for later waves. Happily they remained in formation and successfully evaded all the new weapons. Moreover, the bombers that had carried these were engaged by Hurricanes and suffered several losses.

As other attacking waves came in, the Fleet Air Arm pilots, with the Hurricanes well to the fore as usual, continued to oppose them, shooting down some enemy aircraft, damaging others and breaking up formation after formation. Sub-Lieutenant Lucas of 800 Squadron was killed, another victim of enemy air gunners, but his CO, Lieutenant Commander Bruen, who had earlier shared in the destruction of a Junkers Ju 88, now shared in that of a pair of Italian bombers. Another pilot who deserves mention was Sub-Lieutenant Peter Hutton who, as we saw, had distinguished himself in the defence of the HARPOON convoy, and had also survived the sinking of *Eagle*. Now flying from *Indomitable*, he assisted in downing an Italian bomber and destroyed a Reggiane Re 2001 without the need for any assistance.

Not until the bulk of the assaults had been broken did PEDESTAL's merchantmen come under attack, but then a group of Junkers Ju 88s damaged freighter *Deucalion* with a bomb that passed right through her without exploding and several near misses. With her speed much reduced, she had to leave the convoy to try to make her way to Malta on her own. That evening she was sunk by Italian torpedo-planes.

There was then a brief interval between attacks, during which the Italians sprang the last of their surprises. *Victorious* was preparing to recover her fighters when two 'Hurricanes' suddenly roared in upon her. They were really Reggiane Re 2001s that bore a considerable resemblance to the Hawker aircraft and had been camouflaged in British-style colours. Happily their fragmentation bombs had little effect on the carrier's armoured deck, though splinters caused a few casualties. So complete was the surprise that the Re 2001s escaped without a shot being fired at them as, it must be admitted, they thoroughly deserved to do.

A subsequent raid by Heinkel He 111s carrying torpedoes and escorted by Messerschmitt Bf 110s was driven off by the Hurricanes of 880, although at some cost. The squadron's CO Lieutenant Commander Judd was killed by the rear gunner of one of the Heinkels and the Bf 110s then came down on the Hurricanes from above, killing Sub-Lieutenant Cruikshank. The 110 responsible was promptly shot down by Lieutenant Cork.

It is convenient to mention here that later in the day Cork would also shoot down a Cant Z 1007. His four-cannon machine suffered minor damage and while it was being repaired, Cork took off in a standard Sea Hurricane Z7095 to destroy a Savoia Marchetti SM 79. He was then attacked by a pair of Reggiane Re 2001s but his Hurricane, though so damaged in radiator and rudder that it was 'written off' as unrepairable, still brought Cork back to a safe landing and a subsequent award of the DSO.

A lull in the afternoon gave some welcome relief to PEDESTAL, but at about 1800 another massive raid was delivered, this time from Sicily, again in successive waves. The versatile Italians, in addition to the usual Cant Z 1007s in the reconnaissance role and Savoia Marchetti SM 79s carrying torpedoes, used old Fiat CR 42 biplanes as fighter-bombers and some Junkers Ju 87s were flown by Italian pilots. The Germans contributed larger numbers of Stukas and some Ju 88s, and all formations were strongly protected by Messerschmitt Bf 109s, Macchi MC 202s or Reggiane Re 2001s.

Inevitably, therefore, the hard-worked defenders, of which the Sea Hurricanes provided the backbone, found it hard to get at the enemy bombers. Nonetheless, they still managed to break up a few formations and shoot down some Italian bombers and Italian-manned German bombers. Sub-Lieutenant Thomson of 800 Squadron made a particularly effective attack on a group of four Italian Stukas, destroying one and forcing the others to jettison their bombs. He was then engaged by some 109s, but he out-turned one and shot this down also. Only a single Hurricane came down and that was an unintentional victim of the convoy's AA gunners: Lieutenant Fiddes of 880 Squadron had to 'ditch', but fortunately he was quickly picked up.

This time the raiders concentrated not on the merchant vessels but on their escorting warships. A torpedo struck the stern of destroyer *Foresight* and she had to be sunk later. The German Stukas went for *Indomitable*, scoring two hits and three very near misses which buckled her flight deck and wrecked both her aircraft lifts. Just before she was struck, *Indomitable* had launched four more Hurricanes and 800 Squadron's Sub-Lieutenant Ritchie gained some revenge for her by shooting down two of the Ju 87s responsible.

Indomitable's injuries were serious enough to render her incapable of operating her aircraft and those airborne were therefore directed to *Victorious* instead. Among the pilots affected was Lieutenant Cork, as also was Lieutenant Hutton who would thus at different times fly from all three of PEDESTAL's carriers. Sadly, a number of Hurricanes had to be thrown overboard since there was simply not enough room for them. Even so, *Victorious*, having set out on PEDESTAL with five Sea Hurricanes and sixteen Fulmars, returned to Gibraltar with eight Sea Hurricanes, ten Fulmars and three of *Indomitable*'s Martlets.

At about 1900 on 12 August, Vice Admiral Syfret withdrew his major warships – in *Indomitable*'s case ultimately to a repair yard in the United States – leaving a force of cruisers and destroyers under Rear Admiral Burrough to escort the convoy the rest of the way to Malta. The Fleet Air Arm's part in the battle was over. A number of its aircraft had been 'written off' for various reasons, and in combat, besides the Hurricane casualties already mentioned, it had lost three Fulmars and six Fulmar crewmen and one Martlet and its pilot. Its achievements, however, had been immense.

It is difficult to assess the defending fighters' victories exactly. No doubt as usual some exaggerated or duplicated claims were made and it must be stated that enemy records are clearly incomplete. To take the case of Lieutenant Cork, for example, his last victim, a Savoia Marchetti SM 79, is not recorded, yet Cork observed its crew in their dinghy and photographed them with his camera-gun; it was while doing so that he was caught by surprise by the Re 2001s and owed his life to the sturdiness of his Hurricane. The Bf 110 Cork had claimed earlier is also not recorded, but its destruction is even more certain. Not only did it crash close to *Indomitable* before the eyes of many of her cheering crew, but its pilot baled out and was rescued by a destroyer.

It should be noted, however, that David Brown, a former naval airman and at the time a member of the Ministry of Defence's Naval Historical Branch – he became its head shortly afterwards – made a thorough check of Allied and Axis records for his book *Carrier Fighters*. He concluded that PEDESTAL's aerial defenders should be credited with three 'kills' on 11 August – the Ju 88 downed by Judd and two successes by Fulmars – and thirty-five more on 12 August: four by Martlets, seven by Fulmars and twenty-four by Sea Hurricanes.

In any event, whatever the correct number of 'kills', no one, surely, could dispute David Brown's final verdict:

> By any standards the shipboard fighters had scored a victory. The enemy had held the initiative throughout 12th August, attacking in great strength, with an escort which always outnumbered the defenders. Not until the third raid did the fighters manage to subdue the tired naval pilots, most of whom were flying their third or fourth sorties of the day. Even then, the sixty-one attack aircraft managed to obtain only two really damaging hits and they neglected the convoy, which was of far greater strategic significance.

How successful and how important the carrier-fighters had been is demonstrated by the fact that while they were guarding PEDESTAL, the one merchantman lost was *Deucalion* and she only after having to leave the protection of the convoy. In contrast, PEDESTAL's subsequent experiences read like a horror story created to illustrate all possible perils of war at sea.

With dusk on 12 August came the first disaster in the form of a salvo of torpedoes from the Italian submarine *Axum*. These crippled Rear Admiral Burrough's flagship, the light cruiser *Nigeria*, which had to limp back to Gibraltar, sank AA cruiser *Cairo*, once a defender of the HARPOON convoy, and tore a huge hole in *Ohio* as well as starting a raging fire that the tanker's crew somehow managed to extinguish. During the night PEDESTAL was beset with more air-raids that sank two freighters and damaged a third, the *Brisbane Star*, which had to proceed independently. The night also provided cover for German E-boats and Italian MAS-boats which proved more dangerous than those that had tried to penetrate Grand Harbour; they sank light cruiser *Manchester* and four more freighters.

Dawn on the 13th found only six merchantmen in PEDESTAL and before they could come under the protection of long-range Beaufighters from Malta, they were subjected to another series of air attacks.

Waimarama was hit and blew up. *Dorset* was crippled and finished off later. *Rochester Castle* was damaged but kept going. *Ohio*, the main target, suffered terribly. Hit by a bomb that blew her engine room to pieces, shaken by some twenty near misses, one of which split her stern open, and struck by two doomed enemy aircraft, first a Junkers Ju 88 and then a Ju 87 dive-bomber, both of which crashed onto her deck, she dropped behind the convoy and came to a halt, dead in the water.

Yet the 'good start' the carrier-fighters had given once more proved just good enough. That evening *Port Chalmers*, *Melbourne Star* and the damaged *Rochester Castle* entered Grand Harbour, where they were joined the next day by *Brisbane Star*. The 32,000 tons of stores that these ships brought provided half of Malta's needs. The other half was still at sea on a tanker that was slowly sinking, but *Ohio*'s crew, volunteers from vessels that had gone down earlier and the warships escorting her were all determined that she should be saved.

Their resourcefulness equalled their resolution. With destroyers *Bramham* and *Penn* lashed on either side of *Ohio* to stop her breaking in half or sinking, destroyer *Ledbury* secured to her stern to assist in steering her and minesweeper *Rye* steadily towing her onwards, this handful of little ships toiled all through 14 August and all the following night. They did not strive in vain and at 0800 on 15 August, it seemed that the entire population of Malta was there to roar its welcome as the unconquerable *Ohio* entered Grand Harbour, the sea washing over her main deck but her precious cargo virtually intact. Captain Dudley Mason had won a George Cross, and Malta, twenty-three days from surrender, had been saved.

Notes

1. Brown could personally attest to this, for he tells us that 'in Hurricanes, I did 200 landings with no incidents.'
2. It was certainly not easy to distinguish between these types. All of them had the same distinctive three engines and the SM 84 was a development of the SM 79.
3. For a time, the carrier *Furious* also accompanied the convoy but not as part of its protection. Her task was to fly off a batch of Spitfires for Malta. This she duly did on 11 August, after which she returned to Gibraltar with her own eight escorting destroyers.

Chapter Eleven

Jubilee

Exactly a week after the Sea Hurricanes had fought a series of actions to ensure that the PEDESTAL convoy got its 'good start', other Hurricanes would be engaged in very different activities over the coast of occupied France. This day would see the culmination of another campaign and emphasize a fundamental change in the role of the Hurricane as a weapon of war.

The campaign in question was called 'leaning forward into France'. This was the declared policy of Air Marshal Sir William Sholto Douglas, former Deputy Chief of Air Staff, who had succeeded Air Marshal Sir Hugh Dowding as head of Fighter Command, and Air Vice-Marshal Trafford Leigh-Mallory, who had replaced Air Vice-Marshal Keith Park as head of No. 11 Group in the south-east of England. Their intention was to move from the defensive to the offensive, at least in the hours of daylight, and their aggressive attitude inevitably won the approval of Winston Churchill.

Their offensive measures took two forms. These were the 'Circuses' in which British bombers, usually Blenheims but also Hampdens and, from July 1941, four-engined Stirlings, were directed against specific targets, either on land, in which case they were called 'Ramrods', or against enemy shipping when they were 'Roadsteads'. Mainly, though, the Circuses were intended to entice German fighters into the air where they could be attacked, preferably by superior numbers. The bombers were usually given a close escort of Hurricanes to act as their protection, a role that they performed with considerable success, while top cover was provided by Spitfires, ready to swoop down on the enemy aircraft from above.

More significant for the future were sorties by British fighters only. These were either directed against specific targets or intended to engage whatever targets opportunity might offer. They began on New Year's Day 1941, when three Hurricanes from No. 1 Squadron, led by Flight Lieutenant Clowes, strafed enemy positions between Calais and Boulogne for twenty minutes, unhindered by German fighters. If made by a small number of aircraft, these raids were mysteriously code-named 'Rhubarbs'. When made at squadron strength, they were known as 'Rodeos'; if at wing strength, they were 'Rangers'.

These various missions enjoyed mixed fortunes. Losses of aircraft were about equal, but the Germans had the advantage that any RAF pilot who baled out would usually become a prisoner of war, whereas any of their own men who escaped by parachute could fly and fight again. However, the sorties did inflict damage on airfields, factories and shipping; kept airmen, aircraft and AA guns on the Channel coast when they could otherwise have been sent to the Mediterranean or, after June 1941, to Russia; and showed the occupied countries that Britain was undefeated, inspiring the first flickers of organized resistance.

Among the Hurricane squadrons taking part in this offensive, mention should be made of No. 71, the first 'Eagle' squadron. Volunteers from the United States had fought in the Battle of Britain with various fighter units, but the winter of 1940–41 saw the formation of 71, a squadron made up of American citizens, albeit led by a succession of British commanding officers. Equipped first with Hurricane Is, it received IIAs in May 1941, and during June, July and early August would engage in 'leaning forward into France' on numerous occasions. In this period it participated in twenty-eight Rhubarbs, five Rodeos and twelve Circuses, during one of which, on 21 July, Pilot Officer William Dunn shot down a Messerschmitt Bf 109 over Lille to give No. 71 its first confirmed victory.

Of course, other Hurricane squadrons also downed the occasional enemy aircraft in the course of these various raids. In addition, throughout 1941 and the first half of 1942, Hurricanes were operating more and more often at night, seeking out German bombers returning from attacks on Britain over their own aerodromes.

All these events foreshadowed a new career for the Hurricane, different from that of its former comrade-in-arms, the Spitfire. The more modern if more complicated design of this enabled it to remain a front-line fighter throughout the war, with more and more powerful engines being put into its nose. Apart from night operations where the cloak of darkness masked the Hurricane's performance deficiencies, the Hawker fighter could not hope to continue longer in this role, at least on the Channel front. Fortunately, a warplane as adaptable and versatile as the

Hurricane could always prove valuable for other tasks. Air Marshal Peter Wykeham in his *Fighter Command* sets out the situation and its most important development:

> The Hurricane… [was] unable to match the enemy in climb, dive, or top speed, but relying on its manoeuvrability for its continued success. Manoeuvrability is unfortunately not the foremost quality when fighting on the enemy's ground, since you cannot manoeuvre for ever but must start home at some time or other. The Hurricane was therefore kept in service mainly for defence and in special strike roles. It was invaluable for 'Rhubarb', so much so that the purist fighter pilot was further offended when it was equipped to carry one 500lb bomb under each wing. From this stage its progress followed the same path, and it can be called the Royal Air Force's first true fighter-bomber, with its attention increasingly directed towards the ground and the enemy targets that stayed there.

As early as 18 April 1941, a Hurricane I had flown while carrying a pair of 250lb bombs. In the following month, a Mark IIB was given a similar armament and it was quickly found that this version was ideal for the purpose, since its speed was reduced by only 20 mph and its manoeuvrability and excellent handling characteristics were unaffected, even when one of the bombs had been dropped and the aircraft was technically unbalanced. Incidentally, it was also found helpful to omit two of the IIB's twelve machine guns, one from each wing, to allow space for the bomb-racks and their associated wiring. In practice, however, many pilots preferred to ignore this idea, retaining all their guns for protection after the bombs had been used.

Thus was born the 'Hurribomber' and once started, the process proceeded at speed. The Mark IIC was also adapted to carry the 250lb bombs. Then, as Air Marshal Wykeham notes, both IIBs and IICs were given two 500lb bombs. This extra weight admittedly did cause a fairly considerable reduction of speed, particularly in the case of the IICs with their heavy cannons.

Early in October 1941, the Hurribombers of 607 Squadron, led by Squadron Leader Craig, began attacks on Axis shipping in the Channel, hoping to disrupt this supply line, thereby increasing the burden on the enemy's road and rail systems. They joined forces with the Hurricane IICs of 615 under Squadron Leader Gillam[1] which had already begun raids on enemy vessels with their 20mm cannons during the previous month. On 30 October, 607 also made the first Hurribomber strike on land, damaging a transformer station at Tingry and a road bridge at Saumur. Next day, it bombed another transformer station at Holque and barges on a nearby canal. The day after, the Hurribombers of 402 Squadron[2] joined in, hitting an airfield at Berck-sur-Mer, a railway bridge near Étaples, railway wagons and gun posts.

Hurribomber sorties continued into 1942, both on anti-shipping strikes and on raids over enemy-occupied territory, including the whole of the Low Countries and a generous area of northern France. Targets on land varied widely: in addition to those mentioned earlier, they included railway stations, factories, depots and distilleries. The favourite objectives, though, were enemy aerodromes.

The culmination of the intruder missions came on 19 August 1942 with the raid on the French port of Dieppe. There was no intention of making any permanent lodgement in France; only of destroying as many enemy installations as possible in the course of a single day. In addition, it was hoped that the raid would bring up large numbers of enemy aircraft that would be decimated by Leigh-Mallory's heavily reinforced No. 11 Group.

Unhappily, Operation JUBILEE, as the raid was code-named, would give little cause for jubilation. As was perhaps easier to see in retrospect than at the time, Dieppe was not a good place for this type of assault. It was heavily defended on both sides of the harbour, with high cliffs dominating the narrow beaches onto which a murderous crossfire could be delivered, and which, being of steeply sloping shale, were in any case not well suited for landing craft or for tanks once ashore. Moreover, the main landings were entrusted to Canadian troops who, although admirably eager, were inexperienced, and the weight of firepower of their supporting naval forces was utterly insufficient.

Nor were the defenders unaware of British intentions. The Dieppe Raid had originally been planned for July, but bad weather had caused it to be cancelled and enemy Intelligence, as Churchill has confirmed in his book *The Second World War*, had learned of 'the threat to the Dieppe sector', though not the exact date or location of the attack. The Germans had therefore increased the number of their soldiers and the strength of their fortifications in the Dieppe area.³

Not surprisingly, therefore, despite their gallantry, the Canadians were pinned down on the beaches, gained hardly any of their objectives and could only be evacuated with difficulty. There was only one consolation but an important one: lessons were learned; mistakes were not repeated; defects were remedied. As a raid, JUBILEE was a disaster. As a preparation for later greater amphibious operations, it was extremely valuable.

It might be said that the RAF's objective was achieved, for during the morning and early afternoon of 19 August, German warplanes did appear in large numbers. Their attempts to harm the ground troops, landing craft and supporting naval vessels were all thwarted and they lost twenty-five bombers and twenty-three fighters. Sadly, though, the price the RAF paid was just over 100 of its own aircraft shot down or 'written off'. This was a higher total than the Luftwaffe had suffered on any one day during the Battle of Britain, and while it included casualties among Boston and Blenheim light bombers and Mustang reconnaissance machines attached to No. 11 Group for the operation, the heaviest loss was that of more than sixty Spitfires.

The Spitfires' task had been to provide protection from the Luftwaffe. The duty of the eight Hurricane squadrons that participated in the operation was to make low-level attacks over the heads of the Allied soldiers, at first assisting them to advance and then providing covering fire while they were evacuated. Apart from the risk of being attacked by any German fighters that got past the top cover of Spitfires, the Hurricanes would be the targets of every anti-aircraft gun the enemy possessed. Yet their unenviable role seems to have caused little concern to their superiors. Flight Lieutenant (later Air Commodore) John Ellacombe, a member of one of the Hurricane squadrons – No. 253 – tells us in Brian Milton's *Hurricane: The Last Witnesses* that when Leigh-Mallory briefed its pilots, he blandly stated: 'There are a lot of guns placed around. I have told the light bombers from Bomber Command that I don't want them. I want to take out all the defences with my Hurricanes and my Hurricane fighter-bombers. I don't mind losing 50 per cent of them.'

'This was us he was talking about,' exclaims Ellacombe, with justifiable indignation. No wonder he considered that 'Leigh-Mallory was a most unpleasant man'.

Of the Dieppe Hurricane squadrons, two were equipped with Mark IIB Hurribombers and were very experienced in their use on low-level missions. These were 174 and 175 Squadrons and it is an indication of the way in which the Hurricane was changing from an interceptor to a strike aircraft that both were entirely new units that had only come into existence on 3 March 1942 and been formed specifically to be Hurribomber squadrons. They were based respectively at Manston, previously the home of 607 which had been sent to the Far East, and Warmwell, 402's old base. For its motto 175 had chosen 'Stop at Nothing' and 174 the even more direct 'Attack'.

Both squadrons did their best to live up to these slogans, though 174 was quicker to become operational. It had inherited seventeen Hurribombers and eight experienced pilots from 607 and perhaps this gave it a head start. At any rate, its first mission was flown on 28 March when it bombed the aerodrome at Berck-sur-Mer, whereas 175 delivered its first attack – on Maupertus airfield – only on 16 April. Strikes against shipping soon followed. Perhaps the most praiseworthy was that by 175 on 15 May against three German minesweepers. These carried a heavy AA armament, yet the Hurribombers sank two outright and so damaged the third that it went down later. Although 174 could not quite match this achievement, it did have notable successes of its own; for instance, on 29 June it hit a large freighter so badly that this had to be beached.

By contrast, the other six squadrons of Hurricanes that took part in the Dieppe Raid – 3 and 87 with IICs; 32, 43, 245 and 253 with a mixture of IIBs and IICs – had had no experience of low-level missions, having been engaged on night-fighter duties, both on the defensive and in the intruder role. On being notified of their planned participation in JUBILEE, the first thing their personnel had to do was to cover their machines' black camouflage with the more colourful markings of the day-fighter squadrons.

The Hurricanes' part in JUBILEE began at 0425, when 43 Squadron, under Belgian Squadron Leader 'Roy' Du Vivier, took off from Tangmere with six Mark IIBs and six IICs. At first light some fifteen minutes later, 43 came in above the Canadians' landing craft as these headed for the beaches. The Squadron Diary reports the strike with the usual maddening reticence:

No. 43 Squadron was the first to go into the attack against gun positions on the beaches and in the buildings to the west of the harbour. These were the main landing beaches of our troops and were very heavily defended with machine guns and light and heavy flak. Two attacks were made and all pilots reported hits on gun posts, buildings, wireless masts, etc. However, of the 12 who went out only five came back untouched. F/Sgt Wik is missing from this operation. Plt Off Snell was missing after being heard to say over his R/T that he was baling out, but later he was picked up by air-sea rescue and was unhurt. Flt Lt Lister had the underside of one wing badly shot up by a cannon shell and had to make a wheels-up landing at Tangmere, but was unhurt. The Squadron landed at 0620 hrs.

Yet if two Hurricanes were missing and five were unharmed, then five others must have been damaged. So they were, and some of them provided further examples of the Hurricane's remarkable ability to survive the severest punishment. The Squadron Diary does not even mention the experience of Australian Pilot Officer Trenchard-Smith. Fortunately, his account is preserved in *No. 43 Fighting Cocks Squadron* by Andy Saunders:

We went in at nought feet, pouring everything we could into the beach and promenade, then we were over the town, roof-hopping and flat out trying to dodge the flak. It was hopeless, and before we could reach the smoke cover, and in spite of the way I threw my kite around, in and out of streams of fire, I was hit just in front of the rudder by an explosive cannon shell which blew off the fin and tore a huge hole in the tailplane. I was lucky, as I saw the lad in front of me [Flight Sergeant Wik], who had been flying Number 2 to the CO, get hit in a bad way, and that was the last I saw of him.

Despite its damage, Trenchard-Smith's Hurricane got back to base and landed safely, whereupon 'the tail section just fell apart'. The pilot flew three more sorties that day and was known henceforth as 'Tail-less Ted'.

Even the Squadron Diary makes mention of the experience of Flight Lieutenant 'Freddy' Lister which would prove still more harrowing than that of Trenchard-Smith. As it states, one of the wings of Lister's Hurricane IIC – the port wing in fact – was mauled by a cannon shell. It carried him back to Tangmere, but experiments on the return flight had demonstrated that he would lose control if he did not maintain a high speed, and a glance at the shattered wing convinced him that it would be highly dangerous to attempt to lower the undercarriage or the flaps. It might have been wiser to bale out, but Lister had no intention of abandoning his faithful 'mount'. With his airspeed indicator showing 210 mph, he therefore made a spectacular crash-landing, vividly described by James Beedle in his *43 Squadron*:[4]

> Most aeroplanes of that period, hitting the ground at such speeds, would simply have disintegrated; others, dug in the nose, flipped over on to their backs and crushed the skulls of their unfortunate occupants. The Hurricane, possessed of no such venomous streak, just kept going straight and level, ripping open the green turf beside the runway and spewing out the brown clods to either side until, with the radiator wrenched away, it slid to a halt, close to the boundary fence and the sunken road beyond. The air intake had gone, the propeller blades were all sheared at the roots, the spinner was stove in, the bottom cowlings torn. The wheel bay and cannon muzzles were packed with hard-driven earth, and the port wing was a scarcely cohesive jumble of twisted metal and torn skin. But from out of it stepped, quite unhurt though a little stunned by his good fortune, one very valuable flight commander.

Like Trenchard-Smith, Lister flew three more sorties that day and earned the award of a Distinguished Flying Cross. 'No bad effort after that kind of landing,' declares James Beedle, 'and no slight recommendation for the Hurricane either.'

On their return to Tangmere, 43 Squadron's undamaged Hurricanes were hastily refuelled and rearmed and replacements were provided for those machines in urgent need of repair. At 0750 the squadron was airborne again, this time in a search for E-boats reported to be threatening the landing area. Presumably this was a false alarm for no E-boats were sighted, but 43 still had one more mission to fly that morning. At about 1115, its Hurricanes attacked a strongpoint to the east of Dieppe harbour from which heavy shellfire could be directed on the beaches. They found the AA fire weaker, perhaps as a result of earlier strikes, and incurred no losses.

Reverting to the Hurricanes' early dawn attacks, 43 was closely followed by 3 and 245 Squadrons, each of which also made two sweeps against buildings containing guns that threatened the landing beaches. Naturally they came under heavy AA fire, though 3 Squadron escaped comparatively lightly, losing only one aircraft, together with its pilot, the Canadian Sergeant Banks. The squadron subsequently joined with 43 in its vain search for E-boats and its 1115 sortie; in No. 3's case attacking gun positions to the west of Dieppe harbour. Like 43, it suffered no serious casualties.

It was a different story in the case of 245, which found the German flak gunners extremely accurate and lost three pilots killed, while several other Hurricanes were damaged, made forced-landings and were rendered temporarily unserviceable. It was not until the early afternoon that the squadron could fly another mission and that with a strength of only seven aircraft. These attacked the eastern gun positions and had four more Hurricanes hit by AA fire; happily, though, all of them were able to get back to base.

At about the time that the initial attacks by the close support Hurricanes went in, the IIB Hurribombers of 174 and 175 Squadrons were taking off, a few carrying two 250lb bombs but most with two 500lb bombs, fitted with delayed-action fuses so that the later ones to attack would not be blown up by the explosions of those weapons dropped earlier. The target for 174 was a battery of four heavy guns on high ground to the rear of Dieppe which could shell the beaches and the approaches to them: it was code-named the 'Hitler' battery. That of 175 was the 'Göring' battery, similar to 'Hitler' but nearer to Dieppe; in addition 175 was ordered to bomb the headquarters of the local German army division.

In this instance the flak was comparatively light and though many of the Hurricanes 'were found to have a few holes in them', none were lost during the attacks themselves. That on 'Hitler' was considered very successful: a number of hits were scored and on their return home 174's pilots strafed a nearby aerodrome and some motor transport. 'Göring', however, was covered by a thick smokescreen and little if any damage was inflicted on this or on the German headquarters. At least 175 had the satisfaction of getting all its aircraft safely home, which unfortunately was not the case with 174.

For the attack on 'Hitler', 174 had been commanded by Squadron Leader Emile Fayolle, a Frenchman who had made his way to Britain from Oran, Algeria when his country had surrendered in 1940. He came from a distinguished military family for he was the son of an admiral and the grandson of Marie Emile Fayolle who in 1921 had been created a Marshal of France. He had flown Hurricanes with 85 Squadron in the latter days of the Battle of Britain and later with 242 Squadron, and had been awarded a Distinguished Flying Cross. He had only taken control of 174 on 1 August and was leading it into action for the first time.

After its attack on 'Hitler', 174 had split up as its pilots headed for England separately. All arrived except Fayolle who was never seen again. For many years his fate was unknown, though it was thought he may have fallen victim to a hostile fighter. Christopher Shores, in his book *Those Other Eagles*, now confirms that this was indeed what happened but that Fayolle 'either collided with or deliberately rammed' his attacker, a Focke-Wulf Fw 190, and this also went down.

Close on the heels of the Hurribombers came the Hurricanes of 32 and 253 Squadrons; their targets were the gun positions west of the harbour. The former was fortunate enough to return without serious damage. It was promptly ordered out again to engage guns located in the cliff face to the east of the harbour. This it did effectively and again suffered minimal harm from the return fire. Then at about 1115, 32 was once more in action, striking at the western gun positions. Here its luck finally ran out. The target put up a heavy AA barrage and was covered in thick smoke and in the confusion two of 32's aircraft collided. Flight Lieutenant Connolly crashed in flames and was killed but Sergeant Stanage was able to get back to base, although 3ft of his Hurricane's port wing was missing.

In its first attack, 253's luck lay mainly in the strength of its aircraft. It shot up houses along the Dieppe front, but came under fire from positions further to the west. Flying Officer Seal's Hurricane was hit and crashed but, amazingly, he survived with only minor injuries, though as a prisoner of war. The Hurricane of American Flight Sergeant Tate was also hit and damaged sufficiently to cause it to be 'written off' but not to prevent it bringing its pilot home safely.

A second sortie by 253 early that morning brought the pilots scant satisfaction for they believed they had caused little damage, though at least they suffered no casualties. A third in the early afternoon was more dramatic. As 253 crossed the coast, it was attacked by Focke-Wulf Fw 190s but the pilots used their Hurricanes' manoeuvrability to evade these and, though widely separated, did considerable harm to several gun posts. Flight Lieutenant Ellacombe and Pilot Officer Dobson engaged some mobile guns, leaving a trail of wrecked weapons and dead gunners, until Ellacombe's Hurricane was badly hit by AA fire. He managed to get back over the coast before having to bale out and though fired at from the shore, he was unhurt and was taken back to England by a landing craft.

The last Hurricane unit in action early on 19 August was No. 87, led by Squadron Leader Denis Smallwood, who went by the neat nickname of 'Splinters' and would later become Air Chief Marshal Sir Denis Smallwood, Commander-in-Chief of Strike Command which included all Britain's NATO Air Forces. His squadron successfully attacked gun positions west of Dieppe harbour and on the cliffs, but the AA fire proved very accurate and two Hurricanes were brought down. Flying Officer Waltos, a Polish pilot, was killed but Pilot Officer Baker baled out to land directly onto the foredeck of a friendly warship.

Having got going, Smallwood's men were eager to make up for lost time and were quickly airborne once more, attacking the eastern gun positions. They had no casualties on this sortie, but on a final one that afternoon, in which they strafed not only gun positions but German soldiers in a convoy of lorries, they suffered the further loss of Sergeant Ronald Gibson.

The Hurribomber squadrons continued to have a hectic day. Shortly after 1000 the pilots of 175 took off for their second sortie, armed with two 250lb bombs each as the 500lb weapons were already in short supply. Their target was another heavy gun battery, this one to the south-east of Dieppe, code-named 'Rommel'. They found that their lighter bombs were more accurate than the 500lb ones and, ignoring the inevitable AA fire, they struck 'Rommel' accurately and effectively. They also showed that their IIBs were useful fighters as well as bombers, for Flight Sergeant Meredith shot down a Heinkel He 111 that flew across his path, while Pilot Officer Peters was so unlucky as to encounter some Focke-Wulf Fw 190s but damaged a couple and escaped unhurt.

Following the disappearance of Squadron Leader Fayolle, 174 was led by Flight Lieutenant McConnell, an Irishman who was shortly promoted to be the squadron's CO, a post he would hold until February 1944. The squadron's first attack under his direction was made on the eastern gun positions at 1100. It found the targets covered in smoke, through which it launched the 500lb bombs that, unlike 175, it was still carrying. Sadly, no results could be seen and the mission cost 174 three pilots killed or taken prisoner.

By this time the Canadians' position was clearly hopeless and it was decided to withdraw them. This was far from easy for they were pinned down by murderous fire from the town and its supporting gun positions. Large numbers of troops fell into German hands and when, in the early afternoon, the landing craft began to move away from the beaches they were still being shelled, so the Hurricanes continued to provide covering fire.

Naturally the two Hurribomber squadrons played their part. First on the scene at 1330 was 175 which successfully attacked the western gun positions and army posts further inland. Pilot Officer Stevenson was hit by flak and had to bale out into the Channel, where he was rescued by a destroyer. He had previously dropped his bombs on a church, which seems a somewhat improper act until it is recorded that gunfire had been pouring from it and there is no doubt that it was a legitimate target.

While 175 was attacking, 174, still led by Flight Lieutenant McConnell, was just taking off. By this time it too was down to using 250lb bombs, with which it successfully attacked the eastern gun positions and enemy troops and transport beyond them. This was a really low-level attack and when the Hurricane flown by Pilot Officer du Fretay, a Free Frenchman who loathed Germans, was hit and caught fire, it is reported that he plunged, perhaps deliberately, straight into a group of armoured vehicles. Another pilot, Flight Sergeant (later Flight Lieutenant) John Brooks, formerly of 607 Squadron, would later report in Chaz Bowyer's *Hurricane at War*:

> I flew straight at some transport and troops with my guns going and skipped my bombs at them. I passed over the top at a couple of feet and brought back with me a souvenir – the whip aerial of a German tank wedged in my radiator. I wasn't sorry to get out of that lot.

Almost immediately afterwards, the final strafing raid took place east of Dieppe, carried out by the Hurricanes of 3 and 43, acting together yet again. At least six gun positions were struck and no losses caused by flak, but on this occasion the Focke-Wulfs were able to break past the protective 'umbrella' of Spitfires. The Hurricanes of 43 Squadron escaped with minor damage to Sergeant Bierer's aircraft, but 3 Squadron suffered a grievous blow. Squadron Leader 'Alex' Berry, the immensely popular New Zealander who had joined No. 3 on 27 September 1940 and become its CO in April 1942, was shot down in flames by a Focke-Wulf and killed instantly.

Thereafter the Hurricanes flew defensive patrols over JUBILEE's naval forces as they withdrew across the Channel: 245 and 253 doing so in the late afternoon; 245 again and 32 in the evening. For the Hurricanes it had been an exhausting, dangerous and lethal day but in no way a discreditable one.

In the first place, the Hurricanes had been extremely effective. They had bombed or strafed gun batteries, troop positions, wireless stations, tanks, lorries and buildings of various kinds. All Canadian accounts and reports by the covering Spitfires confirm the value of this assistance, describing bombs bursting on the designated targets, flames springing up, and the volume of gunfire from positions that had been strafed decreasing dramatically. The Hurricane squadrons had had every reason to be proud of their achievements.

Equally remarkable had been the sheer toughness of the Hurricanes. Though twenty had fallen or been 'written off', mercifully Leigh-Mallory's estimate of a 50 per cent loss came nowhere near being fulfilled. Though fifteen men were dead or prisoners of war, a succession of Hurricanes had crash-landed on their airfield, on a beach or on a golf course, without injury to their pilots. Still more had somehow come home, though part of a wing or one of the flaps had gone, though the elevators were partly missing and wholly shredded, though three-quarters of the elevator wires were broken, though the rudder controls had been shot away, though the underside of the aircraft could be described as 'pulp', let alone the injuries suffered by the Hurricanes of Flight Lieutenant Lister and Pilot Officer Trenchard-Smith.

That the authorities were more than satisfied with the services the Hurricanes had rendered on 19 August is unarguable. They were acknowledged by the award to Hurricane pilots of fifteen Distinguished Flying Crosses and one Distinguished Flying Medal, this last to 174's Flight Sergeant John Brooks.

There was only one complaint that could be made about the Hurricanes' part in Operation JUBILEE: that their 20mm cannons and even their bombs had proved unsuitable for knocking out really big gun emplacements. Not that Hurricanes had been designed for such a purpose; it was just that by this stage of the war it was generally expected that Hurricanes could and should be capable of doing anything. Yet this was not as unfair as it might appear, for even while JUBILEE was being fought, developments were under way that would complete the Hurricane's transformation from interceptor to ground-attacker.

As early as 18 September 1941, a new Hurricane version, the Mark IID, had flown. This carried only two 0.303in machine guns that fired tracer ammunition, but their purpose was to assist in the aiming of the IID's major weapons, a pair of 40mm anti-tank cannons. In May 1942 these aircraft entered service with No. 6 Squadron, which, however, was based in Shandur, Egypt. They equipped only one squadron in Britain, No. 184, which did not receive them until December 1942 and never took them into combat. They did, though, equip squadrons in both the Middle East and Far East in which they would become the scourge of the Axis armour.

As early as 23 February 1942, a Hurricane IIA had flown with six rocket projectiles, three under each wing. By May it had become clear that Hurricanes could easily be adapted to carry these weapons and although somewhat inaccurate, they might have proved devastating in the Dieppe Raid. Priority for their provision was, however, given to Coastal Command for anti-shipping strikes. In consequence it was not until the following year that Hurricanes were armed with rockets. Their arrival coincided with that of another new Hurricane version, originally called the Mark IIE but, with the installation of later engine types, chiefly the Merlin 27, redesignated the Mark IV,[5] the first of which flew on 14 March 1943.

Like the IID, the Hurricane IV had only a couple of 0.303in machine guns but, unlike it, was designed to carry almost every possible variety of weapons for ground-attack duties: two 250lb bombs; two 500lb bombs; a large number of smaller fragmentation bombs for use against personnel or road vehicles; two Smoke Curtain Installations for providing cover; two 40mm anti-tank guns; and best of all, rockets, now eight of them, four under each wing. These had either a 25lb solid armour-piercing shot or a 60lb high-explosive shell. They were fired electrically from the cockpit and the pilot could use them either in pairs, one from each side, or in a salvo of all eight of them. The effect of this last was considered the equivalent of a full broadside from a light cruiser.

Mark IVs re-equipped 184 Squadron in the spring of 1943 and it made its first attack with rockets on shipping near the Dutch coast on 17 June. Quickly joined by 137 and 164 Squadrons, 184 used its new aircraft and weapons against several different targets on land and sea. Hurricane Mark IVs also equipped squadrons in Italy and on the India/Burma front, and in both areas they continued in action until the end of the war. In North-West Europe, Hurricanes had been replaced by the end of March 1944 with Hawker Typhoons, but the ground-attack exploits of these, especially in Normandy, owed a good deal to the missions flown by their predecessors; yet another long-term benefit derived from the grim experiences of Operation JUBILEE.

Notes

1. Douglas Bader, in his *Fight for the Sky*, hails Denys Gillam as 'the unrivalled maestro of the low-level attack technique'. Gillam, incidentally, was in turn a great admirer of the Hurricane in this role.
2. Formerly No. 2 Squadron Royal Canadian Air Force. This had been renumbered 402 on 1 March 1941 to avoid confusion. On the same day, No. 1 Canadian Squadron became No. 401.
3. In this connection, mention should surely be made of the soapflake advertisement that appeared in the *Daily Telegraph* on 15 August, referring to a 'beach coat from Dieppe'. Then on the 17th, 'Dieppe' appeared in the same newspaper's crossword. A security investigation followed, but established that these were merely weird coincidences. The advertisement, incidentally, reappeared on 20 August, but this time made no mention of Dieppe or beaches which by then had acquired an ugly sound.
4. The full title of this is *43 Squadron Royal Flying Corps, Royal Air Force. The History of the Fighting Cocks 1916–1966*. At the time of the Dieppe Raid, Beedle was an engine-fitter with No. 43, holding the rank of sergeant, and witnessed the return of the battered Hurricanes to Tangmere.
5. The Hurricane Mark III was a version proposed in late 1941, which would use the Merlin 28 engine then being produced in the United States. This, it was felt, would guard against the possibility of Rolls-Royce Merlins falling below the level required. In fact this danger never materialized, so neither did the Hurricane Mark III.

Chapter Twelve

Ground Attack in Tunisia

Unfortunately, no amount of future benefits could alter the fact that JUBILEE had been a disaster. Churchill's immediate reaction was that 'The large-scale air battle alone justified the risk.' This, though, was because exaggerated claims by No. 11 Group's Spitfires had suggested that German casualties had been about the same as British, and Intelligence reports had wrongly estimated that the Luftwaffe had lost more than three times the number of warplanes than was really the case. In fairness also, Churchill was not in a good position to make a judgement. At the time of the Dieppe Raid he was in Egypt where reliable Intelligence had warned that before the end of August, Rommel was planning a final offensive against the Eighth Army that would carry him to the Nile.

It was a prospect viewed with some trepidation because, contrary to later myth, no fresh Allied troops had reached the Eighth Army for a month, whereas Rommel had received reinforcements of men – including a new German division, a new Italian division and a new German brigade – tanks – including some Mark IV Specials that for the first time gave him an armoured vehicle superior to any in the Eighth Army – anti-tank guns and aircraft. Indeed, as Captain Liddell Hart points out in his *History of the Second World War*: 'The strength of the two sides was nearer to an even balance than it was either before or later.'

To meet this threat, General Auchinleck, who as well as being C-in-C, Middle East had taken personal command of the Eighth Army, had approved a plan, the 'essence' of which, as he would declare in his Official Despatch, was 'fluidity and mobility'. The Eighth Army's infantry divisions would retire to strongpoints some way to the rear of the existing front line, where they would split up into battle groups, some of which would man these, while others, together with supporting artillery, would manoeuvre between them. Meanwhile, the armoured formations would cover the infantry retirements and make counter-attacks. Since this was

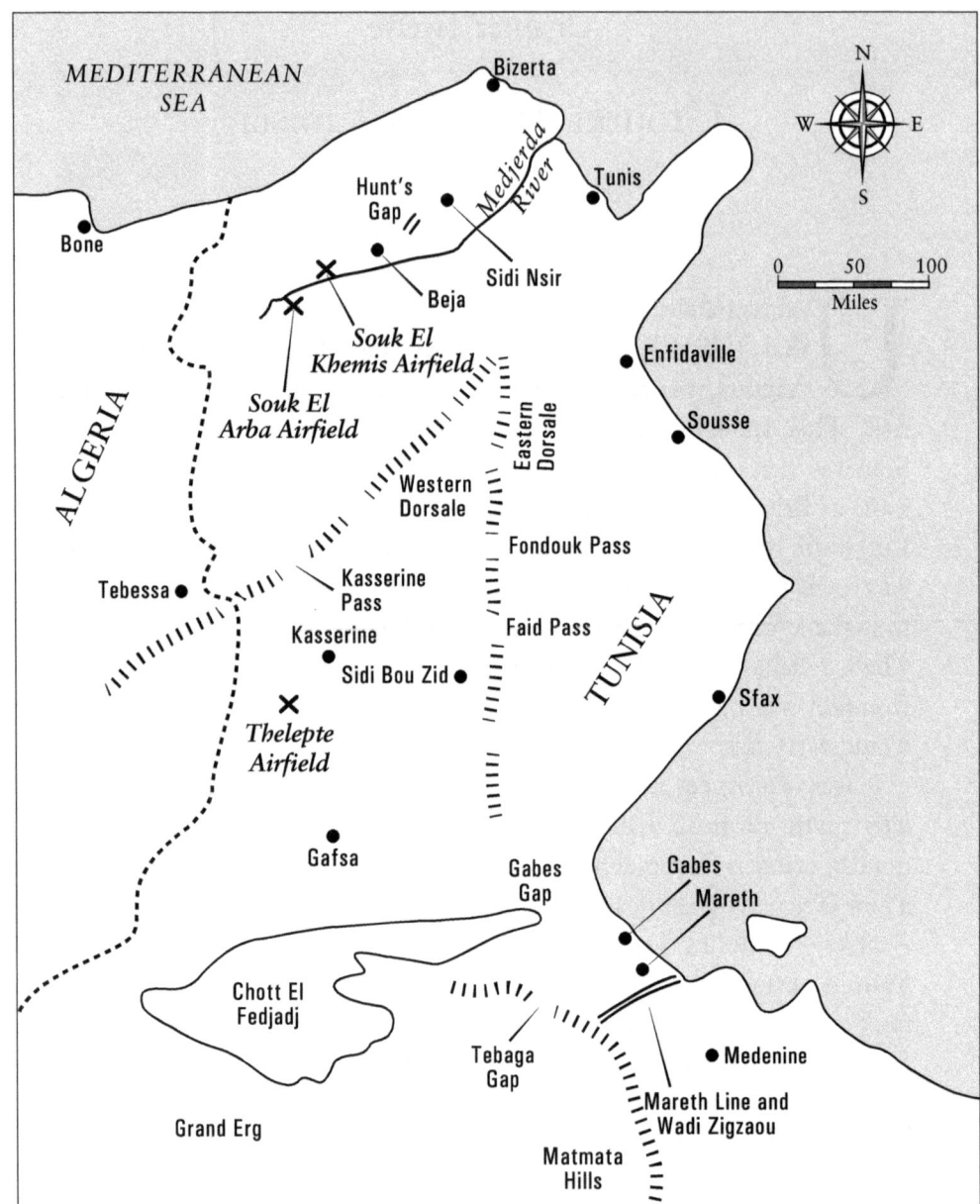

Map 4: Hurricane operations in Tunisia.

just the sort of action at which Rommel's men excelled, it did little to provide reassurance.

Fortunately the plan would never be put to the test. Auchinleck was replaced by General Sir Harold Alexander as commander-in-chief and by Lieutenant General Bernard Law Montgomery as head of the Eighth Army, and Montgomery's ideas were very different. He decreed that the infantry and the artillery should retain their integrity, and the tanks should fight in positions of their own choosing, hull down and supported by anti-tank guns. There should be no retirement from the existing defences, and to strengthen these he brought forward troops left by Auchinleck to guard the cities of Egypt. He also restored co-operation with the Desert Air Force which had been allowed to lapse and laid extensive minefields in which no previous interest had been shown: nothing, after all, is less 'fluid and mobile' than a mine.

As a result, in the Battle of Alam Halfa which began on 31 August 1942, Montgomery not only gained a victory but, as all could see, gained it by just those changes that he had made in the previous plan. The confidence that this inspired was crucial. When Montgomery began his own offensive, the Battle of El Alamein, late on 23 October, his men had to assault fixed positions, protected by half a million mines and every kind of lethal booby-trap. It was a formidable undertaking, but their new-found confidence inspired the Eighth Army's soldiers to persevere until their objectives were attained. The effects of their triumph were felt throughout the Mediterranean, not least at Malta, where the recapture of the Martuba airfields provided the fighter cover that enabled a convoy from Alexandria to bring the siege to an end, and in Vichy French North Africa, where another planned offensive had been deliberately delayed until victory at Alamein had been won.

This was Operation TORCH, which began on 8 November 1942 when Anglo-American troops under the overall command of General Dwight Eisenhower landed at Casablanca, Oran and Algiers. There was considerable confusion, but happily the Alamein victory had its desired effect. Admiral Darlan, heir apparent to the aged Marshal Pétain as Vichy's head of state, was in Algiers to visit his son who was dangerously ill with polio. His aversion to the British was notorious and his first response to TORCH was to arrest the US Consul General Mr Robert Murphy. He was, however, a realist who accepted that in North Africa at least the tide of war had turned. He therefore ordered all French resistance to cease at 1120 on 10 November.[1]

Thereafter, reinforcements quickly expanded the British First Army of Lieutenant General Sir Kenneth Anderson which, aided by further seaborne and airborne landings, pushed on eastward. By 27 November, it had come within 30 miles of Bizerta in the coastal area, while further inland in the valley of the Medjerda River which leads to Tunis, it was only 20 miles short of the capital. If the Allies could take Tunisia, they could strike at Tripoli from the rear, thus dooming Rommel's men. With North Africa secured, they could then invade Italy, described by Churchill as a 'soft underbelly' and by Hitler as 'the groin of Fortress Europe'.

Hitler, in short, was well aware of the dangers presented by an Allied conquest of Tunisia, which he was determined to prevent or at least delay for as long as possible. This was a big risk, for the forces he would need could only come from those earmarked for or already serving on the Russian front, but Hitler, always a gambler, was prepared to take it.

During November, therefore, ten German and six Italian divisions invaded unoccupied France which was quickly subdued. Axis soldiers also poured into Tunisia by sea and air: 15,000 Germans and 9,000 Italians who formed the basis of what would be called the Fifth Panzer Army since it included the 10th Panzer Division. In addition, 400 warplanes together with large numbers of aerial transports were transferred from Russia to the Mediterranean area. On 27 November the redoubtable Field Marshal Kesselring arrived in Tunis. He sternly forbade any further withdrawals and retained control until 8 December when he handed over to General Jürgen von Arnim, a harsh, grim man who had commanded a corps in Russia. On the previous day the weather had broken, choking the Allied communications with thick, clinging mud.

These actions greatly assisted the Russian counter-offensive at Stalingrad and subsequently greatly hampered German attempts to supply the forces that had been trapped there. Even so, Hitler could find some consolation in the thought that he had successfully balked the Allied advance into Tunisia, where, by the end of the year, the battle-front had stabilized on a line running southward from the sea, much of it along a mountain range called the Eastern Dorsale.[2]

The landings at Algiers and Oran had been protected by Sea Hurricanes on three escort carriers and from the first day of TORCH land-based Hurricane fighters had also been present. They would include 32, 43, 87 and 253 Squadrons, all of which had taken part in JUBILEE. As at JUBILEE also, two Hurribomber squadrons would aid the Allied soldiers, not only on ground-attack duties but, in this campaign, by tactical reconnaissance missions as well. Their importance was indicated by the fact that both of them were led by wing commanders.

Wing Commander Millington's 225 Squadron flew from Gibraltar to Maison Blanche airfield, Algiers on Friday, 13 November. On the 17th, the squadron moved forward to Bone, only some 50 miles from the Tunisian border. On the same day it lost its first pilot when Flying Officer Rodwell was shot down and killed by 'friendly' anti-aircraft fire when returning from a reconnaissance sortie.

From then until mid-December, 225 was employed solely on 'recce' duties, flying from either Bone or Souk el Arba, a forward landing strip inside Tunisia that had been prepared by the Royal Engineers. These missions frankly disappointed the pilots, who recognized their value but were eager to 'get at' the enemy with their bombs. Moreover, the Tac R flights were made at a very low level that made the aircraft vulnerable to flak and enemy fighters and cost 225 the lives of four more pilots. The Luftwaffe was also dominant at this time and in one bombing raid by Junkers Ju 88s on Bone airfield after dark on 28 November, five Hurricanes were totally destroyed. Nor were bombs the only unpleasant objects dropped, as we learn from Squadron Leader Bryan Colston, then one of 225's flight commanders, in his *Recollections of Wartime Experiences*: 'The most evil and frightening weapons they [the Germans] used were personnel bombs in the form of fountain pens, which when picked up exploded and tragically many hands were lost or severely injured as a result.'

At least 225's pilots had cause to be thankful for their Hurricanes' strength. Their wide, sturdy undercarriages were particularly welcome after Tunisia's bad weather closed in, as they made the aircraft easier to operate than other fighters, even in conditions like those at Souk el Arba which became little more than a sea of mud and lacked proper maintenance facilities. The Hurricanes' sturdiness also saved several pilots' lives. On 3 December, for instance, two of 225's aircraft were badly shot up by enemy fighters, but both pilots were able to crash-land. Pilot Officer Short did so in Axis-occupied territory and was taken prisoner, but Flying Officer Sharman got back to the Allied lines before coming down at some 200 mph. He walked away from his wrecked Hurricane unhurt.

Finally, on 14 December, much to the pilots' delight, 225 was allowed to act as a Hurribomber unit. Flight Lieutenant Bryan Colston nonchalantly informs us that 'We attacked and destroyed enemy transport and men. We were greeted by a hail of anti-aircraft fire but we all managed to return safely to base.'

Other Hurribomber strikes were made by 225 throughout most of December, again without any losses. At least without any losses on Hurribomber missions, for on 19 December, Pilot Officer Tyson was killed when, for reasons never explained, he crashed while flying from Bone to Souk el Arba. However, on 29 December, it was decided that the squadron – which on the previous day had strafed enemy tanks and other vehicles with its Mark IICs – should be rested; it retired temporarily to Constantine in eastern Algeria.

Some of 225's machines, though, remained at Souk el Arba where they reinforced the Hurribombers of Wing Commander Barker's 241 Squadron. This had flown to Maison Blanche from Gibraltar on 30 November. It was equipped at that time with Hurricane IIAs, but soon received IIBs and IICs instead. It had then moved on to Constantine and had arrived at Souk el Arba on 21 December, where it joined 225 in attacking Axis army units. Atrocious weather continued to handicap the Hurricanes' efforts and 241 lost its first pilot on Christmas Day when Flight Lieutenant Harrap 'failed to return'; he was later reported a prisoner of war.

After 225's departure on 29 December, 241 continued to make Hurribomber strikes, plus an occasional reconnaissance flight, in early January 1943. Targets attacked included troops, road and rail transport, a vehicle repair depot and a gun battery. Enemy opposition was fierce. During the attack on the battery on 6 January, Pilot Officer Beckwith was shot down by Messerschmitt Bf 109s and killed; while in a raid on the railway on the 8th, Pilot Officer MacMurray was hit by flak but managed to get back to the Allied lines before baling out safely.

These sorties were the more commendable because conditions at Souk el Arba remained deplorable. Fortunately an area of flat, hard sand was discovered at Souk el Khemis, north of Souk el Arba, and here the army sappers prepared a number of firm landing strips that were much more suitable. To these 241 moved on 16 January and over the next two or three days 225 returned to join them, both squadrons forming part of 324 Wing.

It was now accepted that Hurricanes were very vulnerable when used on reconnaissance duties. Accordingly, first 225 and later 241 received

Spitfires which thereafter flew most of the Tac R missions, though not without their own losses of men and aircraft. Both squadrons, however, continued to fly Hurricanes on fighter-bomber sorties and for the remainder of January and early February, they would be found striking at Axis troops, tanks and transport. On one attack on enemy lorries on 31 January, Pilot Officer Baker of 225 Squadron was hit by anti-aircraft fire, but managed to crash-land in Allied-held territory without injury. More dangerous were strafing raids on Souk el Khemis by enemy fighters and a number of 225's aircraft were destroyed or damaged on the ground.

The value of Hurribombers would soon become even more apparent. On 23 January Tripoli, once considered the target of the TORCH forces, was in fact captured by Montgomery's Eighth Army, just three months after the start of the Battle of El Alamein. The disadvantage of this success was that Rommel's troops now fell back into Tunisia where they were protected from Montgomery's men by the formidable defences of the Mareth Line, designed by the French specifically to thwart any attempted attack from Libya.

Now that German and Italian forces were holding the Mareth Line and further encouraged by his junction with his comrades in Tunisia and the prospect of engaging foes less experienced than the veterans of the Eighth Army, Rommel, who had shown little resolve recently, recovered his former aggressive spirit. He proposed to strike at Gafsa at the extreme south of the Allied line, held by the II US Corps. Von Arnim, by contrast, wanted his Fifth Panzer Army to assault the Americans further north at Sidi Bou Zid, using not only his own 10th Panzer Division but also 21st Panzer which Rommel had recently transferred to him. Kesselring, the Axis commander-in-chief in Tunisia, therefore decided that von Arnim should attack first, but then hand back 21st Panzer to assist an advance by Rommel.

On 14 February the Fifth Panzer Army, under the command of von Arnim's Chief of Staff Lieutenant General Heinz Ziegler, thrust through the Faid Pass in the Eastern Dorsale. Sadly, intercepted signals – the famous 'Ultra' Intelligence – had indicated that the advance would be made through the more northern Fondouk Pass. In consequence, not only were the Americans taken by surprise but reinforcements were held back in the belief that this was only a diversion and the main assault would come later.[3] Ably supported by Kesselring's dive-bombers, Ziegler inflicted shattering losses, and by 17 February had reached an outlying range of hills called the Western Dorsale.

Ziegler's advance had also compelled the Americans to evacuate Gafsa where vast stores of petrol and ammunition were abandoned. Rommel promptly moved up to secure these. Then with 15th and 21st Panzer, the latter reluctantly returned by von Arnim, and the Italian Centauro Armoured Division, he proposed to break through the Kasserine Pass in the Western Dorsale and threaten the main Allied supply dump at Tebessa.

This was the alarming prospect that opened before General Alexander who arrived at Algiers on 15 February to be Eisenhower's deputy and head of Eighteenth Army Group, coordinating the armies of both Montgomery and Anderson. He immediately sent reinforcements to the Western Dorsale, requested Montgomery to put pressure on Rommel from behind, and established a tight control over the First Army's tactical operations as he thought Anderson was not giving firm enough leadership.[4]

On 20 February Rommel broke through the Kasserine Pass, but could make no further progress against fierce resistance. He was also increasingly worried by Montgomery who was overrunning all Axis positions south of the Mareth Line. Then on the 22nd, 225 Squadron made a successful Hurribomber attack on his supply vehicles. Rommel had had enough. Next day he fell back, spurred on by another Hurribomber strike by 225, whose pilots defied heavy anti-aircraft fire to inflict 'considerable damage'.

Rommel was probably not consoled by Kesselring now appointing him head of Army Group Afrika, with control over both von Arnim's Fifth Panzer Army and his own original command which was now designated First Italian Army. This was entrusted to General Giovanni Messe who had previously led an Italian corps on the Russian front with sufficient ability to earn the award of a Knight's Cross from Hitler.

Kesselring's decision had been made, in part at least, because he was disgusted with the totally unco-operative attitude of von Arnim, who, despite express orders, had given minimal assistance to Rommel. Instead he embarked on a full-scale offensive of his own in northern Tunisia on 26 February, sending seventy-seven tanks against a vital Allied communications centre at Beja. After some initial success, he was halted on the 27th in a narrow marshy valley known as 'Hunts Gap' by British anti-tank guns, with the support of a raid by twelve of 241's Hurribombers that would have a special significance.

Among von Arnim's tanks were fourteen Panzer Mark VI 'Tigers'. These monsters were armed with the 88mm gun that had proved a deadly anti-tank weapon in the desert. They weighed 56 tons and carried up to 102mm of armour, yet could come across country as fast as most other gun-armed tanks. They had first been spotted in Tunisia by 225 Squadron on 27 November 1942, but the shells from its 20mm cannons had literally bounced off them.

The 250lb bombs used by 241 Squadron on 27 February 1943, however, were capable of harming a Tiger if they scored a direct hit. This admittedly was not easy to achieve – by far the most accurate and effective weapons against enemy armour were the two 40mm anti-tank guns carried by the Hurricane IIDs – but 241 was very capable and on this occasion hit three tanks. One of these was a Tiger, previously immobilized but still in action; 241's bombs ended its useful life and killed the entire crew.

During the next few days, both 225 and 241 Squadrons made repeated assaults on von Arnim's tanks and transports; the ground crews meeting the returning Hurricanes at the end of the runway to service, refuel and rearm them in only eight minutes, ready for another mission. On 28 February, 241's Pilot Officer Richmond was shot down and killed by flak, but both squadrons, undaunted, flew forty-two sorties between them on 1 March without loss. There were more casualties the next day. Flying Officer Marshall of 225 crashed on take-off, destroying the Hurricane and injuring the pilot who had to be taken to hospital. Pilot Officer Gould of 241 was injured by AA fire; he got his damaged Hurricane back to base, but he too went to hospital.

By the end of 2 March, twenty-two of von Arnim's tanks were total losses and forty-nine more had been disabled in one way or another. Rommel was openly contemptuous of the whole affair, and now took advantage of his appointment as head of Army Group Afrika to halt the offensive. However, neither 225 nor 241 had finished with von Arnim, making several more Hurribomber assaults in early March. In one of these on the 6th, 241's Flight Lieutenant Nicholl was hit by flak; he crash-landed within the Allied lines and escaped unhurt.

Also on 6 March, Rommel attacked the Eighth Army at Medenine with the 10th, 15th and 21st Panzer divisions, two German and two

Italian infantry divisions and as much artillery as he could assemble, only to find that Montgomery had prepared a perfect defensive position. Rommel gained not a yard of ground and lost some fifty tanks, mainly to the British artillery. It was his last move in Africa. He left for Germany, sick and disillusioned, three days later.

On 14 March, decisions were taken that would greatly influence the fortunes of both 225 and 241. The latter squadron, which had in any case carried out few reconnaissance missions recently, ceased them altogether to concentrate on its Hurribomber role. By contrast, 225 became a purely Tac R squadron, receiving first more Spitfires and later Mustangs for this work and gradually passing over its Hurricanes to 241.

Not all of them, however. Bryan Colston, among others, regretted parting with 'our dear old Hurricanes' and has left us a description of his last operational flight in one of them:

> Towards the end of the month [March 1943] the weather improved and...in one of the Hurricanes that we retained for photographic reconnaissance, I took vertical photographs along the Beja-Sidi Nsir road, known to all pilots as 'Flak Alley'. It was a hazardous task as I had to fly backwards and forwards over the area, straight and level, and keeping my height at exactly 10,000 feet.... A few days later I saw my photographs at the Intelligence Officer's Unit and they were excellent and gave the Army a tremendous amount of information, so it was all worthwhile.

By now, though, attention had switched from northern Tunisia to the extreme south of the country. The First Army may have repulsed the attacks of Rommel and von Arnim, but still seemed unable to break through the Eastern Dorsale to the central Tunisian plain. Alexander therefore pinned his hopes on the very experienced Eighth Army, although this was faced with an impressive series of natural and man-made obstacles.

For a start, all progress was blocked by a vast trackless salt marsh known as the Chott el Fedjadj that left only a small 'gap' between it and the Mediterranean north of the little town of Gabes. Even before the Eighth Army could reach this, its path was hemmed in between the sea and the Matmata Hills that ran parallel to the coast and it was here that the French had sited their Mareth Line. It was possible to outflank the hills to the west, but at their northern end marshes and an impassable sea of sand called the Grand Erg blocked any further advance northward, forcing a turn eastward to the coast through the narrowest 'bottleneck' of all, the 4-mile wide strongly-defended Tebaga Gap.

Both Alexander and Montgomery were confident that they would at least be able to break through the Mareth Line without difficulty, because Ultra intercepts had reported that Rommel and von Arnim had favoured withdrawing from this to Gabes or even Enfidaville on the northern edge of the Tunisian plain. Unfortunately, Ultra had not revealed the far more significant information that neither Hitler nor Kesselring nor Messe had any intention of abandoning the Mareth Line without fighting their hardest for its retention.

When the Battle of the Mareth Line began on 20 March, Montgomery sent a flanking force west of the Matmata Hills as if threatening the Tebaga Gap, but really only to distract attention from his main attack in the coastal areas. His infantry crossed the Wadi Zigzaou, forming the 'moat' of the defences, but his tanks had difficulty in following them, the enemy armour counter-attacked and as a crowning misfortune, on 22 March bad weather grounded the Desert Air Force's light bombers that had been ready to meet any Axis thrust. Early on the 23rd, it became clear that the coastal assault had failed.

Montgomery, who it is fashionable to portray as a cautious, unimaginative general, reacted with superb flexibility. He switched his main weight to his subsidiary outflanking attack, rushing men and armour to it in a move to become known throughout the Eighth Army as the 'Left Hook'. It was impossible to provide the additional artillery necessary to break through the Tebaga Gap, but the Desert Air Force under the inspired leadership of Air Vice-Marshal Harry Broadhurst, once the CO of 111 Squadron, the very first unit to receive Hurricanes, made good this deficiency. Starting on 23 March, it would give close support at very low level, and among Broadhurst's squadrons may be mentioned No. 6 which had been the first to see combat with Hurricane IIDs and No. 241 which had been sent south by Alexander to assist.

On 23 March 241's Hurribombers flew to the airfield at Thelepte, north-west of Gafsa and south-west of Kasserine, from which at 1710 twelve of them made the squadron's first strike on Axis positions near

Tebaga. Though successful, this deprived 241 of the services of Pilot Officer Davis who was hit by flak and compelled to force-land in enemy territory, but only temporarily. Captured by the Italians, he was taken to a prisoner-of-war camp in the port of Sfax, but was able to escape from this and rejoined his squadron on 2 April.

Further Hurribomber attacks on enemy troops and tanks were made by 241 on 24 and 25 March. Flak claimed one Hurricane on each of these days but both of the pilots were able to crash-land and returned safely to their squadron. The aerial activity reached its culmination on 26 March when 241, like the rest of Broadhurst's men, supported the Eighth Army's assault on the Tebaga Gap. The result has been reported by Montgomery with simple directness: 'Brilliant and brave work by the pilots completely stunned the enemy; our attack broke through the resistance and the battle was won.'

The Eighth Army followed the defenders of the Mareth Line as these retired at speed to avoid being cut off. On 6 April the Gabes Gap was secured and the Eighth Army quickly made contact with II US Corps. It then struck northwards, taking the port of Sfax on the 10th, that of Sousse on the 12th and the whole of the central Tunisian plain by the evening of the 13th. The area still remaining to the enemy was now within easy range of the Allied air forces, which took full advantage of the situation.

Among those doing so were the Hurribombers of 241 Squadron, which had returned to Souk el Khemis on 1 April. On the 4th, they again attacked enemy positions, while on the 5th twelve of them varied their targets with a raid on Enfidaville aerodrome. This destroyed a number of Axis fighters, apparently Italian Macchi MC 202s.

Further attacks on airfields on 11 April were successful, but an attempt to strafe Axis troops and transport vehicles in the Enfidaville area was met with exceptionally heavy AA fire that hit three Hurricanes. At least their strength protected their airmen's lives. Pilot Officer Millward got back to the Allied lines; he crash-landed but was unhurt. Both the other pilots baled out over enemy territory; they also survived but as prisoners of war.

By 22 April the situation of the Fifth Panzer Army and First Italian Army had become hopeless. The Royal Navy had complete command of the sea and could prevent any seaborne evacuation. Attempts to supply the Axis soldiers by air had resulted in ruinous losses, and most of the remaining Axis warplanes now withdrew to Sicily while there was still time, leaving von Arnim and Messe largely unsupported.

This meant that 241 Squadron rarely encountered hostile fighters, but the enemy's AA gunners were still plentiful and by now very experienced. Moreover, some of the squadron's airmen had apparently exhausted their luck. During the following week, they attacked Axis ground troops, strongpoints, tanks and field guns, all effectively but at the sad cost of three more pilots dead. What might have been the saddest misfortune came on 25 April when Flying Officer O'Brian, returning from a successful raid, was shot down by 'friendly' AA fire. Mercifully he was unhurt.

The final Allied offensive was launched in the Medjerda valley on 6 May, and in the afternoon of the 7th, British armoured cars entered Tunis, while Bizerta fell to the Americans at almost the same moment. On the 8th, 241 Squadron flew its last Hurribomber mission. It was successful, but as the pilots returned to base they were unlucky enough to encounter one of the few Messerschmitt Bf 109 units still in Tunisia. This shot down Flying Officer Connors, who baled out, becoming a prisoner of war.

Connors was not held captive for long. He was released on 13 May, by which date von Arnim, Messe and the whole of the Fifth Panzer and First Italian armies had surrendered. The number of men in prisoner-of-war camps was later recorded as more than 238,000 but no doubt many of these had been taken earlier and the final surrenders are estimated to have been more than 100,000 Germans – more than at Stalingrad – and almost 90,000 Italians. Just nine months had passed since Alexander had become C-in-C, Middle East and Montgomery had taken charge of the Eighth Army.

Notes

1. Darlan would gain no personal benefit from his action. On Christmas Eve he was assassinated by Bonnier de La Chappelle, a youthful anti-Vichy fanatic who was himself hastily court-martialled and shot two days later.
2. Furthermore, the Germans recovered with remarkable resilience from their disaster at Stalingrad and on 21 February 1943 were able to commence a new offensive in Russia that culminated in their recapture of Kharkov on 15 March.

3. More orthodox Intelligence had estimated the Germans' intentions correctly, but Ultra was considered sacrosanct in some quarters, then as later.
4. Alexander was so doubtful of Anderson's ability that he enquired if one of the Eighth Army's corps commanders could be spared to take his (Anderson's) place. Since this proved impossible, Anderson remained at the head of the First Army for the rest of the Tunisian campaign. He would later hold other important posts, but no further command in the field.

Chapter Thirteen

Close Support: Kohima and Imphal

Splendid as were the activities of the Hurribombers at Dieppe or in Tunisia, their greatest achievements would come later and thousands of miles away. They would come on the north-west frontier of Burma where this abuts on Assam and the beautiful little state of Manipur, the capital of which is Imphal, in the months from March to early July 1944, when the Hurribombers would help to win the decisive battle of the India-Burma campaigns.

Hurricanes were no strangers to combats in this theatre. In the early months of 1942, they had fought valiantly but vainly against overwhelming odds as the Japanese overran Burma. Later that year they defended Calcutta from Japanese bombers based in Burma, and in the early months of 1943 they would be found assisting a British advance into the Arakan, as Burma's coastal area was called, and protecting the subsequent British retreat. In the course of this, if at some cost, they gained a supremacy in the air that would never be forfeited. As Lieutenant Colonel Frank Owen reports in *The Campaign in Burma*:[1] 'They gripped the Japanese air power and repelled its offensive, offsetting the reverses on the ground.'

At the same time, the Hurricanes proved their worth in another role. On the night of 14 February 1943, 3,200 men under Brigadier (later Major General) Orde Wingate crossed the Chindwin River to operate in Japanese-held territory until mid-April. During this period, Wingate's 'Chindits' – who took their name from the mythical creature, half-lion, half-griffin, that guarded the Burmese pagodas – were supplied by parachute drops from Allied Douglas Dakotas and these in turn were protected, most effectively, by Hawker Hurricanes.

Though the visible results of Wingate's raid were not impressive and its casualties were high, its long-term benefits were immense. The news that British and Indian soldiers could outfight and outwit the Japanese in the jungle caused a dramatic rise in morale, while the use of aerial transports showed the way in which the superior Japanese manoeuvrability could be

180 Hurricanes in Action Worldwide

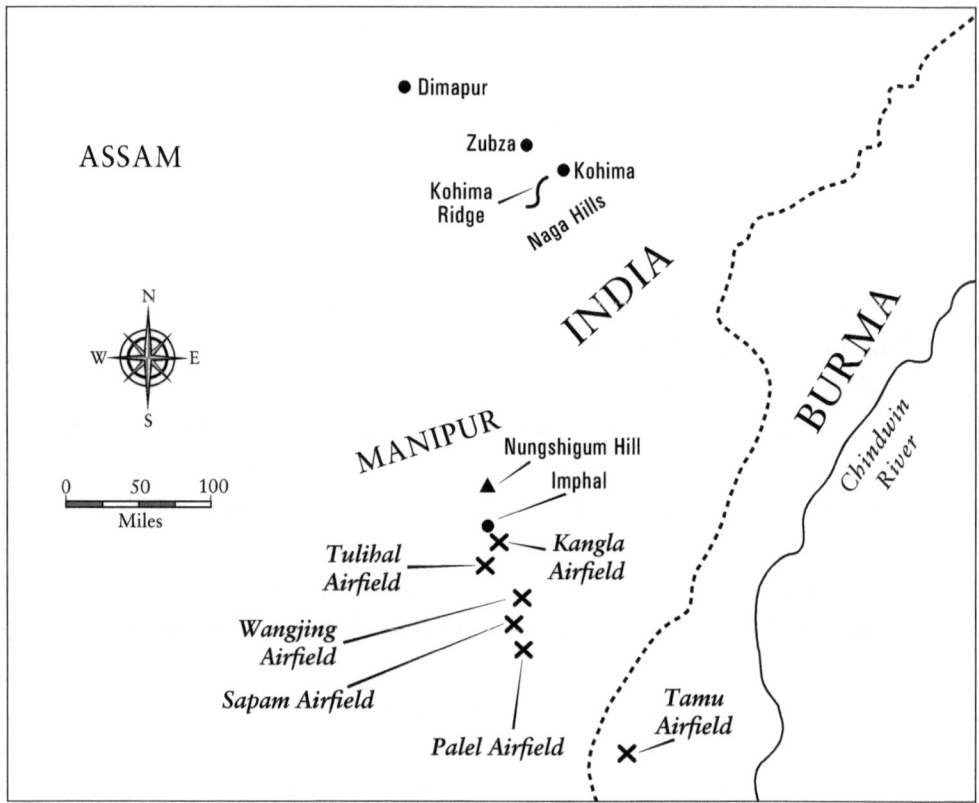

Map 5: Hurricane operations around Kohima and Imphal.

countered successfully. From this raid stemmed all future successes and it is very sad that it should later have been denigrated, not least by the officer who had most cause to be grateful for it.

About six months after Wingate's death – in an air crash on 24 March 1944 – Lieutenant General William Slim, commander of Britain's Fourteenth Army responsible for the defence of the frontier, paid him a fulsome tribute, declaring him to have more than one 'attribute of genius' and to be 'irreplaceable'. Yet when Field Marshal Viscount Slim, as he then was, produced his much-praised reminiscences *Defeat Into Victory* in 1956, his attitude was completely different and it seems he had become jealously resentful of the praise given to Wingate's part in turning the tide of the India-Burma campaigns.[2]

Thus Slim belittles Wingate personally, though his account of clashes between them is described as 'decidedly inaccurate' by eye-witnesses including 'neutral' RAF officers. Worse still, he dismisses the Chindit raid as 'an expensive failure' and damns with faint sneer its benefits as arising from 'somewhat phoney propaganda' that was 'skilfully handled'.

Slim also declares that the raid 'had no immediate effect on Japanese dispositions and plans'. Certainly its effects were not 'immediate', but ultimately they were profound because the raid warned the Japanese that the Chindwin River was not the secure barrier that they had believed. They would therefore decide, in early 1944, that it would be desirable to gain a better defensive position by seizing the Imphal plain. This, incidentally, was exactly the move Slim was hoping they would make and he had been pondering endlessly on how to provoke it. He need not have troubled; the Chindits had done so for him.

In the meantime, there had been several changes in the constitution of the Allied Air Forces in this theatre and these had had a considerable effect upon the Hurricane squadrons, and not only those of the Royal Air Force. In August 1943 No. 6 Squadron of the Indian Air Force received Hurricanes, as did seven other Indian units over the next few months. In all, some 300 Hurricanes served in the IAF, usually on undramatic but vital tactical reconnaissance duties. Though the Japanese airmen rarely interfered with these missions, hostile terrain, inadequate landing grounds and violent weather made them extremely hazardous, while it took highly skilful observations to spot enemy positions for which almost perfect camouflage had been provided. During the remaining campaigns in Burma, the pilots of these 'recce' Hurricanes flew more than 16,000 sorties, losing 50 aircraft but gaining 44 decorations for gallantry.

They gained only one aerial victory, however, when Flying Officer Verma of 6 IAF shot down a Nakajima Ki-43 Oscar in February 1944. This was symbolic of the change being made in the roles of the Hawker fighters. The pure interceptor versions that had 'gripped the Japanese air power' were replaced in these duties from early October 1943 by Spitfires or Mustangs. On the other hand, during the latter half of 1943, a number of Blenheim units gave up their valiant old light bombers and received Hurricane IIBs and IICs: 60 Squadron in July; 11 and 34 in August; 113 in September; 42 in October. All were specifically detailed to be Hurribomber squadrons, were equipped usually with two 250lb bombs but sometimes with two 500lb bombs, and during the Imphal campaign would earn more praise from army personnel than any other warplane.

As a preliminary to their Imphal offensive and in the hope of diverting attention and troops from the Imphal area, the Japanese, on 4 February 1944, attacked Allied forces that were again slowly advancing in the Arakan. The 7th Indian Division[3] was surrounded and engaged from all sides at a place called Sinzweya in what was to be known as the 'Admin Box'. In the past this would probably have caused panic, but not now, for the defenders knew they could be supplied from the air, as indeed they were by a swarm of Dakotas, so well-protected by Hurricanes that only one was lost, while other Hurricanes made strafing attacks on Japanese positions.

By 11 February the Japanese, lacking any aerial support and relying for supplies on inadequate jungle tracks, were already short of food and ammunition. They could still have retired in good order but, with a folly that would shortly be repeated on a greater scale elsewhere, they continued to make desperate attacks until 24 February, when the 5th Indian Division broke through to relieve the Admin Box. The Japanese then fell back in disorder, having lost 5,000 men to the Allies' 3,500.

Allied morale was further raised by this episode and Slim calls it 'one of the historic successes of British arms' and 'the turning-point of the Burma campaign'. In *Battle for Burma*, Brigadier 'Birdie' Smith offers a more restrained reminder that 'In reality five British and Indian divisions, supported by an enormous air effort, had been fully stretched to withstand the invasion of 8,000 Japanese.' When one recalls Slim's belittlement of the Chindits' achievements, it is a delicious irony that Smith adds that the Admin Box affair was 'not nearly as great a victory as was claimed in the glowingly phrased communiqués issued'.

Since their preliminary move had at least directed Allied interest and Allied reserves to the Arakan, the Japanese were not too discouraged by their reverse. They continued with their plans for Imphal, apparently not appreciating that the Allied aerial transports could quickly return those reserves to the Imphal area if necessary.

The assault on Imphal was entrusted to the grandly entitled Fifteenth Japanese Army of Lieutenant General Renya Mutaguchi, but this contained just three divisions and in practice therefore was equivalent only to an Allied army corps. It was accompanied by the 'Indian National Army' formed by Subhas Chandra Bose, once president of the Congress Party, from Indians the Japanese had taken prisoner and had changed sides.[4] It was intended that, once on Indian soil, they would call on their countrymen to rise against the British, but the Japanese, who were openly contemptuous of them, did not believe for a moment that they would be of more than nuisance value. Their contempt was justified, for Bose's followers deserted whenever opportunity offered.

Both sides at different times would declare for propaganda reasons that the Japanese assault was 'a march on Delhi' and Slim assures us that it was intended to seize the 'glittering prize' of India and 'change the whole course of the world war'. Had this been the case, the coming clash would have been still more important than it was. In reality though, the Japanese intentions were strictly limited, as Slim was well aware.

In his *Defeat Into Victory*, Slim complains that: 'I had not at my disposal the sources of information of the enemy's intentions that some more fortunate commanders in other theatres were able to invoke. We depended almost entirely on the Intelligence gathered by our fighting patrols.' Yet in works like Michael Smith's *The Emperor's Codes*, it is revealed that in the Imphal campaign, the Allied code-breakers were 'providing Slim with a wealth of information' that included 'a complete order of battle of the Japanese forces' both on the ground and in the air.

Among the 'wealth of information' that Slim received was confirmation that the aim of this offensive was strictly limited. It was intended to capture Imphal with its airfields and supply depots and Kohima on the road from Imphal to the main Allied base at Dimapur on the Bengal-Assam railway; here the road crossed the Naga Hills at an altitude of about 4,700ft and was at its most vulnerable. Yet Dimapur itself, the fall of which would have given the Japanese food and equipment and deprived the Fourteenth Army of the base for a counter-offensive, was not among the enemy's objectives. Mutaguchi did urge its capture, but the overall Japanese commander in Burma, Lieutenant General Masakazu Kawabe, refused permission because this would mean too deep an advance into India.

Mutaguchi's own supply lines were terrible and his situation was made no easier by the start of the second Chindit operation on 5 March 1944. Slim would again speak slightingly of this, but Mutaguchi would declare that it 'put a great obstacle in our Imphal plan' and 'had a decisive effect on our operations'. The Japanese had now to capture Imphal and its supplies or starve. On the night of 7/8 March, the campaign began as Mutaguchi's men broke over the Chindwin River. His 33rd Division made a wide sweep to attack Imphal from the south and west; his 15th Division struck directly at Imphal from the east and also moved north of it to cut the road to Kohima; his 31st Division raced directly for Kohima itself.

It was an extraordinarily daring, not to say reckless move. Not only was the Fourteenth Army aware of its enemy's plans, but it enjoyed an infinitely better supply line, a great superiority of manpower, an immense superiority of artillery, a colossal superiority of armour both in quantity and quality and, most decisively, an almost total command of the air. Sadly, while Slim had been warned that the Japanese would make their assault in early March, he did not believe they could be ready before the middle of the month. He had forgotten their ability to advance rapidly over the most difficult terrain.

Consequently Mutaguchi's opening moves achieved surprise, his warriors soon gained their preliminary objectives, and the three divisions of Britain's IV Corps retired to the wide plain south of Imphal, where they were joined by the bulk of a fourth, hastily ferried by air from the Arakan. As Captain Liddell Hart rather sourly remarks: 'Japanese nimbleness and thrustfulness had once again thrown their numerically superior opponents off balance and put them in an awkward plight.'

Happily for IV Corps, not only could it be supplied from the air, but the Imphal plain contained airfields or at least landing-strips at Tulihal, Wangjing, Sapam, Kangla, Palel and Imphal itself, on which were stationed the warplanes of 221 Fighter Group RAF. This was led by Air Commodore (later Air Vice-Marshal) Stanley Vincent who had controlled the Hurricanes' brave but unavailing fight in the East Indies. He would now conduct an equally gallant but far more successful campaign, and once again Hurricanes formed the backbone of his command. There were the Hurribombers of 11, 34, 42 and 113 Squadrons, the tactical reconnaissance Hurricanes of 28 Squadron and 1 Squadron IAF – these could also be adapted to carry bombs at short notice – and 5 Squadron which had done great work in the Arakan with anti-tank Hurricane IIDs but was now short of 40mm shells, so mainly used Hurricane IICs for escort duty or strafing attacks.

During the first three weeks of the Imphal campaign, the Hurricanes achieved little and suffered casualties. No. 5 Squadron lost two machines and their pilots in accidents, while 28 Squadron lost two Hurricanes through enemy action: Warrant Officer Walker was shot down by Japanese fighters but baled out; Flying Officer Perry was killed by AA fire. The most tragic incident occurred on 22 March, when three Hurricanes of 113 Squadron apparently got lost and landed at Tamu airfield not knowing that it had just been evacuated on the approach of the enemy. While looking for assistance, the pilots were attacked by a Japanese patrol and two were killed. Flight Sergeant Clement, though, escaped into the jungle and ultimately somehow got back to Imphal. Next day, Hurricanes from 34 Squadron strafed and destroyed the three grounded aircraft.

By 29 March Imphal's situation was becoming perilous. The Imphal plain was threatened on all sides by the Japanese, and on this day they cut the road to Kohima. Then at 1800 a reconnaissance Hurricane flown by Squadron Leader Arjan Singh sighted a complete Japanese battalion only 10 miles north of Imphal airfield and heading straight for it. He promptly sent warning to the squadrons based there – 28, 34 and 42 RAF and his own 1 IAF – and their Hurricanes were given their first chance to play a vital part in this vital battle. The airmen's reactions are described in Volume III, *The Fight is Won*, of the RAF Official History:

> Pilots and crews had already been dispersed for the night; some were eating their supper, others in their canvas baths. One and all made at once for their aircraft, those who had been bathing dressing as they ran. Within ten minutes nine Hurricanes had taken off, and in all thirty-three Hurricanes, accompanied for some unexplained reason by an elderly Harvard trainer, presently arrived over the area through which the Indian officer had reported the enemy to be passing. In the almost gathered dusk nothing could be seen but the dim outlines of trees and scrub; but the leading aircraft, flying very low, turned on their landing lights, and in their beams the Japanese column was clearly descried. The squadrons went in with bombs, cannon and machine-gun fire, and though they could see no apparent result no enemy appeared in the environs of Imphal. It was only later that they learnt from captured documents that 220 Japanese, including 14 officers, had met their ends that evening.

Since the Hurricanes had only a short distance to fly, almost all of them got back to their base before nightfall, but one straggler had to land in the dark without the aid of a flare-path and did so perfectly.

Despite this success, however, the fact remained that the Imphal plain was now encircled and it would not be the only area under siege for very long. While two of Mutaguchi's divisions concentrated on Imphal, his 31st Division under Lieutenant General Kotuku Sato was speeding – with astonishing rapidity considering the difficulties of the terrain – towards Kohima, which it reached late on 4 April. Sato's orders were to capture it and then hold it as a barrier protecting the rear of the Japanese forces assaulting Imphal.

It had been assumed by Slim that the main Japanese objective in Assam would be Dimapur, as indeed it should have been. He therefore allotted only 1,500 combatant troops under Colonel Hugh Richards to the defence of Kohima in the belief that they would encounter only minor enemy forces. When they were confronted by an entire Japanese division, they abandoned Kohima village and fell back westward to Kohima Ridge. The Japanese followed up, surrounded and isolated the ridge and also swung past it to block the road to Dimapur at a place called Zubza.

Thus the battle raged round two separate areas. On the Imphal plain the Japanese attacked IV Corps from all directions. At Kohima the situation was more complicated, for as the men of Japan's 31st Division tried to roll up the defenders of the ridge by pressure at its southern end, they also had to resist pressure on themselves from the north-west as Britain's XXXIII Corps, which had been brought forward from India and reinforced by units flown in from the Arakan, advanced against them from Dimapur.

In both areas, the struggle became one of savage attrition. It has been said that more casualties were suffered in proportion to the numbers engaged than in any other action in the Second World War and participants on both sides have compared it with the brutal bloodbaths of the First World conflict. These observations say little for the generalship shown, but they do emphasize the extraordinary courage, endurance and tenacity of the ordinary soldiers; British, Indian and Japanese alike.

What turned the struggle in favour of the British and Commonwealth soldiers was not their superiority in men and equipment but the Allied possession of command of the air and particularly of two types of aircraft. One was the Dakota aerial transports. These not only evacuated some 35,000 sick and wounded from the Imphal area but, throughout the long siege, kept IV Corps' remaining 120,000 men supplied with every requirement, especially food: it was the besiegers and not the besieged who would starve. At Kohima the siege was shorter and the much smaller garrison did not run low on food, but the Dakotas had to and did provide them with ammunition, with medical supplies and, after 6 April when the Japanese captured a crucial reservoir, with water.

In their missions the Dakotas were frequently escorted by that other vital aircraft type, the Hurricanes. So effectively was this task performed that not a single Dakota was lost when under Hurricane protection. The Hawker fighters also acted as escorts for Vultee Vengeance dive-bombers in strikes on Japanese troops or supply lines, and their numbers were increased in early April by the Hurricane IICs of 123 Squadron. As well as escort duties, these flew tactical reconnaissance sorties, losing two of their pilots in the course of them during the month. That they were never used as Hurribombers is perhaps somewhat surprising since it was in that role that the Hurricanes were of most value to the Fourteenth Army, especially in early April when the Japanese came closest to victory at Imphal.

On 6 April the Japanese gained a footing on a large hill called Nungshigum that rose abruptly from the Imphal plain. This was little more than 6 miles north of the Imphal airfield on which were immense supplies of food, ammunition and petrol. The threat was obvious and the Hurricanes set about thwarting any further advance. On the 7th Flight Sergeants Guy and Draycott of 28 Squadron sighted and strafed a Japanese column, though Draycott was killed by ground fire. Hurribomber attacks on Nungshigum followed, causing so many casualties that an Allied attack drove the Japanese off the hill without much difficulty. The danger, however, was far from over.

On 11 April the enemy attacked in strength, not only from the north but from the south-east where the attack was directed at another crucial airfield at Palel. This was now the base of 42 Squadron's Hurribombers, which were concealed in bays cut in a nearby hillside, and the pilots and ground crews were at readiness from dawn to dusk. The advance was made from positions established only 2 or 3 miles away but the defenders, supported by 42's Hurricanes, checked the attack and then counter-attacked and took the forward Japanese positions, again with the assistance of Hurribomber strikes, one of which was seen to blow up a Japanese bunker with direct hits.

At Nungshigum the Japanese were more successful, taking both the hill's two peaks. Counter-attacks and raids by Hurribombers on

11 and 12 April failed to dislodge them, and a major effort was ordered for the 13th. At 1030 Hurribombers blasted the enemy positions with great effect, observers noting that 'clouds of earth, shattered branches of trees and mangled bodies were flung into the air'. Then the British and Commonwealth infantry attacked, aided by artillery fire and by tanks which had to be winched up the steep slopes, while overhead Hurricanes strafed the hill, diving 'almost into the tree-tops' it was said, and interspersing their strikes with 'dummy runs' to 'keep the defenders' heads down'. Both Nungshigum's peaks were taken, admittedly with heavy casualties, and never again fell into Japanese hands.

Nor did the Hurricanes neglect the Kohima front. They carried out strafing attacks and the undramatic but essential tactical reconnaissance missions. Once again, however, it was the Hurribombers that were the most valuable; 11, 34, 42 and 113 Squadrons between them flying more than 2,200 sorties in the Kohima area alone during April 1944. They supported XXXIII Corps' 2nd Division as it attempted to break past the enemy defences at Zubza; struck at Sato's 31st Division as it tried to overrun the Kohima Ridge. Since these operations were carried out close to the trapped garrison, they gave this tremendous encouragement.

It was greatly needed, for the Japanese were slowly and painfully but steadily capturing the British defences on the ridge. By nightfall on 17 April, Colonel Richards held only the extreme north of the ridge, his positions forming a rough circle of only some 500 yards in diameter. Clearly urgent action was needed and early on the 18th, the 2nd Division's artillery delivered an intense bombardment, which was followed by Hurribomber attacks. In the course of one of these, 34 Squadron hit a Japanese bunker, but Canadian Flight Lieutenant 'Jimmy' Whalen, bravely but unwisely coming back for a second strike when the defenders had been alerted, was shot down and killed by AA fire. Under cover of these assaults, however, a company of Punjabis was able to get through to reinforce a grateful Colonel Richards.

'Reinforce' but not 'relieve'. Japanese troops in front of and on the flanks of the 2nd Division still prevented major forces reaching the Kohima Ridge. For the remainder of 18 April and throughout the 19th, therefore, the 2nd Division's artillery and Hurricanes bombing and strafing pounded the enemy flanking forces. In the course of these two days, two more Hurricanes were lost while making strafing attacks and their pilots killed: Flight Lieutenant Thomas of 5 Squadron by flak; Flying Officer Murcott of 1 IAF by hitting a tree. Flying Officer McPherson of 28 Squadron also came down, behind enemy lines. He was injured and temporarily knocked out, but was rescued and cared for by friendly Naga tribesmen, of whose country Kohima is the heart.[5] He recovered, was guided to safety, and rejoined his unit on 5 May.

These assaults drove the Japanese from their advanced positions and cleared the 2nd Division's line of communications. On 20 April it was ready for a final effort. At 0900 Hurribombers struck at the enemy in the vicinity of Kohima Ridge and the raid followed by a heavy artillery bombardment was so effective that at 0945, British infantrymen reached the defensive perimeter held by Richards. The siege of Kohima was over.

Nonetheless, Japan's 31st Division continued to hold high ground near Kohima and resisted determined attempts to drive it from this. There was thus no chance yet of a British advance southward to Imphal. This remained under siege and throughout the rest of April savage fighting continued to rage and the Hurricane units mourned the death of pilots from 5, 34 and 1 IAF, all victims of flak. To add to their problems, two more Hurricanes were lost when one of their 20mm cannons, for reasons unexplained, exploded while strafing. Mercifully, Flight Lieutenant Shannon of 34 Squadron baled out and was unhurt, while 28 Squadron's Flight Lieutenant Johnson was injured but survived when he crash-landed.

On the other hand, in late April three more Hurricane squadrons were transferred to airfields on the Imphal plain. No. 9 Squadron Indian Air Force carried out tactical reconnaissance duties, but two RAF units had more aggressive sorties in mind. No. 20 was equipped with Hurricane IIDs fitted with two 40mm anti-tank guns. In the absence of their most favoured targets, the pilots originally also flew reconnaissance missions but with unhappy results. On 23 April Pilot Officer McPhail suffered engine failure and was injured when he crash-landed, while on the 25th Flight Sergeant Whitehall apparently lost control of his aircraft and was killed when it plunged into a river. On 28 April, however, the squadron joined in the attacks being made on the Japanese lines of communication, possibly with some relief.

Last and perhaps most welcome of the new arrivals was 60 Squadron RAF. This was another Hurribomber unit and it wasted little time before embarking on Hurribomber missions. On 28 April twelve of its aircraft successfully attacked enemy motor vehicles in the neighbourhood of Palel. Their achievement, though, was marred by a sad mishap. Warrant Officer Pritchard was forced to bale out, presumably hit by ground fire. He attempted to make his way back to his own lines, but early next morning he encountered a 'friendly' patrol who thought he was Japanese and tragically opened fire, killing him.

It was also at the end of April that the Hurricanes clashed with enemy fighters (usually the concern of Spitfires or Mustangs) as these attempted to engage the Allied bombers or the omnipresent Dakotas that the Hurricanes were protecting. So effective was that protection that the Hurricanes did not lose a single one of their charges, though occasionally suffering damage themselves. On 26 April, for instance, 5 Squadron was escorting Vengeance dive-bombers when it was attacked by Oscars which hit Flying Officer Mann's Hurricane. It showed the usual Hurricane toughness and Mann retaliated, probably downed his attacker and returned safely to base.

On the same day, 11 Squadron was escorting Dakotas when a group of enemy warplanes was sighted, obviously on an offensive mission. A section of three Hurricanes led by Flight Lieutenant 'Chris' Ditmas was ordered to engage this. Ditmas was so unlucky as to be unable to release his long-range drop-tanks, yet despite this handicap he damaged one bomber. His aircraft was then hit by fire from the escorting Oscars but he dived to low level where, as he explains in *Air War for Burma* by Christopher Shores:

> For all of fifteen minutes I flew between, under and almost through trees, hills and occasionally huts. The technique was to fly sideways with maximum slip, and it seemed to work. It's always hard to sight and fire at a twisting target within a few feet of the ground. Add considerable slip and gauging deflection becomes even more difficult. Anyhow, I can vividly recall the tracer passing just to one side, over and over again.

Ditmas eventually escaped, or his enemy ran out of ammunition, for he got home safely. His damaged Hurricane crash-landed, but its pilot walked away unharmed.

On 28 April a group of Oscar fighter-bombers attacked Allied positions in the Zubza area but hastily retired when some Hurricanes appeared, much to the disgust of Japanese infantrymen watching from neighbouring hills. This was the last Hurricane-Oscar encounter for some three weeks, but the Japanese fighters would be back.

On the ground, the bloodstained battles of attrition dragged on seemingly endlessly during May into early June, as Mutaguchi repeatedly attempted to take the Imphal plain. All his concentrations, however, were revealed by 'recce' Hurricanes and were broken and dispersed by repeated Hurribomber strikes.

It was in an attempt to end this intolerable situation that the Oscars reappeared. Patrols of them would fly over their own lines with orders to ignore large Allied formations but to pounce on any single or pair of Hurricanes they sighted since they would know these were on reconnaissance duties. Other Oscars were instructed to make snap intruder raids over Allied airfields in the hope of catching Hurricanes as they took off or landed.

These tactics began on 20 May. In the Imphal area, nine Oscars shot down two of 5 Squadron's Hurricanes that had just taken off, killing both pilots. Next day, two Hurricanes of 1 IAF were engaged by half a dozen Oscars while on reconnaissance. Pilot Officer Masih was shot down in flames and killed. Flying Officer Cheeseman's Hurricane was also set on fire, but only in a long-range fuel tank. Cheeseman was able to jettison this and escaped at low level.

On 23 May nine Oscars attacked a couple of 11 Squadron's Hurricanes, hitting them both. Warrant Officer Bowden was killed, but Flight Lieutenant Page evaded his opponents and returned safely to base. A damaged Oscar with a wounded pilot at the controls crash-landed at its airfield. Since Page made no claim for this, Bowden was presumably responsible.[6] As late as 8 June Oscars engaged a pair of reconnaissance Hurricanes from 28 Squadron. Both were hard hit, but Warrant Officer Baker was able to return to his airfield unhurt. Flying Officer Muff's aircraft was set on fire and he crash-landed at 240 mph. Though suffering from burns, he was able to walk away from his wrecked machine: one more pilot who owed his life to the strength of his Hurricane.

That, though, was the last day when Hurricanes were troubled by hostile fighters. Indeed, during late May and early June, they were probably more hindered by adverse weather. The monsoon began on 18 May, and bad weather is believed to have claimed the lives of two pilots from 1 IAF and one each from 11, 20 and 28 Squadrons, all of whom failed to return from reconnaissance or night-intruder sorties. In addition, a pilot from 28 was killed when his Hurricane crashed on take-off. Yet neither the best efforts of the enemy nor the worst effects of the weather proved capable of preventing the reconnaissance Hurricanes from making their crucial reports to the Fourteenth Army.

Of still greater value to the Fourteenth Army were the Hurribomber attacks on Japanese positions, made in both the Imphal region where IV Corps was trying to drive back enemies still dangerously close to the vital airfields and the Kohima area where XXXIII Corps was putting constant pressure on Sato, preventing him from sending part of his strength to assist the assaults on Imphal as Mutaguchi had ordered. During April the Hurribombers had launched a million pounds of bombs onto the luckless Japanese infantrymen and they increased their efforts in May. So highly were they prized that five Wellington bombers were withdrawn from their own operations to ferry the 250lb bombs used by the Hurricanes up to the front line.

The Hurribombers' effectiveness was increased because Air Commodore Vincent and the officers of 221 Group – following precedents set in North Africa and Italy – worked very closely with the Fourteenth Army. It became the practice that after the programme for any day had been drawn up, those Hurribomber or Tac R units not assigned to specific tasks were placed under what was called the Army Air Support Control. To this, the forward ground troops could radio requests for assistance which would be dealt with by the wing commander in charge without reference to Group; in effect, therefore, its aircraft were controlled by the Fourteenth Army. They were supplemented by what was later known as the 'Cab Rank', which consisted of Hurricanes on standing patrol over particularly vital areas, attacking targets of opportunity.

These procedures could help the soldiers whether they were defending or attacking, but in attacks there were additional ways in which the Hurribombers were of assistance. One such would later be called 'Earthquake', which followed the example of the early attacks on Nungshigum. The Hurricanes would first bomb the position being assaulted, then strafe it with cannon-fire, and finally make mock attacks:

these would compel the enemy to seek shelter instead of providing resistance, but at the same time avoid any chance of the attacking infantrymen being harmed by their own aircraft.

To aid the Hurribombers in their supporting role, it became customary for their pilots to visit army units designated to participate in an offensive and study from advanced observation posts the enemy positions at which they would shortly have to strike. With increasing experience they proved able to hit targets only some 170 yards from the front line without endangering their own soldiers. Thus in an attack on 10 May near Palel, the Hurribombers went in so close to the Allied infantrymen that these clearly saw parts of the bunkers that had been hit and the bodies of some of their defenders blasted high into the air, while on 18 May near Kohima, the Hurribombers released their weapons over the Allied trenches, their momentum causing these to sweep on into the enemy bunkers.

Apart from providing close support, the Hurricanes operated well away from the front line. They attacked Japanese ammunition dumps, bases and headquarters when these could be located, one such raid reportedly killing about 100 of the enemy. Mostly, though, they struck at the Japanese lines of communication, their targets including bridges, railway locomotives, river craft of all descriptions and especially road transports. Naturally the Hurribombers were very effective in this respect, a favourite tactic being to drop bombs immediately in front of and immediately behind a column of vehicles, forming craters that blocked their advance and their retreat alike. Then the column itself would be attacked with bombs and cannons and would suffer accordingly.

Perhaps the squadron most successful in this role, however, was No. 5 which did not fly Hurribombers. Instead, under the command of Squadron Leader Guy Hogan, it specialized in strafing attacks on Japanese motor transports. It quickly found the 20mm cannons of its Mark IICs more than adequate to destroy these, especially if they were carrying fuel or ammunition, when they would disintegrate in spectacularly satisfying explosions. When the Japanese changed to travelling at night, 5 Squadron located them because they drove with their headlights full on. When they stopped using headlights and relied on moonlight, 5 Squadron still tracked them by observing the shadows cast by the vehicles across the road.

How effective Hurricane attacks of this kind proved to be would be confirmed by Japanese reports captured later, which referred to their 'frightfulness' and gave harrowing descriptions of burned-out vehicles and dead drivers. Since the Japanese had strictly limited numbers of motor transports in the first place, by mid-May they had become desperately short of food, ammunition and medical supplies. The vile weather completed the ruin of their lines of communication and several of Mutaguchi's subordinates urged him to withdraw his men while this was still possible. Neither he nor the supreme commander in Burma, Lieutenant General Kawabe, would agree and thereby they doomed their valiant Fifteenth Army.

Particularly serious was the condition of Sato's 31st Division; its men were reduced to eating leaves and roots and were outnumbered by at least five to one. Nonetheless, they held on in the Kohima area, though subjected from 24 May onwards to continuous artillery fire and attacks by the inevitable Hurribombers. These reached their culmination on the 31st. It was a sad day for the Hurribombers as Flight Sergeant Taylor was killed by ground fire on 60 Squadron's third raid of the day, but finally the Japanese broke. They fell back from Kohima and many frankly fled, throwing away their weapons. Yet the 2nd (British) Division's advance down the road to Imphal was still opposed by rearguards, who in turn were subjected to more Hurribomber strikes. An aircraft from 113 Squadron was brought down by flak on 5 June, but Warrant Officer Bott baled out safely.

While XXXIII Corps was hammering at Sato, IV Corps at Imphal was still resisting assaults by Mutaguchi's other two divisions. As always, the defenders were assisted by Hurricanes. The Hurribombers were very much to the fore, though 42 Squadron had a bad day on 30 May, losing two of its pilots to anti-aircraft fire. The Hurricane IIDs with their 40mm guns were now showing their worth as well. The Japanese at last brought up tanks, three of them at least. On 26 May they were spotted and 20 Squadron, hitherto operating largely against river craft, destroyed all three.

Throughout June, Mutaguchi's men continued to attack but they were becoming increasingly hungry and exhausted and all their efforts proved futile. The IIDs of No. 20 found more opportunities to strike at tanks. In one of these on 7 June, Flying Officer Brittain was shot down and killed, but during the month the squadron destroyed a total of twelve tanks, the only ones sighted, plus eighteen other motor vehicles, and it was just one of the Hurricane units in action against the enemy.

On 22 June the troops advancing from Kohima at last made contact with their comrades in Imphal and the long siege of Imphal was raised. Still the Japanese fought on and it appears that by now the Hurricane pilots were also becoming exhausted because in just over a fortnight they lost two men from 60 Squadron and one man each from 11 and 34 Squadrons, all to ground fire as the Japanese airmen were conspicuous by their absence. To end the account of their activities on a happier note, however, on 5 July Flight Sergeant Lomax of 42 Squadron hit some trees while attacking enemy soldiers, but his tough Hurricane pulled out of its dive and gained the height and distance needed for Lomax to bale out over friendly territory, which he did safely.

By 8 July, even Mutaguchi had had enough and ordered a general retirement. His losses in men and equipment had been ruinous. Of the men, 30,000 were dead, while a large proportion of the 23,000 wounded died from starvation or disease during their retreat. Astonishingly, only about 600 had been taken prisoner, all but a handful of them either badly wounded or in the last stages of exhaustion or both. Mutaguchi had already removed his three divisional commanders and would himself be dismissed before the end of 1944, as would his superior, Kawabe.

By contrast, the British, who had employed a total of six divisions, not to mention some smaller units, had incurred only 11,700 casualties. Slim and his corps commanders Lieutenant Generals Scoones and Stopford, were knighted on the battlefield by the Viceroy of India, Field Marshal Lord Wavell. They could easily follow up their victory, being delayed far more by the monsoon than by the shattered remnants of Japan's Fifteenth Army.

So great in fact were the Japanese losses that they could never be made good, which in turn meant that there was no possibility of their being able to do more than delay a British reconquest of Burma. Indeed, Brigadier Smith in his *Battle for Burma* goes so far as to suggest that they would have done better to evacuate Burma voluntarily as this 'would have saved thousands of lives without radically changing the outcome of the war in South-East Asia'.

The Hurricanes naturally played a major part in driving the Japanese back to the Chindwin and then out of Burma altogether. By the time the first RAF squadron had landed on a Burmese airfield, Tamu, on 2 November 1944 – it was of course a Hurricane squadron; No. 11 to be precise – the number of pounds of bombs the Hurribombers had dropped had risen to 5.5 million, and they would drop plenty more later. During the summer of 1945, however, all Hurribomber squadrons were converted to Thunderbolts. The pilots, who considered the Hurricane the ideal close-support aircraft and the Thunderbolt a big ugly brute that needed half of Burma in which to make a turn, were not pleased.

Nonetheless, when on 2 September 1945 the Japanese formally surrendered aboard the US battleship *Missouri* in Tokyo Bay, 20 Squadron RAF, its Hurricane IIDs now supplemented by rocket-firing Mark IVs and 28 Squadron RAF with its trusty Tac R Mark IICs, still flew the Hawker fighters, as did eight Indian Air Force squadrons. On the last day of the Second World War, as on the first, the Hurricane was a front-line warplane.

Notes

1. This work was prepared for South-East Asia Command by the Central Office of Information. Owen was the editor of the theatre newspaper *SEAC*.
2. Slim's original tribute to Wingate appeared in a booklet prepared by the *SEAC* newspaper. It is repeated in full, along with a detailed account of Slim's subsequent changes of attitude in *Wingate and the Chindits: Redressing the Balance* by David Rooney, a former senior lecturer at Sandhurst.
3. Really British-Indian. As mentioned earlier, it was general practice for the brigades in 'Indian' divisions to contain two battalions of Indians or Gurkhas and one battalion of British soldiers.
4. The Gurkhas, it is hardly necessary to mention, remained loyal to a man.
5. The Nagas were fiercely loyal to the British. They ignored alike threats from the Japanese and anti-British pamphlets from the Indian Congress Party. When India was granted independence, they were bitterly unhappy and rebelled unsuccessfully soon afterwards.
6. The Japanese airmen reported a fight with two 'Spitfires'. Clearly 'Spitfire snobbery' could affect Orientals as well as Europeans.

Last Word

That, then, was the Hawker Hurricane, perhaps the most valuable Allied aircraft of the Second World War.

There are three main grounds on which this claim can be made. First are its achievements in the Battle of Britain. These have been discussed earlier, but let it be recorded here that in that conflict Hurricanes made 80 per cent of successful interceptions and downed more enemy aircraft than all other British fighters – principally Spitfires, but the Blenheims and Defiants should not be forgotten – and all forms of ground defence put together. That fact cannot be repeated too often, if only because it is too often ignored, at least in the country to which it brought salvation; oddly enough in the United States it is the Hurricane that holds pride of place.

A charming example of this is revealed in Dr John W. Fozard's *Sydney Camm and the Hurricane*. Since Dr Fozard began a brilliant forty-five-year career in aviation as a member of Camm's design staff, his admiration for the Hurricane was perhaps natural, but it was exceeded by that of an American wife who arrived in Britain in 1985, just in time for the Hurricane Jubilee Symposium commemorating the 50th anniversary of the prototype's first flight. As her husband relates:

> Since then she has become the most vociferous of US nationals who correct the popular misconception that the Spitfire won the Battle of Britain. Gloria convinces everyone, from US Senators downwards, that the Battle of Britain was won by Hurricanes and Spitfires but that *the Hurricane played the dominant role*.

Another American who held the same opinion was Drew Middleton who was a war correspondent stationed in London in the summer of 1940. In his book *The Sky Suspended*, he bluntly states: 'It was the Hurricane, marvellously adaptable and very hard to hurt, that played the major role in Fighter Command's battle.'

This compliment to the Hurricane's adaptability and strength indicates the other two grounds on which its value can be judged: it could do anything and it could go anywhere.

With regard to the former, apart from its own exploits the Hurricane demonstrated what could be done, inspiring others to follow the paths it had indicated. It was the first modern British fighter to fly from aircraft carriers. It was the only modern British fighter to be catapulted off merchant ships. As Air Marshal Wykeham confirms in *Fighter Command*, it was the RAF's 'first true fighter-bomber'. It was also the RAF's first fighter to carry rockets and the only RAF fighter to carry the deadly 40mm anti-tank guns.

With regard to the latter, it could be sent wherever it was needed and would operate there safely and successfully, regardless of climate or conditions. In the stern waters of the Atlantic Ocean, the mountains and monsoon of Assam and Manipur and the jungles of Sumatra and Java, everywhere this aircraft could be found. Francis K. Mason in *The Hawker Hurricane* thus reflects on the service it gave: 'It fought on more fronts, in more countries, and in more theatres than any other fighter in history. The Royal Air Force was glad to get the Spitfire….it HAD to have the Hurricane!'

Bibliography

Allwood, Maurice, *Hurricane Special* (Ian Allen, 1975)
Ash, Bernard, *Norway 1940* (Cassell, 1964)
Bader, Group Captain Sir Douglas, *Fight for the Sky: The Story of the Spitfire and Hurricane* (Sidgwick and Jackson, 1973)
Barker, A.J., *Eritrea 1941* (Faber & Faber, 1966)
Barker, Ralph, *The Hurricats* (Pelham Books, 1978)
Beedle, James, *43 Squadron* (Beaumont Aviation Literature, 1966)
Bickers, Richard Townshend, *Ginger Lacey: Fighter Pilot* (Robert Hale, 1962)
Birtles, Patrick J., *Hurricane: The Illustrated History* (Patrick Stephens, 2001)
Bishop, Edward, *Hurricane* (Airlife Publishing Limited, 1986)
Bishop, Edward, *The Battle of Britain* (George Allen & Unwin, 1960)
Blackah, Paul, Lowe, Malcolm V. & Blackah, Louise, *Hawker Hurricane* (Haynes Publishing, 2010)
Bowyer, Chaz, *Hurricane at War* (Ian Allen, 1974)
Brown, David, *Carrier Fighters* (Macdonald & Jane's, 1975)
Cameron, Ian, *Red Duster, White Ensign: The Story of the Malta Convoys* (Frederick Muller, 1959)
Chorlton, Martyn, *Hawker Hurricane Mk I-V* (Osprey, 2013)
Churchill, Winston S., *The Second World War* (Cassell, 1948–1954)
Collier, Basil, *The Battle of Britain* (Batsford, 1962)
Colston, Bryan P., *Recollections of Wartime Experiences* (Privately published, 2004)
Cotter, Jarrod (ed.), *Hurricane Salute* (Key Publishing, 2008)
David, Group Captain Dennis, *Dennis 'Hurricane' David* (Grub Street, 2000)
Dibbs, John & Holmes, Tony, *Hurricane: A Fighter Legend* (Osprey, 1995)
Dibbs, John, Holmes, Tony & Riley, Gordon, *Hurricane: Hawker's Fighter Legend* (Osprey, 2017) (Note: This is a totally different work from the previous one.)
Dick, Air Vice-Marshal Ron, *Hurricane: RAF Fighter* (Airlife Publishing Limited, 2000)
Donahue, Flight Lieutenant A.G., *Last Flight from Singapore* (Macmillan, 1944)
Evans, General Sir Geoffrey & Brett-James, Anthony, *Imphal: A Flower on Lofty Heights* (Macmillan, 1962)
Fozard, Dr John W., *Sydney Camm and the Hurricane* (Airlife Publishing Limited, 1991)
Franks, Norman L.R., *The Greatest Air Battle: Dieppe 19th August 1942* (Kimbers, 1979)
Hastings, Max, *Operation Pedestal* (Collins, 2021)

Hiscock, Melvyn, *Hawker Hurricane Inside and Out* (Crowood Press, 2003)
Holmes, Ray, *Spy Sky* (Airlife Publishing Limited, 1989)
Holmes, Tony, *Hurricane Aces 1939–40* (Osprey, 1998)
Jackson, Robert, *Hawker Hurricane* (Blandford Press, 1987)
Jackson, Robert, *Strike from the Sea: A History of British Naval Air Power* (Arthur Barker, 1970)
Jacobs, Peter, *Hawker Hurricane* (Crowood Press, 1998)
Johnson, Brian, *Fly Navy* (David & Charles, 1981)
Kelly, Terence, *Battle for Palembang* (Robert Hale, 1985)
Kelly, Terence, *Hurricane and Spitfire: Pilots at War* (Kimbers, 1986)
Kelly, Terence, *Hurricane over the Jungle* (Kimbers, 1977)
Kelly, Terence, *Nine Lives of a Fighter Pilot* (Airlife, 2003)
Lewis, Peter, *Squadron Histories: RFC, RNAS & RAF since 1912* (Putnam, 1959. New edition, 1968)
Liddell Hart, Captain B.H., *History of the Second World War* (Cassell, 1970)
Lucas Phillips, Brigadier C.E., *Springboard to Victory* (Kohima) (Heinemann, 1966)
MacIntyre, Captain Donald, *Narvik* (Evans, 1959)
MacIntyre, Captain Donald, *The Battle for the Mediterranean* (Batsford, 1964)
March, Peter R., *The Hurricane Story* (Sutton Publishing, 2007)
Mason, Francis K., *Battle over Britain* (McWhirter Twins, 1969)
Mason, Francis K., *Hawker Hurricane Described* (Kookaburra Technical Publications, 1970)
Mason, Francis K., *The Hawker Hurricane* (MacDonald, 1962. Revised edition, Aston Publications Limited, 1987)
Masters, David, *So Few* (Eyre & Spottiswoode, 1943)
McKinstry, Leo, *Hurricane Victor of the Battle of Britain* (John Murray, 2010)
Menzies, Sir Robert, *Afternoon Light* (Cassell, 1967)
Middleton, Drew, *The Sky Suspended* (Secker & Warburg, 1960)
Milton, Brian, *Hurricane: The Last Witnesses* (Andre Deutsch, 2010)
Moorehead, Alan, *The Desert War* (Hamish Hamilton, 1965)
Moyes, Philip J.R., *Hawker Hurricane I* (Vintage Edition Publications, 1978)
Neil, Wing Commander T.F., *Onwards to Malta* (Airlife, 1992)
Owen, Colonel Frank, *The Campaign in Burma* (HMSO, 1946)
Perowne, Stewart, *The Siege within the Walls: Malta 1940–1943* (Hodder & Stoughton, 1970)
Poolman, Kenneth, *Faith, Hope and Charity* (Kimbers, 1954)
Popham, Hugh, *Sea Flight* (Kimbers, 1954)
Richards, Denis & Saunders, Hilary St. G., *Royal Air Force 1939–1945* (HMSO, Volume I, *The Fight at Odds*, 1953. Volume II, *The Fight Avails*, 1945. Volume III, *The Fight is Won*, 1954)
Robertson, Bruce & Scarborough, Gerald, *Hawker Hurricane* (Patrick Stephens, 1974)
Rooney, David, *Wingate and the Chindits: Redressing the Balance* (Arms & Armour, 1994)

Roskill, Captain S.W., *The War at Sea* (HMSO, 1954–61)
Rybin, Yuriy, *Soviet Hurricane Aces of World War 2* (Osprey, 2012)
Rys, Marek, *Hawker Hurricane* (Mushroom Model Publications, 2006)
Saunders, Andy, *No. 43 'Fighting Cocks' Squadron* (Osprey, 2003)
Shacklady, Edward, *Hawker Hurricane* (Tempus Publishing Limited, 2000)
Shankland, Peter & Hunter, Anthony, *Malta Convoy* (Collins, 1961)
Shores, Christopher & Williams, Clive, *Aces High* (Grub Street, 1994. Supplemental Volume II by Shores, Christopher, Grub Street, 1999)
Shores, Christopher & Massimello, Giovanni, *A History of the Mediterranean Air War 1940–1945* (Grub Street. Volume I, *North Africa: June 1940–January 1942*, 2012. Volume II, *North African Desert: February 1943–March 1943*, 2012. Volume III, *Tunisia and the End in Africa: November 1942–May 1943*, 2016)
Shores, Christopher, *Air War for Burma* (Grub Street, 2005)
Shores, Christopher & Cull, Brian with Izawa, Yasuho, *Bloody Shambles* (Grub Street. Volume I, *The Drift to War to the Fall of Singapore*, 1992. Volume II, *The Defence of Sumatra to the Fall of Burma*, 1993)
Shores, Christopher, *Dust Clouds in the Middle East* (Grub Street, 1996)
Shores, Christopher & Ring, Hans, *Fighters Over the Desert* (Neville Spearman, 1969)
Shores, Christopher, Ring, Hans & Hess, William N., *Fighters Over Tunisia* (Neville Spearman, 1975)
Shores, Christopher, *Fledgling Eagles* (Grub Street, 1991)
Shores, Christopher, *Hawker Hurricane Mk I/IV in Royal Air Force & Foreign Service* (Osprey, 1971)
Shores, Christopher & Cull, Brian with Malizia, Nicola, *Malta: The Hurricane Years 1940–41* (Grub Street, 1987)
Shores, Christopher & Cull, Brian with Malizia, Nicola, *Malta: The Spitfire Year, 1942* (Grub Street, 1991)
Shores, Christopher, *Those Other Eagles* (Grub Street, 2004)
Slim, Field Marshal Sir William, *Defeat Into Victory* (Cassell, 1956)
Smith, Brigadier E.D., *Battle for Burma* (Batsford, 1979)
Smith, Michael, *The Emperor's Codes* (Transworld Publishers, 2000)
Smith, Peter C., *Pedestal: The Malta Convoy of August 1942* (Kimbers, 1970)
Stewart, Adrian, *Hurricane: The War Exploits of the Fighter Aircraft* (Kimbers, 1982. Revised edition, Canelo, 2021)
Stewart, Adrian, *Ten Squadrons of Hurricanes* (Pen & Sword, 2016)
Stewart, Adrian, *They Flew Hurricanes* (Pen & Sword, 2005)
Swinson, Arthur, *Kohima* (Hutchinson, 1966)
Thomas, Andrew, *Hurricane Aces 1941–45* (Osprey, 2003)
Townsend, Group Captain Peter, *Duel of Eagles* (Weidenfeld & Nicolson, 1972)
Tsuji, Colonel Masanobu, *Singapore: The Japanese Version* (Mayflower-Dell, 1960. UK edition, 1966)
Vincent, Air Vice-Marshal Sir S.F., *Flying Fever* (Jarrolds, 1972)
Wallace, Graham, *RAF Biggin Hill* (Putnam, 1957)

Wood, Derek & Dempster, Derek, *The Narrow Margin* (Hutchinson, 1961. Revised edition, Arrow Books Limited, 1969)
Woodman, Richard, *Malta Convoys 1940–1943* (John Murray, 2000)
Wykeham, Air Marshal Sir Peter, *Fighter Command* (Putnam, 1960)

Also the following booklets prepared by the Ministry of Information:
The Abyssinian Campaigns (HMSO, 1942)
The Air Battle of Malta (HMSO, 1944)

Index

Note: The ranks of the service personnel are those held at the time of the incident or incidents described.

Abotsinch (Airfield), 3
Abyssinia, 41, 44–5, 48–50, 52–4
Addis Ababa, 52–3
'Admin Box', 182
Afmadu (Airfield, Italian Somaliland), 48
Agordat, 46–7
Aircraft Types:
  American:
    Airacobra (Bell), 95–6
    Boston (Douglas), 184
    Buffalo (Brewster), 104
    Dakota (Douglas), 179, 182, 186–7, 190
    Harvard (North American), 84, 185
    Hudson (Lockheed), 104, 107
    Kittyhawk (Curtiss), 95–6, 98, 110, 115, 135
    Martlet (Grumman), 141, 147–8
    Maryland (Glenn Martin), 58, 116
    Mohawk (Curtiss), 54
    Mustang (North American), 154, 174, 181, 190
    Tomahawk (Curtiss), 53, 95
    Thunderbolt (Republic), 70, 98, 196
    Vengeance (Vultee), 187, 190
  British:
    Audax (Hawker), 70
    Beaufighter (Bristol), 125, 148
    Beaufort (Bristol), 36
    Blenheim (Bristol), 15–16, 18, 21, 31, 36, 104–107, 119, 150, 154, 181, 197
    Defiant (Boulton Paul), 16, 197
    Fulmar (Fairey), 58–9, 73, 75, 136–8, 141–2, 147–8
    Fury (Hawker), 43
    Gauntlet (Gloster), 46
    Gladiator (Gloster), 3, 5, 7, 9, 11–12, 16, 43–4, 46, 55–6, 70
    Hampden (Handley-Page), 150
    Hurricane (Hawker), *see* Hurricane
    Magister (Miles), 60
    Skua (Blackburn), 3, 56–7
    Spitfire (Supermarine), 12–13, 15–16, 18, 21, 24–5, 29, 31, 34, 36–9, 125–32, 134, 136, 149–51, 154, 162, 165, 174, 181, 190, 196–8
    Stirling (Short), 150
    Sunderland (Short), 56–7, 59, 117, 124
    Swordfish (Fairey), 11, 58, 61, 64, 69, 117
    Tempest (Hawker), 115
    Typhoon (Hawker), 115, 164
    Walrus (Supermarine), 10
    Wellington (Vickers), 58, 61, 64, 192
    Whirlwind (Westland), 16
  German:
    Dornier Do 17, 15, 17, 31–3, 37, 40
    Dornier Do 18, 136
    Dornier Do 26, 5, 6, 8
    Focke-Wulf Fw 190, 157–60, 162
    Focke-Wulf Fw 200 (Condor), 8, 17, 71–83
    Heinkel He 59, 18, 23
    Heinkel He 111, 7, 8, 17, 21, 36–7, 63, 93, 142–6, 160
    Heinkel He 115, 3
    Henschel Hs 126, 89
    Junkers Ju 86, 43, 48
    Junkers Ju 87 (Stuka), 9, 17–20, 22–5, 56–9, 61–2, 64, 118, 127, 129, 138, 146–7, 149
    Junkers Ju 88, 5, 8, 17–18, 20, 58–63, 91, 95, 120–3, 125, 127, 129–30, 137–8, 142–6, 148–9, 169
    Messerschmitt Bf 109, 16–30, 32–6, 38–9, 60–5, 87–91, 93, 95–7, 120–2, 124–7, 129–30, 144, 146, 151, 170, 177
    Messerschmitt Bf 110, 17, 20, 22–4, 26–40, 59, 61–3, 93, 126–7, 144–7
  Italian:
    Cant Z 506, 59
    Cant Z 1007, 137–8, 144–6, 149

Caproni Ca 133, 43–4, 47–8, 50
Fiat BR 20, 68
Fiat CR 32, 43, 50–4
Fiat CR 42, 44, 46, 48–57, 59, 62, 137–9, 146
Macchi MC 200, 58–9, 68–9, 177–8
Macchi MC 202, 116–18, 138, 144, 146, 176
Reggiane Re 2001, 138, 144–7
Savoia Marchetti SM 79, 46–7, 49, 53, 55–6, 64, 68, 98, 137–8, 144–7, 149
Savoia Marchetti SM 81, 44, 46
Savoia Marchetti SM 84, 138, 144, 149
Japanese:
Babs (Mitsubishi), 110
Kate (Nakajima), 109
Lily (Kawasaki), 105–106, 112–13
Nate (Nakajima), 100, 108–109, 112
Nell (Mitsubishi), 103
Oscar (Nakajima), 100–102, 105–107, 109, 114, 181, 190–1
Sally (Mitsubishi), 107
Topsy (Mitsubishi), 107
Zero (Mitsubishi), 99–102, 110–15
Aircraft Carriers:
Argus, 56–7, 87, 119, 125, 129, 132, 136–8
Ark Royal, 3, 56–7, 61–2, 64–8, 119, 132–3
Eagle, 125–7, 130, 136–3, 141–5
Furious, 64, 67–8, 136, 149
Glorious, 3, 4, 9–14, 67
Illustrious, 58–9, 61
Indomitable, 103, 141–7
Victorious, 87, 141–7
Wasp (USS), 128, 130–1
Aircraft Transports:
Athene, 105–108
Langley (USS), 110
Alamein, Battle of, *see* El Alamein
Alam Halfa, Battle of, 167
Alexander, General Sir H., 166–7, 172, 175, 177–8
Alexandria, 59, 133–5, 140
Algeria, 145, 159, 167–70, 172
Allard, Sergeant G., 29
Allen, Wing Commander J., 63
Allen, Sergeant J. Sandeman, 110, 113
Amba Alagi, 42, 53
Anamaet, Lieutenant R., 104
Anderson, General Sir K., 167, 172, 178
Anderson, 2nd Lieutenant M., 112
Andir (Airfield, Java), 112
Andrews, Pilot Officer E., 127

Anson, Sergeant P., 90
Aosta, Duke of, 41–2, 46–8, 52–3
Archangel, 86
Arnim, General J. von, 168, 171–7
Asmara, 47, 51–2
Atlantic, Battle of, 71–84, 136
Auchinleck, Lieutenant General, later General Sir C., 5, 118, 165–7
Auger, Flying Officer H., 62

Bader, Squadron Leader D., 68, 124, 142, 164
Baker, Pilot Officer I., 171
Baker, Flying Officer T., 160
Balden, Squadron Leader P., 56
Ballentine, Sergeant R., 122
Banka Island, 106, 108
Banks, Pilot Officer N., 8, 74
Banks, Sergeant S., 158
Bantam Bay, 110–11
Barber, Flight Sergeant J., 105
Barber, Flight Lieutenant R., 55
Bardufoss (Airfield, Norway), 3–5, 7, 11
Barentu, 46–7
Barker, Wing Commander J., 170
Barnwell, Pilot Officer D., 68, 117
Barton, Pilot Officer A., 33
Barton, Flight Lieutenant, later Squadron Leader R., 39, 64
Barwell, Squadron Leader P.R., 3, 12–13
Batavia, 104, 109–10, 113
Beazley, Flying Officer J., 69
Beckwith, Pilot Officer E., 170
Beedle, Sergeant J., 164
Berck-sur-Mer (Airfield, France), 153, 155
Berg, Flight Lieutenant V., 87, 91
Berry, Squadron Leader A., 162
Bierer, Sergeant E., 162
Biggin Hill (Airfield), 12, 20, 33
Birrell, Sub-Lieutenant M., 75–6
Blake, Flight Lieutenant R., 44, 46
Blanchard, Pilot Officer M., 121
Boltenstern, *Hauptmann* W. von, 34, 36
Bone (Airfield, Algeria), 169–70
Bordeaux, 71, 78, 80–1
Bose, Subhas Chandra, 182–3
Bott, Warrant Officer J., 194
Bowden, Warrant Officer N., 191
Boyd, Pilot Officer J., 131
Bradbury, Flight Lieutenant H., 60
Branston, Sergeant R., 63
Brink, Major General G., 45
Britain, Battle of, 12–13, 15–25, 27–40, 57, 59, 62, 64, 75, 81, 84, 88, 104, 107, 124, 142, 151, 154, 159, 197–8

Brittain, Flying Officer W., 194
Broadhurst, Air Vice-Marshal Sir H., 175–6
Brooker, Squadron Leader R., 106–107, 109, 111–13, 115
Brooks, Flight Sergeant J., 161–2
Brothers, Flight Lieutenant P., 20
Brown, Captain E., 136, 149
Brown, Flight Lieutenant, later Wing Commander H.M., 32, 117–18
Bruen, Lieutenant Commander J., 144–5
Brunier, Lieutenant J., 104
Bullivant, Lieutenant B., 138
Bulmer, Sub-Lieutenant G., 20
Bunker, Pilot Officer G., 10
Burgham, Sub-Lieutenant A., 136
Burma, 44, 97–8, 164, 179–86, 194–6
Burrough, Rear Admiral H., 147–8
Bush, Pilot Officer B., 90

Cameron, Pilot Officer N., 88, 93
Campbell, Sergeant B., 87
Campbell, Pilot Officer J.A., 110
CAM-ships (Catapult Aircraft Merchantmen):
  General, 73–5, 84
  Individual vessels:
    Empire Darwin, 83
    Empire Foam, 79
    Empire Heath, 81–2
    Empire Moon, 81
    Empire Rainbow, 76
    Empire Tide, 83
    Michael E., 75–6
Carpenter, Flight Lieutenant J., 121
Carver, Lieutenant R., 144
Catania (Airfield, Sicily), 123
Cavan, Flying Officer B., 121
Ceylon, 108–109, 115, 119
Chaffe, Squadron Leader R., 124
Chamberlain, Neville, 14–15, 26
Cheeseman, Flying Officer I., 191
Chindwin River, 179–81, 184
Churchill, Winston, 14–15, 21, 26, 72–3, 83, 85, 97, 118, 128, 150, 153, 165, 168
'Circus' Missions, 150–1
Clawson, Corporal H., 123
Clement, Flight Sergeant H., 185
Clowes, Flight Lieutenant A., 150
Coetzer, Lieutenant J., 51
Coffin, Pilot Officer J., 121–2, 125–6
Colston, Flight Lieutenant B., 169–70, 174
Comiso (Airfield, Sicily), 117–18, 123
Connolly, Flight Lieutenant M., 159
Connors, Flying Officer J., 177

Connors, Flight Lieutenant S., 33
Constable-Maxwell, Pilot Officer W., 37
Constantine (Airfield, Algeria), 170
Convoys:
  BOOTY, 29
  BOSOM, 18–20
  BREAD, 15
  DERVISH, 87
  HARPOON, 135–40, 145, 148
  MC9, 61
  PEDESTAL, 140–50
  PEWITT, 21–4
  VIGOROUS, 135–6
Cork, Lieutenant R., 141–2, 144–7
Cowles, Pilot Officer, later Flying Officer R., 3, 4, 10
Cox, Flight Lieutenant P.A.N., 20
Craig, Squadron Leader G., 152
Craig, Sergeant J., 33
Crosley, Sub-Lieutenant M., 137–8
Cross, Squadron Leader K., 3, 4, 7–12
Crossley, Flight Lieutenant M., 33, 40
Croydon (Airfield), 32–5, 40
Cruikshank, Sub-Lieutenant I., 146
Cunningham, Lieutenant General Sir A., 45, 48–50, 52–3
Cunningham, Admiral Sir A., 55, 59, 70, 133–5
Cunnington, Sergeant W., 57
Cyrenaica, 45, 59, 118, 123, 130

Dafforn, Squadron Leader R., 129
Dalton-Morgan, Flight Lieutenant T., 23
Darlan, Admiral J., 167, 177
David, Flying Officer J., 104
David, Group Captain W.D., 25
Davidson, Pilot Officer H., 76
Davies, Sergeant M., 64
Davis, Pilot Officer H., 176
Denmark, 1, 17, 31
Derna, 123, 133
Desert Air Force, 59, 167, 175
Dessie (Airfield, Abyssinia), 53
Dieppe, Raid on, *see* Operation JUBILEE
Dietl, General E., 1–2, 5–6, 89
Digby (Airfield), 3
Dimapur, 183, 186
Diredawa, 49–50, 52–3
Ditmas, Flight Lieutenant C., 190
Dobbie, General Sir W., 134–5
Dobbyn, Flight Lieutenant H., 110
Dobson, Flying Officer G., 160
Donahue, Flying Officer A., 108
Dönitz, Admiral K., 71, 78, 80, 83
Doorman, Rear Admiral K., 110

Douglas, Air Marshal Sir W. Sholto, 150
Dowding, Air Chief Marshal Sir H., 29, 38, 150
Dowland, Wing Commander J., 117
D'Oyly-Hughes, Captain G., 10
Draycott, Flight Sergeant K., 187
Dredge, Pilot Officer A., 63
Driver, Captain K., 46–7, 51
Drummond, Pilot Officer J., 7–10, 13
Dudley, Lieutenant L., 49
Du Fretay, Pilot Officer M., 161
Duncan, Lieutenant A., 51
Dunn, Pilot Officer W., 151
Duthie, Sub-Lieutenant H., 137–9
Dutton, Flight Lieutenant R., 24
Du Vivier, Squadron Leader L., 155
Dymond, Sergeant W., 33

Eastern Dorsale, 168, 171, 174
Ebner, *Feldwebel* F., 37
Egypt, 41–5, 52–5, 61, 64–5, 125, 131, 133–5, 163, 165, 167
Ehekercher, *Feldwebel* R., 34
Eighteenth Army Group, 172
Eighth Army, 53, 118, 165, 167, 171, 173–8
Eisenhower, General D., 107
El Alamein, Battle of, 167, 171
Ellacombe, Flight Lieutenant J., 154, 160
Emmerton, Pilot Officer L., 106
Enfidaville (Airfield, Tunisia), 176
Eretatwetan, 110–12
Eritrea, 41, 45–7, 50–3
Escort Carrier:
  Nairana, 136
Etchells, Flight Sergeant F., 65–6, 70, 132
Everett, Lieutenant R., 77–9

Farina, Lieutenant Colonel G., 138
Farnborough (Airfield), 75
Farthing, Flight Lieutenant H., 103
Fayolle, Squadron Leader M.E., 159–60
FC (Fighter Catapult) Ships:
  General, 73
  Individual vessel:
    Maplin, 74, 77–9
Fenton, Squadron Leader H., 23
Fiddes, Lieutenant D., 146
Finland, 1, 85–6, 93–4
Finlay, Sergeant C., 131
Finlay, Flight Sergeant W., 68
First Army, 167, 172–4, 178
Fleming, Sergeant J., 112
Fletcher, Pilot Officer J., 129
Flynn, Pilot Officer P., 83
Forrest, Lieutenant J., 142

Fourteenth Army, 44, 180, 182–95
France, Battle of, 25, 29, 31–2, 37, 62, 77, 101
Frost, Captain J., 46, 48–50, 52–3
Frost, Pilot Officer, later Flying Officer P., 3–4, 10

Gallabat, 42, 44–5
Ganes, Sergeant N., 131
Gavrilov, Lieutenant P., 93
Gela (Airfield, Sicily), 118
Gibraltar, 78, 80–2, 119, 133, 135, 137, 139, 147–9
Gibson, Sergeant R., 160
Gillam, Squadron Leader D., 153, 164
Girdwood, Sergeant A., 39
Gobwen (Airfield, Italian Somaliland), 48
Gondar, 54
Göring, Hermann, 17, 21, 29, 31, 36
'Göring' Battery, Dieppe, 158
Gort, General Lord, 135, 140
Gosport (Airfield), 75
Gould, Lieutenant C., 44
Gould, Pilot Officer G., 173
Grand Harbour, Malta, 58–9, 61, 68–9, 121, 131, 134, 139, 149
Gray, Pilot Officer C., 63
Greenhalgh, Sergeant W., 118, 132
Griffiths, 2nd Lieutenant B., 43
Gross, *Oberleutnant* A., 82
Grundy, Flight Lieutenant K., 22
Gura (Airfield, Eritrea), 47
Guy, Flight Sergeant G., 187

Haley, Sergeant A., 117
Hal Far (Airfield, Malta), 59, 61, 63, 67, 129
Halifax, Edward Wood, Earl of, 14–15, 21
Hallowes, Sergeant J., 23
Hamilton, Flight Lieutenant H., 29
Hankey, Sub-Lieutenant M., 144
Hare, Sergeant M., 67
Harrap, Flight Lieutenant C., 170
Harstad, 2, 4, 10
Harvey, Captain N., 49
Harvey, Sergeant R., 122
Harwood, Admiral Sir H., 135
Haw, Flight Sergeant C., 38, 89–91
Hawkinge (Airfield), 31
Haworth, Flying Officer J., 18
Hemingway, Pilot Officer J., 34
Hesselyn, Sergeant R., 126
Higgins, Sergeant W., 20
Hintze, *Oberleutnant* O., 28, 30, 38–40
Hitler, Adolf, 16–17, 21, 25–6, 36, 58, 69, 71, 85, 118–20, 130, 132–3, 135, 168, 175

Index   207

'Hitler Battery', Dieppe, 158–9
Hogan, Squadron Leader G., 193
Hogan, Squadron Leader H., 19
Holmes, Pilot Officer R., 88
Howarth, Sub-Lieutenant R., 136
Howetson, Lieutenant J., 53
Hunton, Sergeant C., 117
'Hunt's Gap', 172–3
Hutton, Sub-Lieutenant P., 138, 145, 147
Hurricane (Hawker):
  Individual Aircraft:
    Z2585, 94
    Z4642, 142, 146
    Z5584, 113
    Z7095, 146
  Squadrons:
    No. 1, 31–2, 40, 60, 62, 101, 117–18, 150
    No. 3, 155, 158, 161–2
    No. 5, 184, 189–91, 193
    No. 6, 163
    No. 11, 181, 184, 188, 190–2, 195–6
    No. 17, 29, 31, 39, 86–7, 98
    No. 20, 189, 192, 194, 196
    No. 28, 184–5, 187, 189, 191–2, 196
    No. 32, 20, 33, 155, 159, 162, 168
    No. 34, 181, 184–5, 188, 195
    No. 42, 181, 184–5, 187–8, 194–5
    No. 43, 18, 23–4, 155–8, 161–2, 164, 168
    No. 46, 3–13, 67, 74, 85
    No. 56, 18, 20, 37
    No. 60, 181, 189–90, 194–5
    No. 69, 116–17, 122
    No. 71, 151
    No. 79, 75, 80
    No. 80, 54
    No. 81, 86–92, 97
    No. 85, 24, 29, 34–5, 159
    No. 87, 25, 155, 160, 168
    No. 111, 16, 32–3, 175
    No. 113, 181, 184–5, 188, 194
    No. 123, 187
    No. 126, 67–9, 116–17, 120–2, 125
    No. 134, 86–92, 98
    No. 137, 164
    No. 145, 22–4
    No. 151, 28
    No. 164, 164
    No. 174, 155, 158–61
    No. 175, 155, 158, 160–1
    No. 184, 163–4
    No. 185, 62, 67–9, 116–17, 121, 124–7, 129–31
    No. 213, 64, 98
    No. 225, 169–74
    No. 229, 64, 127, 129, 131
    No. 232, 102–109
    No. 238, 18, 22–3, 36
    No. 241, 170–7
    No. 242, 68, 109–14, 119–20, 124, 142, 159
    No. 245, 16, 155, 158, 162
    No. 247, 80
    No. 249, 39, 64–9, 116–17, 120, 124–5
    No. 253, 154–5, 159–60, 162, 168
    No. 257, 22, 39
    No. 258, 101, 103–109, 114–15, 119
    No. 261, 56–65, 67, 70
    No. 274, 64
    No. 303, 38
    No. 335, 98
    No. 401, 164
    No. 402, 153, 155, 164
    No. 488, 104, 106, 109, 111
    No. 501, 18–20
    No. 504, 37, 86–8
    No. 601, 18, 35–6, 81
    No. 605, 109–12, 114, 119–20, 129
    No. 607, 40, 152–3, 155, 161
    No. 615, 20, 153
    No. 800, 141, 144–7
    No. 801, 137–9, 141–2, 144
    No. 804, 73, 75
    No. 813, 137–8, 141, 144
    No. 835, 136
    No. 880, 136, 141–6
    No. 885, 141, 144
    No. 22 Finnish Air Force, 85
    No. 1 IAF, 184–5, 189, 191–2
    No. 6 IAF, 181
    No. 9 IAF, 189
    No. 1 RCAF, 164
    No. 2 RCAF, 164
    No. 53 Rumanian Air Force, 85
    No. 1 SAAF, 43–7, 50–2
    No. 2 SAAF, 43–4, 46
    No. 3 SAAF, 43–4, 46, 48–50, 52–4
    No. 41 SAAF, 54
  Normandie (Free French), 94–5
  Units other than squadrons:
    No. 263 Flight, 16
    No. 418 Flight, 56
    No. 1435 Flight, 68, 116–17, 121–3, 125, 129, 131
    Malta Fighter Flight, 55–6
    Malta Night Fighter Flight, *see* 1435 Flight
    Merchant Ship Fighter Unit, 75–84
Hutcheson, Flight Lieutenant J., 106–107

Imphal, Battle of, 179–95
India, 94, 97, 179–96, 198
Italy, 41, 54, 89, 164, 168, 192

Jameson, Flight Lieutenant P., 5–6, 10–11
Java, 103–15, 119, 198
Java Air Force (Dutch), 104, 109–11
Johnson, Flight Lieutenant R., 189
Jordan, Sergeant P., 64
Judd, Lieutenant Commander F., 136, 142, 144, 146, 148

Kaberov, Colonel I., 95
Kalaja, Captain H., 86
Kalidjati (Airfield, Java), 112
Kangla (Airfield, India), 184
Kassala, 42, 45–6
Kawabe, Lieutenant General M., 183, 194–5
Kayll, Squadron Leader J., 20
Keeble, Flight Lieutenant P., 56
Keedwell, Pilot Officer R., 105
Keg Ostrov (Airfield, Russia), 87–8
Kellett, Squadron Leader R., 38
Kelly, Sergeant T., 101–102, 106–107, 110, 114–15
Kenley (Airfield), 20, 32
Kenya, 41–6, 48
Keren, Battle of, 47, 50–1
Kershaw, Lieutenant R., 50
Kesselring, Field Marshal A., 17, 120–1, 123, 128, 130, 132–4, 168, 171–2, 176
King-Joyce, Lieutenant T., 137
Knight, Flying Officer H., 10–11
Kohima, Battle of, 183–6, 188–9, 192–5
Kok, Lieutenant J., 46
Kravchenko, Lieutenant V., 93
Kuharenko, Captain A., 92
Kunii, Lieutenant M., 106
Kursk, Battle of, 97
Kuttelwascher, Flight Lieutenant K., 40
Kuznetsov, Major General A., 92–3

Lacey, Sergeant J.H., 19–20, 26
Lambert, Sergeant H., 107
Lambert, Squadron Leader R., 56, 61–2
Landels, Squadron Leader L., 103
Lardner-Burke, Pilot Officer H., 117
Laubscher, Flying Officer C., 64
Lee, Pilot Officer K., 131
Lefevre, Pilot Officer, later Flight Lieutenant P., 3–4, 7, 10, 67, 69
Leggett, Flying Officer G., 65–7, 70
Leigh-Mallory, Air Vice-Marshal T., 150, 153–4, 162

Leotta, Lieutenant Colonel E., 117
Libya, 41, 45, 171
Lintern, Pilot Officer D., 116
Lister, Flight Lieutenant F., 156–7, 162
Lloyd, Air Commodore, later Air Vice-Marshal H., 66–7
Lockwood, Pilot Officer W., 107
Loftus, Lieutenant P., 44
Lomax, Flight Sergeant J., 195
Lowe, Pilot Officer P., 119, 125
Lucas, Sub-Lieutenant J., 145
Luftwaffe:
  Air Fleets (*Luftflotten*):
    Luftflotte 2, 17, 31, 120
    Luftflotte 3, 17, 31
    Luftflotte 5, 17, 31
  Fliegerkorps:
    Fliegerkorps II, 120, 133–4
    Fliegerkorps X, 58, 64, 120
  Geschwader:
    JG 3, 61
    JG 26, 60–3, 70
    JG 27, 20, 22–3, 63
    JG 51, 20
    JG 52, 32
    KG 2, 31
    KG 4, 18
    KG 40, 71, 77–82
    KG 55, 36–7
    LG 1, 22–4
    StG 1, 20, 22
    StG 2, 22
    StG 3, 22
    StG 77, 22
    ZG 26, 28, 36–7
  Gruppe:
    Erprobungsgruppe 210, 27–40
Luqa (Airfield, Malta), 56, 59, 61, 63, 67, 122, 128
Lutz, *Oberleutnant*, later *Hauptmann* M., 30, 36, 38
Lydall, Flying Officer W., 5, 8
Lympne (Airfield), 31

MacCaw, Flying Officer D., 23
Mackie, Pilot Officer A., 122
MacLachlan, Flight Lieutenant J., 57, 59–60
MacMurray, Pilot Officer W., 170
Macnamara, Flying Officer G., 107
Macnamara, Pilot Officer T., 121
Madagascar, 136
Maguire, Wing Commander H., 104–107, 111–13, 115
Maison Blanche (Airfield, Algeria), 169
Malaya, 102

Index 209

Malta, 7, 55–71, 116–36, 139–40, 145, 148–9, 167
Malta Convoys:
  Individual Convoys, see Convoys
  Supply ships in:
    Breconshire (Naval Auxiliary), 134
    Brisbane Star, 148–9
    Burdwan, 136, 139
    Chant, 136, 139
    Deucalion, 145, 148
    Dorset, 149
    Essex, 58
    Kentucky (Tanker), 136, 139–40
    Melbourne Star, 149
    Ohio (Tanker), 141, 148–9
    Orari, 136, 139–40
    Port Chalmers, 149
    Rochester Castle, 149
    Tanimbar, 136–7
    Troilus, 136, 139–40
    Waimarama, 149
    Welshman (Minelayer), 131, 136
Mann, Flying Officer A., 190
Manston (Airfield), 31, 34, 155
Mareth Line, Battle of, 171–2, 175–6
Martlesham Heath (Airfield), 31, 34
Martuba (Airfield, Cyrenaica), 123, 133, 135, 140, 167
Martyn, Lieutenant W., 144
Masih, Pilot Officer N., 191
Mason, Captain D.W., 141, 149
Mason, Flying Officer, Later Squadron Leader E.M., 63–4, 70
Massawa, 1, 47, 52
Matmata Hills, 174
Maupertus (Airfield, France), 155
Maynard, Air Commodore, later Air Vice-Marshal F., 55, 67
McConnell, Flight Lieutenant, later Squadron Leader W., 160–1
McIntosh, Sergeant W., 111
McPhail, Pilot Officer J., 189
McPherson, Flying Officer T., 139
Mearns, Sub-Lieutenant S., 136
Medenine, Battle of, 173–4
Mee, Flying Officer M., 7, 10
Mendizabal, Pilot Officer A., 112
Menzies, Sir Robert, 72–3
Meredith, Flight Sergeant J., 160
Messe, General G., 172, 175–7
Metemma, 44
Miller, Squadron Leader A., 86, 91–2
Millington, Wing Commander E., 169
Millward, Pilot Officer C., 176
Mitchison, Leading Aircraftsman E., 128

Mogadishu, 49
Montgomery, Lieutenant General, later General Sir B.L., 167, 171–2, 174–7
Moore, Group Captain M., 10
Moran, Sergeant D., 120–1
Mould, Flight Lieutenant, Later Squadron Leader P., 62, 116
Moulton-Barrett, Wing Commander E., 75
Moyale, 42
Muff, Flying Officer J., 191
Muntok (Airfield, Banka Island), 106, 108
Murcott, Flying Officer N., 189
Murmansk, 86–7, 89, 92–3
Musi River, 106–108
Mussolini, Benito, 41, 43
Mutaguchi, Lieutenant General R., 182–4, 186, 191–2, 194–5

Naga Hills, 183, 189, 196
Nash, Pilot Officer A., 107
Narvik, 1–9, 89
Neale, Sergeant D., 122
Neil, Flight Lieutenant T., 65–6, 70
Ngoro (Airfield, Java), 109, 111
Nicholetts, Group Captain G., 108
Nicholl, Flight Lieutenant E., 173
Nicholls, Sergeant H., 105–106
Normandy, Battle of, 164
North Coates (Airfield), 3
Northolt (Airfield), 104
North Weald (Airfield), 38–9
Norway, 1–12, 14, 16–17, 31, 67, 80, 85
Nungshigum, 137–8, 192

O'Brian, Pilot Officer H., 177
Operational Code Names:
  Allied:
    CRUSADER, 118–20
    HURRY, 56–7
    JUBILEE, 153–64
    TORCH, 167–8
    WHITE, 57, 61
    See also, Convoys
  Axis:
    ADLERTAG (Eagle Day), 21, 29, 31
Oosthaven, 108
Oran, 167–8
Ormrod, Pilot Officer O.O., 119, 127–9
Owen, Flight Lieutenant D., 116

P1 (Airfield, Sumatra), 105–107
P2 (Airfield, Sumatra), 105, 107–108, 114
Page, Flight Lieutenant V., 191
Palel (Airfield, India), 134, 187, 190, 193
Palembang, 105–108

Pare, Lieutenant R., 51
Park, Air Vice-Marshal K., 150
Parker, Flight Lieutenant B., 113
Parkinson, Sergeant C., 18
Peel, Squadron Leader J., 21–4
Perry, Flying Officer F., 185
Pétain, Marshal H.P., 167
Peters, Pilot Officer R., 160
Pettit, Pilot Officer H., 111
Pinkerton, Wing Commander G., 75
Pinna, General P., 47, 50–1
Pladjoe, 107
Plate, River, Battle of, 135
Platt, General Sir W., 45, 47–8, 50–1
Plummer, Pilot Officer R., 3
Popham, Sub-Lieutenant H., 142–3
Portsmouth, 30, 36–7
Pound, Admiral Sir D., 72
Powell-Sheddon, Squadron Leader G., 168
Pritchard, Warrant Officer B., 190

Rabagliati, Squadron Leader, later Wing Commander A., 67, 118
Ramsbottom-Isherwood, Wing Commander H., 86, 91–2
Räty, Lieutenant A.J., 85
Rembang, 110–11
Repnikov, Lieutenant N., 93
'Rhubarb' Missions, 151–2
Richards, Colonel H., 186, 188–9
Richey, Wing Commander P., 101–102, 110
Richmond, Pilot Officer P., 173
Rigby, Sergeant J., 89
Ritchie, Sub-Lieutenant B., 147
Roberts, Sub-Lieutenant G., 144
Robertson, Sergeant F., 56, 61–2
Rodwell, Flying Officer P., 169
Romagnoli, Lieutenant Colonel C., 68
Rommel, General, later Field Marshal E., 45, 118, 120, 123, 130, 133, 166, 168, 171–5
'Rommel Battery', Dieppe, 160
Rook, Squadron Leader A., 86–7, 90–1
Rook, Flight Lieutenant M., 86–7, 91
Ross, Flight Lieutenant J., 87–8
Rössiger, *Oberleutnant* W-R., 30, 38
Roy, Flight Sergeant D., 129
Royal Air Force:
    Groups:
        No. 9 Group, 75
        No. 11 Group, 150, 153–4, 165
        No. 12 Group, 12
        No. 203 Group, 45
        No. 221 Group, 184, 192
        No. 225 Group, 104
        No. 226 Group, 104
        West Group, Java, 108
    Wings:
        No. 151 Wing, 86–95, 97, 99
        No. 266 Wing, 104–106
        No. 324 Wing, 170
Rubensdörffer, *Hauptmann* W., 27–34, 36, 40
Russell, Sergeant J., 122
Russia, 1, 38, 70, 82, 85–99, 120, 130, 151, 168, 174, 197
Russian Air Force Regiments:
    72nd, 92, 96
    78th, 92–3, 96, 98
    152nd, 93
    2nd Guards Combined, 96
Rumania, 85

Safanov, Captain, later Lieutenant Colonel B., 92–3, 98
'Safi Strip' (Airfield, Malta), 67
Sanders, Pilot Officer V., 81
Sapan (Airfield, India), 184
Sardinia, 56, 133, 137–8, 141, 144
Sato, Lieutenant General K., 186, 188, 192, 194
Saunders, Pilot Officer R., 67
Scoones, Lieutenant General Sir G., 195
Scott, Sergeant N., 106
Seal, Flying Officer H., 159
Sgibnev, Major P., 96
Shackley, Flight Sergeant E., 3–4, 10
Shandur (Airfield, Egypt), 163
Shannon, Flight Lieutenant B., 189
Sharman, Flying Officer R., 169
Sharp, Flying Officer N., 111
Sherburne, Sergeant D., 67
Short, Pilot Officer S., 169
Shuttleworth, Pilot Officer Lord R., 24
Sicily, 41, 57–8, 60, 67, 69, 117, 120, 123, 131, 133, 138, 141, 146, 177
Simpson, Sergeant P., 118
Sims, Sergeant J., 90.
Sinev, Lieutenant D., 93
Singapore, 102–103, 114, 119
Singh, Squadron Leader A., 185
Skaanland (Airfield, Norway), 4
Slatter, Air Commodore L., 45
Slee, Flight Sergeant P., 105
Slim, Brigadier, later Lieutenant General Sir W., 44, 180–4, 195–6
Smallwood, Squadron Leader D., 160
Smith, Sergeant N., 89, 91
Snell, Pilot Officer A.E., 156

Index 211

Somaliland:
  British, 42, 50
  Italian, 41, 45, 48–9
Somerville, Vice Admiral Sir J., 57, 141
Souk el Arba (Airfield, Tunisia), 169–70
Souk el Khemis (Airfield, Tunisia), 170–1, 176
Sowrey, Air Commodore W., 45
Spedding, Sub-Lieutenant H., 138
Speke (Airfield), 75–7
Sperrle, Field Marshal H., 17
Spyer, Sergeant R., 57, 61
Stalingrad, Battle of, 168, 177
Stanage, Sergeant H., 159
Steele, Pilot Officer A., 126
Steele, Pilot Officer E., 120
Stevenson, Pilot Officer D., 161
Stewart, Pilot Officer J., 83
Stewart, Flight Lieutenant R., 10
Stopford, Lieutenant General Sir M., 195
Strange, Squadron Leader L., 77
Strelnikov, Captain V., 98
Sudan, 41–6
Sumatra, 103–108, 111, 114–15, 119, 198
Surabaya, 104
Surma, Pilot Officer F., 39
Sydenham (Airfield), 73, 76
Syfret, Vice Admiral Sir N., 141, 147
Sylvester, Pilot Officer E., 19
Syracuse, 69, 117

Takali (Airfield, Malta), 58, 122
Tamminen, Sergeant T., 93
Tamu (Airfield, Burma), 185, 195
Tangmere (Airfield), 156
Taranto, 58
Tate, Flight Sergeant J., 159
Taylor, Sergeant B., 9–11
Taylor, Flight Sergeant K., 194
Taylor, Flying Officer N., 81–2, 34
'Tebaga Gap', 175–6
Tedford, Pilot Officer D., 118, 124–5
Tesei, Commander T., 68–9
Thacker, Pilot Officer P., 60
Thelepte (Airfield, Tunisia), 175
Theron, Lieutenant, later Captain S. van B., 43, 46, 48–9, 52
Thomas, Flight Lieutenant R., 189
Thompson, Squadron Leader J., 32–4
Thomson, Sub-Lieutenant A., 146
Thomson, Squadron Leader J., 107
Tickner, Lieutenant L., 138
Tjilatjap, 111, 113
Tjililitan (Airfield, Java), 109, 112
Tobruk, 118
Townsend, Squadron Leader P., 23–5, 34–5, 40
Trenchard-Smith, Pilot Officer E., 156, 162
Tripoli, 168, 171
Trondheim, 1–3, 14
Troubridge, Captain T., 143
Trumble, Squadron Leader A., 56
Truter, Captain St E., 43
Tsuji, Colonel M., 103
Tulihal (Airfield, India), 184
Tunisia, 55, 97, 133, 137, 141, 168–79
Turnbull, Lieutenant R., 137–9
Turner, Flight Lieutenant D., 29
Turner, Squadron Leader P.S., 124–5
Tyson, Pilot Officer H., 170

'Ultra' Intelligence, 68, 171, 175, 178
Upton, Pilot Officer H., 23

Vaenga (Airfield, Russia), 87–92
Valesi, *Hauptmann* E., 29
Varley, Flying Officer G., 80
Venter, Lieutenant A., 49, 52–3
Verma, Flying Officer J., 181
Vian, Rear Admiral Sir P., 134–5
Viljoen, Lieutenant S. de K., 50
Vincent, Air Commodore S.F., 107–108, 111, 184, 192
Volkov, Lieutenant M., 93

Walker, Warrant Officer A., 185
Walker, Sub-Lieutenant C., 79
Walker, Pilot Officer J., 39
Wallace, Sergeant T., 33
Wallis, Sub-Lieutenant F., 136
Walsh, Pilot Officer J., 60
Walters, Flying Officer A., 160
Wangjing (Airfield, India), 184
Warmwell (Airfield), 155
Waters, Flying Officer J., 55
Watson, Flight Lieutenant G., 60
Watson, Pilot Officer T., 106, 112
Waud, Sergeant K., 89
Wavell, Field Marshal Lord A., 195
Wells, Flying Officer P., 65–6, 69, 70
Westcott, Sergeant J., 121
Western Dorsale, 172
Westmacott, Squadron Leader I., 116, 123, 125, 129
West Malling (Airfield), 38
Whalen, Flight Lieutenant J., 188
Whitehall, Flight Sergeant W., 189
Whittingham, Flight Lieutenant, later Squadron Leader C., 59, 62

Wick (Airfield), 85
Wik, Flight Sergeant H., 156
Wilcox, Sergeant G., 131
Wilmot, Major L., 46, 51–2
Wingate, Brigadier O., 179–80, 196
Winton, Pilot Officer D., 69, 121
Wood, Sergeant J., 125, 129
Woods-Scawen, Pilot Officer A., 23–4
Worral, Squadron Leader J., 20
Worral, Pilot Officer P., 34–5
Wright, Flight Lieutenant, later Squadron Leader E., 109, 111
Wykeham-Barnes, Flying Officer P., 54

Yavello (Airfield, Abyssinia), 43
Young, Sergeant T., 111

Ziegler, General H., 171–2
Zodorozhniy, Lieutenant F., 94
Zomer, Lieutenant Colonel J., 104
Zwik, Gefreiter W., 37
Zubza, 186, 188, 191